William Cunningham

The Churches of Asia

A Methodical Sketch of the Second Century

William Cunningham

The Churches of Asia
A Methodical Sketch of the Second Century

ISBN/EAN: 9783744756754

Printed in Europe, USA, Canada, Australia, Japan

Cover: Foto ©Lupo / pixelio.de

More available books at **www.hansebooks.com**

THE CHURCHES OF ASIA

The Churches of Asia

A METHODICAL SKETCH OF THE
SECOND CENTURY

BY

WILLIAM CUNNINGHAM, M.A.

London
MACMILLAN AND CO.
1880.

PREFACE.

The Kaye Essay for 1879, which is now published, was the occupation of some weeks of vacation, and as such makes no pretension to completeness: whatever interest it may possess is due, not so much to the results, as to the method of historical study which is here imperfectly exemplified.

Unless the course of History is wholly fortuitous, we must recognise that, beneath the confused play of passion which marks every age, definite forces are in operation. To determine the nature and order of these forces is the work of the Philosophy of History, and the true task for the student of any period is that of detecting and delineating the force which was mainly operative at that time, of exhibiting it in conflict with other influences, and of tracing out the results of the struggle.

Those who have adopted a Philosophy of History which leads them to recognise moral forces as the chief factors in the course of the life of mankind, will feel that they cannot understand any epoch of history unless they can recognise an "effective idea," and trace its working in the world. They will notice it first as a conviction or aspiration *impressing* many minds, they will find it also *expressing itself* in the sayings and doings of multitudes of men, and at length *embodying itself* in the institutions of Society: by thus following out the conditions which are necessary for united action, and for the growth of institutions, they will be able to exhibit the progress of events in the order in which they were really brought about, not merely in their chronological sequence. It may even be contended that to learn to apprehend this logical order, as we may call it, of the development of events in any age, is a needful preparation for the "higher criticism" of the documents which survive.

Such is the method I have sought to pursue in dealing with the history and internal development of the Churches of Asia during the second century. I have tried to delineate as clearly as possible, from contemporary evidence, the conviction which impressed all' Christian minds; I have described the conflicts which ensued when it began to express itself, and make itself felt as an effective force in the world; I have sketched the actual institutions which grew up under its influence; and thus I have endeavoured to trace the Christian "idea working itself out" in the planting of the Church. Nor does the correctness of the conclusions appear to be seriously impaired because I have carefully assumed an attitude of indifference to the keenest controversies of literary critics.

This is not the place to attempt a full justification of the method, or of the Philosophy on which it depends: that has already been before the world for years. I can only trust that those who have not well considered the nature of History and the best order of historical investigation will not lightly condemn the method here pursued because they discover erroneous results in a mere occasional Essay.

I have always been careful to state my authorities, though I have not burdened my pages with exact references to well-known passages in Epiphanius, Irenæus, and other Fathers subsequent to the second century, since they can be readily verified from the excellent indices in Migne's *Patrologie*. The Essay has not received a thorough revision before publication, though the sections on the Quarto-deciman controversy have been entirely rewritten, and a few sentences have been added or modified here and there. I have, however, collected in an Appendix a few illustrative extracts from second-century writers. By perusing these original authorities the English reader may obtain a much more vivid conception of early Christian life than by resting satisfied with the most graphic compilations. A table has also been added, in which the chronological sequence of the most important events is roughly indicated.

It has seemed to me worth while to reproduce, as a frontispiece, a design in the Neapolitan catacombs, which illustrates an early allegory of the building of the Church (see p. 79), and incidentally bears witness to the interest it continued to create, for some centuries.

CAMBRIDGE, *July* 1880.

CONTENTS.

	PAGE
FRONTISPIECE (p. 79), TITLE, PREFACE, ETC.,	i.-xvi

Introduction.

STANDPOINT, PLAN, AND SOURCES OF THE INVESTIGATION.

§ 1. Baur, Neander, and Baronius,	3
§ 2. The story of the manifestation of the Christian idea,	8
§ 3. Nature of the evidence required,	14

Part I.

CONCEPTION OF THE CHRISTIAN SOCIETY CURRENT IN ASIA AT THE BEGINNING OF THE SECOND CENTURY.

(1.) *Pre-Christian Conception of the Divine Society.*

§ 4. The Jewish People and the Jewish Church,	23
§ 5. The hope of Israel in the time of our Lord,	27

(2.) *Genesis of the Christian Conception of the Divine Society:* a. *Its nature;* b. *Terms of admission;* c. *Life of its members;* d. *Its organisation.*

§ 6. Evidence of the Synoptic Gospels,	34
§ 7. Evidence of the *Acts of the Apostles*,	41

CONTENTS.

	PAGE
§ 8. Evidence of the *Epistle of S. James*,	48
§ 9. Evidence of the *Apocalypse*,	49
§ 10. Evidence of the *First Epistle of S. Peter*,	53
§ 11. Evidence of the Asian Epistles of S. Paul,	55
§ 12. Evidence of the Fourth Gospel,	58
§ 13. Summary,	62

(3.) *Current Conception as maintained in Sub-Apostolical writings.*

§ 14. Nature of the Christian Society,	64
§ 15. Terms of Admission,	67
§ 16. Life of the Members,	68
§ 17. Organisation: Viceregal Episcopacy,	73
§ 18. Civic Episcopacy — existence of self-regulating bodies,	75

Part II.

THE CONFLICT WITH OTHER INFLUENCES.

(1.) *Non-Christian Elements of Society.*

§ 19. The environment—Gnosticism,	85
§ 20. Judaism: Pharisaic and Essene Ebionitism,	89
§ 21. Essene Ebionites and positive religion—Cerinth,	94
§ 22. Judaism and Christianity about 100 A.D.,	102
§ 23. Survival of Greek political ideas.	104
§ 24. Roman administration,	110

(2.) *Actual Growth of the Church.*

§ 25. Decay of Viceregal Episcopate,	112
§ 26. Functions of Apostles, Presbyters, and Deacons,	117

CONTENTS. xv

		PAGE
§ 27.	Effects of the fall of Jerusalem and deaths of the Apostles, ...	121
§ 28.	Civic Episcopate: actual influence of Greek life, .	127
§ 29.	How far are various theories intelligible ? . .	131
§ 30.	The historical value of the evidence of the *Acts of the Apostles*, ...	136
§ 31.	Growth of heathen antagonism, .	140
§ 32.	The Custom of the Church, ...	144

Part III.

THE NATURE OF THE CHRISTIAN INSTITUTIONS AS REFLECTED IN EARLY CONTROVERSIES.

(1.) *The Discipline of the Church.*

§ 33.	What is real religion ? . . .	151
§ 34.	Marcion—Subjective spirituality, .	153
§ 35.	Montanism—A Christian code, .	159
§ 36.	Stricter discipline. *Disciplina arcani*, . . .	172
§ 37.	The power of the keys. Prophets *v*. Bishops, .	180

(2.) *The Annual Commemoration of the Passion.*

§ 38.	The conflicting traditions, .	186
§ 39.	The rival uses, . . .	193
§ 40.	Different modes of calculation, .	203
§ 41.	History of Quarto-decimanism in Asia,	206
§ 42.	The fundamental agreement,	210
§ 43.	Conclusion, . .	214

Appendix.

A.—EXTRACTS FROM CONTEMPORARY WRITERS, ILLUSTRATIVE OF CHRISTIAN LIFE DURING THE SECOND CENTURY, ... 221

(1.) *Church Organisation.*

1. *S. Clement to the Corinthians*, i. 37-44, . 222
2. *S. Ignatius to the Trallians*, . . . 228
3. *The Pastor of Hermas*, Vision iii., . . . 234

(2.) *Christian Rites.*

4. Justin Martyr's *First Apology*, 61, 65-68, . . 244

(3.) *The Christian Year.*

5. The *Apostolical Constitutions*, v. 13-20, . . 251

(4.) *Christian Sufferings.*

6. The *Martyrdom of S. Polycarp*, . . . 259
7. Eusebius, *History of the Church*, v. 1, . 273

B.—CHRONOLOGICAL TABLE, . . 293

INDEX, . . 295

INTRODUCTION.

A

Introduction.

STANDPOINT, PLAN AND SOURCES OF THE INVESTIGATION.

§ 1. Dr. Baur tells us, at the outset of his work on the *First Three Centuries*, that the standpoint which he has adopted is a purely historical one; but while we agree with the Tübingen school in demanding a strictly scientific investigation of the growth of the Christian Church, we differ from them in our conception of the nature and methods of historical study; for to us it seems incomplete, even if we succeed in placing "before ourselves the materials given in the History, as they are objectively, and not otherwise."[1] Nor can we be satisfied with dissecting out the various interests in which documents were written, or the tendencies they embody, unless we can also show that these tendencies were capable by their co-action of bringing about the state of

[1] Baur, *First Three Centuries*, Preface, vol. i. p. x.

things that was the final result—in fact, unless we can render the course of History intelligible.

There are always two questions which may be asked in looking forward from some starting-point over the struggles of any period—What was the upshot of it all? and, How did that come about? The answer to the first question is given by the writers of the immediately succeeding age when they tell us of their own time; the answer to the second can never be approximately complete, but it may be satisfactory so far as it goes, by showing us historic forces at work that were capable of producing the result which actually occurred; careful criticism of the documents, and stern scrutiny of individual characters, do not rise above the level of literary and biographical studies to that of History, unless they render the actual course of affairs in the world more intelligible, by exhibiting in active operation forces that would tend to produce the very results that came to pass. It is only by viewing them in connexion with the winning forces that we can estimate, not the moral worth, but the historical position of individual men; and so too, it is only by viewing them in connexion with these forces that we can learn to estimate, not merely the literary and evidential value, but the historical import of the writings that are preserved to us; we want to know them—not each in itself, but each in its relation to the real course of the world. Indeed, unless we have some such guiding clew, our criticism is necessarily capricious and arbitrary;[1] it sets itself the hopeless task of showing us some writer in-himself, rather than the truer one of stating clearly what was his relation to his contemporaries. Such criticism tends to exaggerate the signs of personal feeling and passion, and neglects the assertion of truths which were common to all Christian men; for such criticism, each writer ceases to be a witness to God's truth in his own way, and becomes the mere exponent of an abstract tendency which, just because it is abstract, could never have amalgamated with the abstractions upheld by opposite parties. The delineation of such tendencies can never render the course of History intelligible, and no series of mediations and compromises could produce a real reconciliation which would bring such opposing forces into harmonious working. The criticism which Ritschl urged against Schwegler, and which Baur retorts upon the former,[2]

---

[1] G. W. F. Hegel, *Philosophie der Geschichte*, Werke, x. 10, 11.
[2] *First Three Centuries*, i. 100.

seems to be almost equally applicable to the more elaborate theory of the Tübingen professor himself. There may have been an implicit assumption in his mind that some convictions were common to all Christian men, but no attempt is made to show explicitly what these convictions were; and thus, the most important of all the active forces is passed over in silence.

Some sort of conception of the Christian Church underlies Neander's description of its growth, but not a satisfactory one. The apostles are regarded as missionaries who converted a large number of individuals; each of these individuals had a firm faith in his heart, any of them might be endowed with the gifts of the Holy Ghost—all were priests to God. The problem which his history really attacks is that of showing how these aggregates of converted individuals organised themselves; and it almost seems as if he believed that each step that was taken in organising the Christian Society was a departure from the purer life of the past, for the chief influence is ascribed to Judaisers, the ambition of bishops, and the like. To us this account is unintelligible: that these fortuitous elements of ambition and misunderstanding should everywhere lead, sooner or later, and always within a brief period, to the same institution, is simply inconceivable. The idea of atoms thus organising themselves into a society is an unphilosophical one, and the conception of a Church thus built is not only unphilosophical but wholly modern. Though Neander would doubtless have maintained as a verbal proposition that there was a Guiding Hand in all these changes, the belief does not show itself in his work. From its whole tone we should gather that if any deep influence was operating, it was bringing about the decay rather than the development of the Church. He writes as if he believed in the fortuitousness of the development of the various Christian institutions, and looked upon them as evils which were necessitated by the corruptions that overtook the primitive purity of Christian life.

Still less can we accept the view of writers like Baronius, who find a mere identity between the institutions of the past and of the present. If such identity could be proved, it would strike the most terrible blow at any belief in the Church as the divinely commissioned regenerator of the world; for it would show that she had been capable of no new developments to suit the needs of the new æras.

Our Church life of to-day has grown out of that of the first century, but it is fuller and richer, since we possess the religious experience of eighteen hundred years of which the men of that time knew nothing.

§ 2. These remarks have been written, not with the desire of adequately characterising, and still less with any intention of disparaging, works of well-established reputation, but in the hope that a reference to these three great writers of ecclesiastical history may bring into clear relief the view which is adopted, and imperfectly developed, in the following pages. There was, as we believe, a great belief which took hold of the minds of the apostles and their first followers, while succeeding centuries showed the progress made in realising it. There was a great hope—the religious heritage of Israel—there was a positive belief that that hope had been fulfilled in Jesus, and that it lay with his disciples to complete the fulfilment: they had an idea before them, and in the history of the first age of the Church, we see that "idea working itself out." Only when we grasp the idea that possessed its first members, does the growth of the Church become intelligible, for only then can we detect an order in the chaos, or recognise the real course of the events.

The idea of a kingdom of God upon earth had fascinated the apostles, and became the dominant principle in all the thought and conduct of their followers. Here it might be distorted by dull misunderstanding, and disfigured there by petty jealousies; but still it was the dominating principle of their conduct, which, *impressed* upon the minds of all, came to be *expressed* in the Christian institutions of the third century. From Hippolytus, and Clement, and Irenæus, and Tertullian, we can gather a clear idea of the Catholic Church of their day, of its organisation, its worship and its doctrine; and we hold that this was the *manifestation* of that divine conception which the apostles had set themselves to work out. We say the manifestation, not the perfect realisation, of the kingdom of God,—that is yet to come; but the Church of that day did show forth to the world a society which, while in the world, was not of it; where the ties that bound men together, the motives of conduct and the aspirations that were cherished, were wholly alien to those of the rest of mankind. When the kingdom of God was thus manifested among men as an actual institution, it had indeed come with power; true, it had but attained the first stage of its development; it had yet to lose its isolation and lay hold on all sides of secular life, as a kingdom of this world, that through it the kingdoms of this world might become the kingdom of our God and of his Christ.

A very few lines may now serve to indicate the precise nature of the antagonism between the standpoint just described, and each of the three conceptions which have apparently influenced the methods of treatment adopted by the historians named above. We believe that all Christians held firmly to the faith in a divine kingdom which was established in the world—a spiritual Society—call it what you will. The tendencies of which so much is made were not abstract principles which were tenaciously held by men who were out of all sympathy with one another,—they were different opinions which commended themselves to men who had the firmest bond of sympathy, for they shared a common faith. What they had in common was the deepest power that influenced them all, though each man had his personal proclivities; there were many moulds into which the common Faith was cast, but it was one Faith after all. These various personal proclivities are of the deepest interest: they show us what forms the Faith was taking in different minds before it manifested itself in the institutions of the Catholic Church; but the clashing of different opinions does not, in itself, account for the actual growth of the Church on earth,—that is only rendered intelligible by turning our eyes to the Faith in which all were at one.

If, unlike Baur, we hold it of the first importance to portray the common convictions and common sympathies which underlay diverging tendencies, we constantly recognise, as Neander fails to do, a guiding principle, overruling all the conflicts of the time, and so dominating them as to determine the issue. It was thus that a similar result was attained at length in Jerusalem and Rome, in Antioch and Alexandria; different as were the elements of the Christian society in each case, different as must have been the rivalries and struggles, a similar result was found in all: everywhere was the Church organised upon one model.

Once more, we do not, like some Roman writers, recognise an identity of form in the institutions of the Church of all ages: we see rather one eternal principle which has manifested itself in diverse forms. For the Church of Christ on earth has run the course of other institutions,—the one logical process can be traced in its progress. The later stages of the growth of the Society lie beyond our present scope; for we have to do with the earliest phases of development, and to note how the faith began to manifest itself to the world as an actual institution.

A few words may now describe the plan of this Essay; it is purely historical, an attempt to explain what the course of affairs really was, not an attempt to investigate the past as if it were authoritative for guidance in the present; when we know what happened then, we shall best know how far it deserves imitation now; but from our point of view, the Christian Consciousness of to-day, as enlightened by the Holy Spirit present with us now, is the one supreme authority for us;[1] and we investigate the past as a matter of the deepest scientific interest, but not with the vain ambition that any private discussion of past history can enable us to usurp the Church's authority in present controversies as to rites, and dogmas, and discipline.[2]

[1] *Christian Civilisation*, p. 19 *seq.*   [2] Article xxii.

We have already said that the principal force to be considered was the idea of a new society, an idea which worked itself out through the private passions of men.

Our first task must be to describe, as clearly as possible, the nature of this motive force; and that can be done most accurately by tracing the genesis of the conception of the Christian Society, and by taking special pains to determine the form in which it was current in Asia.

We must then notice the opposing influences with which it came in contact, and see it struggling to gain a footing and make itself felt in the world; our researches on this point can be rendered more definite by confining them to the province of Asia.

Lastly, when we have seen the Church firmly planted, we must consider the nature of the institution that had thus grown up; and this we can learn most clearly by attending to the controversies that arose within its pale; we may note too, that while certain discussions were making themselves heard all over the Church, the chief interest with regard to them centred in Asia and the neighbouring provinces. We may thus gain much by rendering our inquiries definite, while yet regarding the history of the Churches of Asia as fairly typical of the general Church development in the second century.

§ 3. The sketch of the plan of the Essay has put us in a position to discuss the sources of evidence; we now know the precise points on which we wish for evidence; it is obvious that sources of information which might be of the highest value in other inquiries are practically valueless in regard to our special subject. The extant writings are, in the first place, of value to us in so far as they enable us to judge of the *current conception* of the Christian Society; canonical writings, being those which were generally received, have of course the chief value for this purpose; of other writings which were not generally received, we can chiefly appeal to those which have some traceable connexion with the province of Asia, and can thus be quoted as evidence of current opinions there.

The one question which may always be neglected is the question of authenticity or authorship; the one which ought to be definitely settled in each case, before our inquiry could be considered complete, is the question of the date of each writing. It is, however, obviously impossible to enter into a thorough discussion of this series of problems, which have met with so many contradictory solutions, and no real attempt will be made to justify the dates here assigned; it may be well to notice, however, that even a serious mistake in regard to the date does not destroy the evidence as to the direction of the growth of the current conception of Christianity; it can, at the outside, only lead to a misapprehension in regard to the rate of development. We use the writings not with the view of quoting the authority of the author for some opinion, still less with the attempt of discovering the purpose with which it was composed. For us, each writing is simply the evidence of a certain conviction as existing about a given date—existing at the very least in the mind of the author, and in the minds of those who readily accepted his teaching. Early writings which were generally received are the documents we wish to study.

The same documents may then be drawn upon for evidence in regard to the *actual growth* of the new kingdom and its relation to its environment; but in addition to them we can make use of the *History* of Eusebius, and of other external evidences of the same kind in pagan histories and documents.

For the discussion of the differences that developed themselves within the Church as an instituted religion, the writings of the defenders of the Catholic Faith against heathens and heretics are of course the chief source of information; though the Asian origin of the *Apostolical Constitutions* renders them valuable too, even if they were not collected in their present form till a later date.

To specify in greater detail. For the purpose of tracing the genesis of the current conception of the Church, the Synoptic Gospels, the *Acts of the Apostles*, and the Pauline Epistles may be accepted without difficulty; as also may the First *Epistle of S. Peter*, and the *Epistle of S. James;* for the doubts as to the authenticity of these writings which are due to modern analysis, and which had no place in ancient tradition, have no bearing on our inquiry: if any of them was a forgery, it was a forgery which received universal assent, and thus bears equal evidence to the current conceptions of the day. In the same way we may at once accept the *Epistle to the Hebrews* without attempting to solve the question of its authorship. Modern inquiry may be regarded as establishing the early date of the *Apocalypse*, even in spite of the doubt in ancient days; the doubts about the *Gospel of S. John* which were felt long ago, and which have prevailed so widely in our own day, need not prevent our appealing to it as, in any case, a monument of early Ephesian Christianity, and this suffices for our immediate purpose.

Turning to the sub-apostolical writings, we find that the reception which was accorded to the (first) *Epistle of S. Clement* of Rome to the Corinthians may allow us to make use of it, even though it has no direct bearing on Asia; the balance of evidence as to its date seems to be in favour of the time of Domitian, and we may place it at something like 97 A.D. The *Epistle of S. Barnabas*, though not improbably somewhat earlier, has hardly been so generally received as worthy of reading in church; its bearing on our subject is however comparatively slight. The *Pastor of Hermas*, though a Roman work, written in all probability somewhat before the middle of the century, attained so early to recognition in Asia, that we may examine it with more confidence.

The *Epistle of Polycarp* we may place, following M. Waddington, about 155 A.D.; and the tangled controversy about the *Ignatian Epistles* must be cut rather than unravelled. Some critics are in doubt as to the authenticity of either the shorter Greek or the Syrian version;[1] there is a practical unanimity in the opinion that the longer recension belongs to a later date. Whether the Syrian or short Greek version is the truer representation of the original we need not say; it suffices for us that we cannot place either writing later than 150 A.D., though the belief that the shorter recension is genuine seems to have gained ground rapidly during the last few years,[2] and if this be true that version cannot be later than 115 A.D.

Many of the fragments and documents embodied in the *History* of Eusebius are of the highest interest, especially the letter from the Churches of Lyons and Vienne; their direct connexion with Asia renders this document of special interest.

On the other hand, when we come to documents which, though possibly older than some of those mentioned above, were never generally received, we have to tread with greater caution. Many of them contain mere legends which have no bearing on our

---

[1] For the sake of shortness, however, I have ventured to avoid the awkward periphrasis, and to speak of the "author of the Ignatian Epistles" as "Ignatius;" so too in similar cases of doubtful authenticity.

[2] *Prolegomena* in Gebhardt, Harnack and Zahn's edition.

inquiries: such are, for the most part, the Apocryphal Gospels and Acts; others, as the *Clementines*, were early stigmatised as Ebionite writings, and they can only be used as supplying us with instructive analogies, rather than as a source from which to derive fuller information about the growth of the conception of the Catholic Church.

PART I.

THE CONCEPTION OF THE CHRISTIAN SOCIETY CURRENT IN ASIA AT THE BEGINNING OF SECOND CENTURY.

Part I.

THE CONCEPTION OF THE CHRISTIAN SOCIETY CURRENT IN ASIA AT THE BEGINNING OF SECOND CENTURY.

(1.) *Pre-Christian Conception of the divine Society.*

§ 4. In trying to trace the growth of a conception it is necessary for us to divest ourselves of the various personal associations which cluster round a given word. Strange as it is, the word Church, in the minds of some who call themselves Christians, has come to be a symbol for a hated mixture of superstition, bigotry, and social superiority. To others, especially in France, it has a close association with the injustice of the Ancien Régime, and the tyranny of the Second Empire. To the great majority of men the Church is a religious institution, and as such has little or nothing to do with "secular politics." Unless we can entirely discard the distinctions which have been forced on modern minds by the history of the last eighteen centuries, we cannot arrive at the primary conception of the Church, far less consider its growth. But as we can hardly expect to free ourselves entirely from these associations, we shall perhaps do best to discard the word for the present, and to look at the hope of Israel, and the way in which Jesus fulfilled it; this may prove the true starting-point for considering the growth of the conception of the Christian Institution.

Even thus we may not wholly free ourselves from the danger of anachronism; we habitually read and hear of the Jewish Church, and we are apt to carry with us the modern idea of a religious institution bearing some ill-defined relationship to the political administration of the country; but the Jewish people was a chosen race, the kingdom of David and the empire of Solomon was a divinely directed institution. It is true that there was a terrible decadence in the monarchy at the time of Manasseh, but was there not also a terrible decadence in the priesthood and among the prophets in the time of Jeremiah? The chosen people were unworthy of their calling, but they were chosen as a people, and as a nation; it may be that, in changing the government from the tribal to the regal form, there was a certain accommodation to the passions[1] of the people, but so there was not less certainly in the enactments of the Law with regard to divorce:[2] in spite of these things we may yet say that the kingdom was divinely instituted, just as the Law was divinely framed: the kingdom of David was for generations the type of the kingdom of the Messiah: in it there was one tribe charged with the performance of religious services; in it, too, as time rolled on, there were schools of prophets maintained, as well as untrained individual witnesses for God; but neither the Levites (still less the priests) nor the prophets, were the "Jewish Church;" that was the chosen nation, which was ruled in accordance with a divine tradition, and in the expectation of a divine triumph. It was to the line of the kings, not to the house of Aaron or the schools, that the hopes of those who waited for God in Israel were turned: it was from the line of the kings that their hopes were at length fulfilled.

Rothe[3] has clearly marked the precise period

---

[1] 1 Samuel xii. 17. [2] S. Mark x. 5.
[3] Anfänge der christlichen Kirche, Einl. p. 69. While acknowledging the great assistance received from Rothe in this and the following paragraphs, I must dissent from his theory of the Church, and still more from the distinction between the Church

when the Jewish kingdom ceased to occupy this position, and became a mere political power which had neither inherited a religious tradition nor cherished a divine hope. So soon as the sceptre passed into the hands of Herod, the people ceased to look to their ruler as the centre of their religious hopes: then began the separation between their civil and religious institutions; and in the time of our Lord, there was a Jewish Church in the modern sense, that is, a religious institution with a definite organisation, apart from, and in some sort of antagonism to, the civil government of the country.

But if there was for a time a Jewish Church— a religious body governed by the High Priest and Sanhedrin,—the expectation of the people had not changed. Still did they look for a divine kingdom; only because the nation was oppressed as a nation, only because their civil independence had gone, did their religious life exist in such an abnormal condition: what they longed for was a resuscitation of

and the kingdom of God, which is closely connected with it. From our point of view, the Church is not merely the means for introducing the kingdom of God,—it really is that kingdom, gradually growing in, and extending around, and embracing the kingdoms of this world. Compare more especially § 12 in Rothe.

the old state, when the divine Law should be the rule of life, and the divine worship should be truly celebrated.

§ 5. Various causes have been at work to prevent the ordinary reader from realising, not only the form which the religious hopes of the Jews took, but the passionateness with which these hopes were cherished: partly, because we have memorials of exceptional Jewish life where the hope was practically extinct; partly because, in other cases, the existence of that passionate hope was such an obvious fact that it was taken for granted rather than expressed.

Of the three sects of the Jews, one—and that one which had no little influence on the Asian Churches—had discarded the hope of Israel as a practical religious power. Living in little communities, apart from the life of the nation, seeking by ascetic discipline to attain to a high standard of individual holiness, the Essenes discarded as much of the religious heritage of their nation as conflicted with their own ideal of holiness. In the sacrifices of their nation they would have no part; while the family life, which was so highly esteemed in Israel, appeared positively sinful to them: nor had they scrupled to add on such Oriental observances, however incompatible with the religion of their forefathers, as seemed to them to tend to edification; such, for example, as the worship of the sun. No wonder that in minds which were devoted to their private religious well-being, and whose view was limited by the bounds of their little congregation, the hope of Israel had nearly, if not entirely, died out.[1] But just because they were separatists, and cut off from the great stream of national life, we may neglect them in estimating the real current of feeling that was at work. A sect whose existence is ignored in the Talmud[2] need not be taken into account here, though the picturesqueness of their life attracted the admiring curiosity of contemporaries, and even though their influence in particular churches was undoubted.

If the hope had died out in the desert round the Dead Sea, it had also ceased to flourish in the active metropolis of Jewish culture at Alexandria. In some of the books of the Antiochian period,[3]

---

[1] Keim, *Jesus of Nazara*, i. 385, and note.
[2] Lightfoot, *Colossians*, p. 159.
[3] Drummond, *The Jewish Messiah*, pp. 227-273.

there is little apparent expectation of a personal Messiah, and in later writings it seems strangely wanting. To the Jews of Alexandria their religion commended itself from a certain sentiment of pride in the history of their people, while its theology, so much nobler when contrasted with the mythologies around them, was attractive to their intellects. As a practical religious power, the hope of Israel seems to have lost its hold upon their minds, even though it is possible to find in their writings some help for the delineation of the kingdom for which their brethren at Jerusalem still passionately longed.

Turning, however, to the real centre of national life, we find in the records of the first seventy years of our era sufficient evidence of the fervour of the popular hopes. Again and again the populace broke out in rebellion under some new leader; nor could even the destruction of their city extinguish the ardour which was fanned into flame by Bar Cochab. These were no fitful uprisings due to foreign oppression: they were eager, successive attempts to resuscitate the old state, and to once more establish a divine kingdom upon earth. Much of the New Testament narrative only becomes intelligible when the existence of this passionate hope is kept clearly in view.[1]

We have thus attempted to indicate the vividness of the politico-religious hope of the Jews: it is necessary, however, to delineate its nature more clearly. Perhaps this can be done in no better way than by compressing, with as little alteration as may be, the already brief summary which Mr. Drummond gives[2] of the results of his careful investigation of the subject.

The Jews regarded all time as divided into two great periods answering to this "age" and the "coming age" of the New Testament. These were separated from one another by the occurrence of the judgment. The Messiah is represented as appearing in the first age, not as a superhuman being, but simply as a being endowed with high spiritual gifts. The heathen peoples should assemble themselves to wage war against the chosen people, but should be utterly destroyed. Then the Messiah should reign as a righteous king over Israel. This kingdom is referred to as the kingdom of God: according to

---

[1] Hence the success of the author of *Philochristus* in depicting the environment of Christ's earthly life.
[2] *The Jewish Messiah*, pp. 388 *seq.*

some authorities, the Gentiles should be converted to the true religion. The scattered tribes of Israel should return: the old Jerusalem be replaced by a new and more glorious city. A final and decisive judgment should take place: but the Messiah is nowhere represented as the agent through whom the judgment is to be administered; for on this awful occasion, God Himself would sit on the throne of judgment, and pronounce the verdict against which none might appeal. On the conflicting opinions as to the nature of a resurrection and the final state of the dead we need not dwell; suffice it to say that in the second age, or time after the final judgment, the just would, it was believed, enter into a glorious existence in the immediate presence of God.[1]

Such is the brief outline of the general features of the expectation which was so vividly present to the minds of the contemporaries of our Lord. The Sadducees rejected the hope[2] of the final glorious existence; they limited their ideal to a secular existence, and it is only natural that their less fervent expectation should kindle but little enthu-

---

[1] Drummond, *The Jewish Messiah*, pp. 360-387.
[2] Compare S. Paul's explanation before the Sanhedrin, *Acts* xxiii. 6.

siasm in their hearts. The Pharisees were the real leaders of the popular enthusiasm; and in the popular mind, the militant Messiah overcoming the Gentiles was the centre of the whole hope. We cannot doubt that multitudes who flocked around our Lord followed Him in the expectation that He would unfurl the standard against the Romans: nor can we doubt that the same conception was constantly before the minds of the apostles; when we read of the half-military, half-civil, functions which were discharged by the different orders of dignitaries in the empire of Solomon,[1] we can best understand the ambitions of the twelve, and the unseemly squabbles to which they gave rise: we cannot forget that there were occasions when the language of Jesus would foster their expectations: "When the Son of Man shall sit in the throne of His glory, ye also shall sit upon twelve thrones judging the twelve tribes of Israel."[2] Only in two points, though these were most important ones, did our Lord's teaching[3] come into direct conflict with the current Messianic idea:

---

[1] Ewald, *History of Israel*, iii. 269 *seq.*

[2] *S. Matt.* xix. 28.

[3] In strict accordance with the current Messianic idea, the kingdom of God is throughout regarded as preparatory to the final bliss: Rothe, on the other hand (*Anfänge*, pp. 93, 94),

He represented the progress of the kingdom as peaceful, but to be accomplished through His death; and He represented Himself as occupying God's throne in the final judgment—this is by far the strongest assertion of His divinity which occurs in the Synoptic Gospels. It was not His part to modify the hope, but rather to fulfil it; and to fulfil the hope, not as it ought to have been in some few selected minds, not only as it had existed among the best of the prophets, but as it did exist in the minds of the common men of His own day. It was because they believed that Jesus could and would realise the best they had ever longed for, that the disciples accepted Him as their king: it was because this hope was present in the heart of every true Israelite, that they too met with a ready audience when they went forth into the synagogues of distant towns to proclaim the kingdom of God.

Such being the expectation, we shall gain a still clearer idea of the nature of the Christian Society if we examine the Synoptic Gospels for their account of the kingdom which Jesus founded.

identifies the kingdom of God with the final bliss, and regards the Church as preparing for the kingdom.

(2.) *Genesis of the Christian Conception of the divine Society:* a. *Its nature;* b. *Terms of admission;* c. *Life of Society;* d. *Its organisation.*

§ 6. *a.* There can assuredly be no doubt that Jesus is represented in the Gospels as professing to satisfy this expectation, and coming to establish the kingdom of God. Two of the Synoptics trace a connexion with the royal line of Judah; all tell of S. John the Baptist as preparing for His coming by announcing that the kingdom of God was at hand; while in His first public appearances our Lord seems to have taken up the Baptist's cry in proclaiming His own mission to His countrymen,[1] and in sending forth His disciples to preach.[2] When we read these words in connexion with the Messianic idea, with which the minds of His hearers were saturated, we can have no doubt that the work of Jesus was presented by Him, to their minds, as that of establishing the divine kingdom which they were expecting.

Nor perhaps should we be wrong if we divided the whole teaching of the Synoptics into two parts: the one *evidential,* and establishing the claim of Jesus to be the Messiah, by recounting the power which He

[1] *S. Mark* i. 14. 15. [2] *S. Matt.* x. 7.

possessed of overcoming the devils and men[1] who resisted Him, with not infrequent references to the prophetic descriptions of the Messiah as additional confirmations; the other we may almost call *legislative*, in which He describes, by parables and direct instructions, the nature of the kingdom He had come to found. It is in the last words of S. Matthew's Gospel that we read the grandest assertions of His kingship;[2] it has been through the Christian Consciousness, enlightened by God's Holy Spirit, that the kingdom has been extended and governed.

b. But little is said in the Gospels of the manner of entering the kingdom, and that little did not at all define the nature of the service that was undertaken. Baptism was the common rite of initiation into a new profession: it was only another way of asserting that He had a mission, when our Lord sent out His disciples to baptize:[3] nor was repentance a new demand upon the recipients of the message; if they expected to be the leaders in a divine kingdom they would think themselves unworthy of the splendid office, and feel the need of turning from

---

[1] *S. Matt.* x. 1; xxii. 46.   [2] *S. Matt.* xxviii. 18, 19, 20.
[3] *S. Matt.* xxviii. 19. According to *S. John* iii. 22, 26, and iv. 2, the disciples baptized, as well as preached, before the Resurrection: but on this the Synoptics are silent.

their sins as a preparation for the part they had to play. So far there is no antagonism between the kingdom as expected and the kingdom as proclaimed.

c. It is when we turn to the parables and discourses which describe the kingdom of God, that we first understand the antagonisms which were roused by our Lord's teaching: the kingdom which He described did not fire the enthusiasm of His followers.

He always represented the kingdom as growing and spreading gradually, not as coming with observation.[1] The parables of the Leaven and of the Tares are also sufficiently explicit on this point: the growth of the kingdom was to be slow and gradual like the growth of any natural organism, not a rapid victory over His foes through a sudden manifestation of His power. This it was that chilled the enthusiasm of those who shouted at His triumph,[2] when they thought the hour for the destruction of the Roman garrison had come at last.[3] To this He opposed the idea of a gradual extension. His new teaching first comes out in the Sermon on the Mount, where He tells His disciples that they are the light

---

[1] *S. Luke* xviii. 20.   [2] *S. Luke* xix. 38.
[3] The same chilling disappointment of their hopes had been experienced by those who at an earlier time would have taken Him by force to make Him king. *S. John* vi. 15.

set on a hill for the good of the world, or the salt whose savour will preserve the whole. The same conception of a principle working outwards, and overcoming the evil, runs through the series of parables.

d. At the same time, we have sufficient evidence that this kingdom was not merely to be an internal principle, a power in the hearts of individuals; there is clear evidence that Jesus designed an actual institution which should do this work: He did not merely preach a doctrine, He founded a Society. He had come to fulfil the expectations of His people and establish a kingdom; men were to become members of it by Baptism and repentance; the disciples were to proclaim it, and to be the chief officers in it. These ideas are everywhere present; there are, however, passages which render them clearer, and show us the model which the writers and readers of the Gospels must have believed that Jesus had before Him: it was the conception of a synagogue, the ordinary religious society of this time. Just as there were synagogues of different nationalities at Jerusalem, so was there to be a Christian synagogue which was to be founded by S. Peter,[1] as was done at the day of Pentecost. Or

[1] *S. Matt.* xvi. 18, 19.

the view may have been somewhat wider: it may rather have been that of a group of synagogues presided over by a Sanhedrin, which should have the power of legislating (binding and loosing), and of enrolling new members or excluding unworthy ones from the Christian Society, just as the Sanhedrin ruled over the Jews in all lands. If the passage in *S. Matthew* xviii. 15-20 be taken along with that just referred to, we can have no doubt that they are both to be understood in the same sense,[1] as true of the new Christian Society which was to spring out of the existing system, originated by S. Peter, but with powers inherent in itself. A fault was to be confessed to the Church, and discipline exercised by the Church; the same body in which prayer was to be made, the same body which was to legislate for itself (bind and loose), was to be able to cut off an unworthy member, in all things exercising over itself the same powers—and herein lies the difference from the religious rule that then held sway—as those which the Sanhedrin exercised over the Jewish

---

[1] Abundant authority can be produced for this interpretation of the later passage (xviii. 15-20), *e.g.* Erastus, Vitringa, Olshausen, as quoted by Rothe, *Anfänge*, p. 93. I can see no grounds for giving a wider significance to the much-disputed passage about S. Peter.

people. Nor can we doubt that our Lord foresaw there would soon be ample need for the use of these powers of discipline which He thus conferred; the parables of the Tares and of the Drag-net sufficiently indicate that many of the members of the kingdom would be unworthy of their calling, like lamps which had gone out, or salt that had lost its savour.

A kingdom which was thus grafted on to the synagogue system, and which was to grow so unostentatiously, was not of a kind to arouse enthusiasm: to many it did not seem worth struggling for: no personal advantage, but a devoted personal loyalty to the king, was the motive which was to work for its realisation. A devotion to Him as He revealed Himself upon earth, a faith in Him as present with His Church even when He ascended, this was the power which was to remove mountains, and in the might of which His people were to conquer. It was thus that faith was set forth as the one essential for service in this kingdom, faith in Him as being what He professed, and as having the powers which He assumed, and which were chiefly shown forth in the Resurrection and also in the Ascension.

Such was the kingdom as depicted in the Synoptic

Gospels—a true kingdom, which, beginning as a mere offshoot of the synagogue, was to grow till it became a world-wide realm. A few words may indicate the relation which it was to have to the existing civil societies. There was to be no open antagonism;[1] it was not of this world, and there was to be no fighting; nor was there to be any repudiation of lawful authority, even if it was exercised by bad men.[2] On the other hand, this passive obedience is not a cringing submission: our Lord stood upon His rights as a Jewish citizen in repudiating the grossly illegal trial to which He was subjected;[3] but this refusal to obey lawless authority does not conflict with the injunction to abide by the law of the land. In the time of Jesus it was still possible to obey the civil rulers from a religious motive; in rendering what was Cæsar's to Cæsar, men were also rendering what was God's to God. It was from the side of the civil rulers, not from that of the Church, that the active struggle between Christ's kingdom and the secular realms commenced.

We have thus tried to delineate the primary idea

---

[1] *S. Matt.* xxvi. 52. See also *S. John* xviii. 36.
[2] *S. Matt.* xxiii. 3.
[3] The illegal character of the trial is clearly shown by Mr. Taylor Innes—*Contemporary Review*, xxx. 393 *seq.*

of the Church as it appears in the Synoptic Gospels: it was to be a kingdom in this world, but not of it, an organised society which was ultimately to become a world-wide rule, but to begin as a mere synagogue at Jerusalem, with self-regulating powers. We have not said that this was the full conception of the Church in the mind of our Lord Himself, but we do say that this was the conception of the Church to which the writers of the Synoptic Gospels had attained, and which had in it the germ of all that was subsequently revealed and realised.

§ 7. It will be convenient to take next in order the *Acts of the Apostles*, and to consider the picture of the Christian Society which is there presented to us, because, though certainly later in date than several of the writings we shall discuss, it gives us a harmonious representation of the Christian life, and this representation afterwards received general assent.[1] Whether this harmony was historically true, or merely portrayed by a mediating writer, we need not stop to inquire, though we shall have a word to say on this below (§ 30). What concerns us is that we have here a representation of the first

[1] The rejection of this book by the Marcionites hardly affects the unanimity of the Christian Church on this matter.

years of the Christian Society which was alike accepted as satisfactory in communities which claimed to follow the traditions of S. Peter, or S. Paul, or S. John; we can then notice more briefly the special details which may be added from a study of the writings ascribed to each of these leaders.

a. The opening chapter at once connects the story of the doings of the apostles with the hope of Israel. It is assumed that the Messiah has come, the only question which the disciples ask (i. 6) is as to the time of the fulfilment of the promise. And on the day of Pentecost S. Peter declares to the multitude that the Messiah had indeed come, and thus proclaims His kingdom. The whole plan of his discourse is an endeavour to prove that in Jesus Christ the hope of Israel was fulfilled, and that therefore the kingdom had come: then it was, that those who gladly received his word were added to the Church.

b. The means of admission to the kingdom were as before,—Repentance, with its outward symbol of Baptism; but now we get the demand for allegiance to this king—they were to be baptized in the name of the Lord Jesus, and thus to profess their willingness to be His faithful soldiers and servants to their lives' end. This was the profession of allegiance which was made when first the gospel was extended beyond the bounds of the sacred city (*Acts* viii. 12, 37). The controversy as to the terms on which the Gentiles should be admitted need not detain us, as we know how it was settled. No further profession, no further rite, was required from them than from the Jews, only a care for the failings of others was enjoined upon them by the Council of Jerusalem.

c. It is when we examine the account which is given of the teaching of the apostles about the nature of the kingdom and of the king, that we find how far they had advanced from the level on which they stood while they were themselves being taught by the Master. The power of their king, as evidenced by that resurrection of which they were witnesses, and as confirmed by their expectations that He would be the Judge of the world, are constantly set forth. These were the two points in which their faith in their Master went beyond the current expectation in regard to the Messiah, and these were the points on which they chiefly insisted; and though they still preached the kingdom of God, they had learned to realise that it was a slowly developing, purifying power, not a force that would suddenly display itself at a given time.

d. While this was the strain of their doctrine, the duties of practical piety were undertaken on a large scale; the voluntary surrender of private property, and the distribution for the maintenance of the poor, were as ordinary incidents of the life of the Church as their daily prayer in the Temple or breaking of bread in their common gatherings. We find, too, that the Christian Society suffered from the presence of unworthy members like Ananias and Simon Magus, and that it assumed the powers of discipline which had been conferred upon it. At the Council of Jerusalem we find the Church "loosing" what the Mosaic Law had "bound," in absolving the Gentiles from many of the ancient requirements; in an earlier day, the Church assumed the power of the keys, in reviewing (and confirming) the admission of Gentile members which had been made by S. Peter (*Acts* xi. 1, 18). The apostles did not merely proclaim a doctrine, they organised the Society which Jesus had founded.

Evidences of the beginnings of this organisation are to be found in the formation of the diaconate; we do not care to argue, against Ritschl,[1] that this was a mere experiment which was temporarily tried

---

[1] *Entstehung der christlichen Kirche*, 2te Aufl. p. 355.

to meet a special emergency; that may have been so, at least the success of the experiment led to the adoption of the same means for meeting the emergency elsewhere; the diaconate of Jerusalem was a type of the order in the Church.

Of greater interest are the hints which are dropped of the method of governing the whole body of Christians; Jerusalem was the centre of Christian life, as it was of Jewish; to that Church the Christians looked for supreme earthly guidance, as the Jews did to the Sanhedrin; from it embassies went out to distant Churches (*Acts* xi. 22; xv. 27), and letters were addressed. The whole organisation was directed from one centre, and at this centre one man was chief. There was no parallel to the position which is accorded to James, the brother of our Lord; and if, as we believe, he was not one of the twelve,[1] his position is all the more striking. We find him specially singled out in xii. 17, and he occupies a decisive position in the first Council (xv. 13). If we compare with this the language of S. Paul in the *Epistle to the Galatians*,[2] we cannot resist the conclusion that James the Just was in a very emphatic sense head of the Church at Jeru-

[1] Lightfoot, *Galatians*, p. 261. [2] *Gal.* ii. 12.

salem, just as the Church at Jerusalem was the recognised authority for the Christians in many other towns, if not in all. We might compare his position to that of the High Priest for the year, but his seems to have been a permanent office, and it is at least a most probable hypothesis if we say that he, the blood-relation of our Lord, of the royal lineage, was held to be the most suitable viceregent, who should act for Him, and in His stead be chief among the officers of God's kingdom upon earth during an absence that they believed would be brief. Presbyters there were in Jerusalem (*Acts* xv. 23), and in every city (xiv. 23), but there was at the time of S. Paul's second missionary journey only one chief pastor, one vice-regent,[1] of the whole Church on earth.

The later chapters of the *Acts*, which tell us of the founding of the Church in Gentile cities, need not detain us; we have always the same course pursued: the church emanates from the synagogue, presbyters are ordained, and there is at least an informal connexion kept up by some of them,

---

[1] While by no means satisfied with this term, I cannot think of another that implies so clearly the ruling of a *kingdom*, and that is therefore so appropriate to this earliest phase of the Christian Society.

though not perhaps by the Churches of Asia, with that Jerusalem which was the mother of them all.

But there are not a few interesting details with regard to the attitude which was assumed towards existing governments by the leaders in the new kingdom. That attitude was never aggressive, but neither was it one of cringing submission. As our Lord had stood upon His Jewish rights, so SS. Peter and John could refuse to bend before an arbitrary exercise of capricious power (*Acts* iv. 3, 16-21), or S. Paul could scorn, as a Roman citizen, to submit to unworthy indignities. In this, as in every other respect, we have a more detailed delineation of the kingdom than occurs in the Synoptic Gospels, but not one of the lines which were there sketched has to be altered. Still is the kingdom set forth as fulfilling the ancient expectations; still are the old terms of admission enforced, with the sole addition of a profession of that loyalty to the king without which there could be no true service; the organisation is developed on precisely the lines which our Lord had suggested, and the position which is taken towards the outside world was exactly that which was maintained by Him.

§ 8. The *Epistle of S. James* bears on its face the fact that it is a letter on practical religion addressed to a specially Jewish audience: it is only incidentally that we can gather information regarding the author's idea of the Christian Society: he makes but one explicit mention of the kingdom (ii. 5), and only hints that its "heirs" are rich in faith: no other qualification for participation is suggested: nor is any allusion made to the events of the Gospel story, as, *e.g.* to the resurrection which justified their faith in the Lord Jesus: we find, however, a mention of the other distinctively Christian doctrine that the Lord would come to be the judge (v. 8_x 9).

The author's great desire is to lay down directions for the life of the members of the kingdom: such directions he describes as a Law, but it is a law of liberty, laid down by the Christian consciousness, when enlightened by the God who gives wisdom, and disciplined by self-denial. The sense, too, that loyalty to the king was incompatible with disrespect to the persons of His poor servants, is a further illustration of the fact that the laws of the kingdom are not external ordinances, but have their source in an internal principle.

We get some few new hints as to the practice of

the early Church: anointing with oil by the presbyters is spoken of as a familiar use. The numerous evils of the time demanded the exercise of discipline, and we find a call to confess their sins to one another, and a suggestion of the priesthood of all Christians in the exhortation to intercessory prayer for absolution (v. 16).

While, then, there is in this epistle no real addition to the delineation of the Church, there is nothing at variance with the picture already drawn.

§ 9. Though the *Apocalypse* presents us with some important modifications of the conception of the kingdom of God, it still adheres firmly to its main outlines. It opens (i. 5, 7) with a reference to the two fundamental beliefs about the person of the king, His triumph over death, and His future coming to judge the earth: it ends with a description of the New Jerusalem which should appear in the second age: but the realm of the blessed is still thought of as a kingdom: there is the throne of God and of the Lamb (xxii. 1, 3, 5), but the writer saw no temple therein (xxi. 22). The main idea is still the same, and its close connexion with the visions of Ezekiel and Daniel brings this clearly into view.

There is however a subsidiary thought which is very noticeable: the new kingdom is a kingdom of priests (i. 6, v. 10, xx. 6). In this there is no departure from the Israelite tradition: the phrase was already familiar to the readers of *Exodus* (xix. 6) and *Isaiah* (lxi. 6), but it was not an idea which had taken hold of the minds of the first disciples, while they still thronged the temple services that were performed by the old priesthood.

With this new conception of the Christian Society as a body of priests, is connected a new view of the nature and work of Jesus: He is no longer merely a king, He is the means of consecrating His people for the priestly office. If we turn to the account in *Leviticus*, viii. 1-32, of the consecrating of Aaron and his sons, we get some sort of help in understanding the view which now comes into prominence. Christ is the sacrifice by which the people are redeemed: it is with His blood that they are washed (*Lev.* viii. 24), and thus it is that they become priests of God, through the Lamb that was slain.

This preliminary investigation would be carried beyond all reasonable limits if we attempted to trace the idea of the Christian Society through all the canonical writings; it is, however, interesting to notice that the maintenance of this—which is the subsidiary view in the *Apocalypse*—is the main thesis of the *Epistle to the Hebrews*. There, the kingdom is barely mentioned (xii. 28): the person of Jesus is magnified, not as a divine king, but as a divine priest, who, just because He was so wholly above the Jewish priesthood, and because His sacrifice was so different from theirs, could take away their sins and make them also priests who should offer spiritual sacrifices to God (xiii. 21, 15; x. 12, 22).

There is one other interesting modification of the view of the kingdom, in the *Apocalypse:* it is set now in clear antagonism to the larger portion of the Jewish people; the kingdom had been announced as the fulfilment of their hopes; it had fulfilled their highest hopes, yet some who had been born to inherit the expectation had held aloof from the Christian Society in which the hope was realised; but such were no true Jews, they were the synagogue of Satan (ii. 9, iii. 9). The true Israel of God was to be found in the Church; the others, Jews though they might be by blood, had cut themselves off from the blessings of the covenant; and thus the traditions of the people of God, like the hopes of the people of God, belonged truly to the Christian, and not by any means to the Jews who rejected the Messiah that had come. In this respect also the *Epistle to the Hebrews* offers an instructive analogy, not in any repudiation of the unbelieving Jew, but by the boldness with which it claims the Jewish tradition as the heritage of the Christians.

In a book of this kind we cannot expect to get a clear picture of the details of Church life; there are, however, some hints in regard to organisation which must not be neglected. The leading position of Jerusalem is not forgotten; it is still "the beloved city" (*Rev.* xx. 9); its glory will be greater than was revealed; but at the time its supremacy seems to have fallen into abeyance, if indeed it had ever been formally acknowledged in Asia, and divine messages are given from the Lord directly to Civic Churches;[1] the supremacy of the Jerusalem Church and the position of its viceregal bishop are practically ignored in the opening chapters; and thus we have the idea of Civic Churches as separate, self-regulating communities, not as mere members of one body which was ruled from Jerusalem. This at least seems no unfair deduction from the tone in

---

[1] This phrase will be justified by the delineation of the actual growth of the Church below, §§ 23 and 28.

which each Christian community is addressed: on the other hand, we cannot feel that when a writer whose mind is teeming with the phraseology of *Ezekiel* and *Daniel* writes of an angel, he can be thinking of anything but a heavenly power, not an earthly officer; the passage does not give us any clear idea of the means by which the administration of each Civic Church was to be carried on.

§ 10. The *First Epistle of S. Peter* is a most beautiful exhortation to the Asian and other Churches, which is full of allusions to the conceptions of the Christian Society which have already been delineated; it contains them all, but in many respects it rises above them, and indeed there is a perfect torrent of mixed metaphor in which the author strives to convey his conception of the gloriousness of the Christian Society. Such phrases as "royal priesthood," the "holy nation" who are to show forth the praises of God, and the idea of redemption through the blood of Christ, need not detain us; with these we are already familiar; there are, however, two or three new phrases which merit our attention. We have the Christian Society figured as a flock fed by the Shepherd and Bishop of our souls (ii. 25), and again as the flocks committed to the charge of the elders (v. 1 and 2). Again there is the analogy between the wanderings and sufferings of the Israelites on their way to Canaan, and the pilgrimage of these "strangers" on their way to their inheritance (ii. 11). But the most striking image is that of the living temple founded on Jesus Christ (ii. 4, 5, 6). The Church is no longer figured as a body of men with a king, or as a body of priests with one High Priest who had consecrated them by His own sacrifice,[1]—there is an organic union between the foundation and the building. A somewhat similar figure had been used by our Lord,[2] but the new interpretation which S. Peter here gives brings out the difference that underlies the resemblance: S. Peter was the first stone laid, our Lord was the eternal basis of the whole. It is the organic union between Christ and the Church which is brought out in this figure of the temple, and which marks an advance upon the writings we have already considered; over and over again is the idea reiterated, with special reference to the communion of the Christians in the sufferings of Christ (ii. 20, 21; iv. 1, 2, 13).

[1] Nor, as also in the *Epistle to the Hebrews*, as a household, where each slave owes obedience to the heir, iii. 6.
[2] *S. Matt.* xvi. 15.

With this infinitely grander conception of the nature of the Christian Society as a true union with Christ, we find a nobler conception of the admission into the body: the admission into that Church is a true regeneration (i. 3), of which Baptism is the outward sign (iii. 21); not that this regenerated Society thus united to Christ was perfect: malice and guile and hypocrisy and fleshly lusts—these were not wholly things of the past; nor was the administration of the Church all that could be wished,—the younger members were unruly, and the presbyters were not free from reproach (v. 2, 5). So far as any light is thrown on Church organisation, the writer's idea of it does not differ from that in the *Apocalypse*,—it presents us with the view of independent Civic Churches, each ruled by their own presbyters, though it adds this important feature, that they at the same time kept up communication with one another.

§ 11. If in turning to the writings of S. Paul we limit our attention to the three Asian epistles, this is not because their authenticity is less unquestioned than the rest, but because they are witnesses of Asian Christianity; for we do not so much want to give a complete picture of S. Paul's teaching, as to notice what was effective teaching in that region: their evidence is amply sufficient. We may say at once that these writings show no advance on the conception of the Christian Society that has been already drawn, but they concentrate the attention on one point alone—the organic union between Christ and the Church. The reference to the relation of husband and wife is a new attempt to portray this union (*Eph.* v. 23); but the apostle's favourite image deserves special attention,—the Church is the body of which Christ is the head. Nothing can more fitly illustrate the organic union than this, and therefore on this he specially dwells, both as illustrating the relations of the body to the head and of the members to one another (*Col.* i. 18; *Eph.* i. 23). In this glorious conception of the body of Christians as partaking in the life of Christ Himself, dying with Him, and rising with Him, all the feebler representations of the Church are lost. We still hear of the kingdom (*Eph.* i. 21), and of the inheritance of the covenant (ii. 12), and of the consecrated priests (*Col.* i. 21-22), but all is lost in the thought of the body of Christ, one with Him, buried with Him, risen with Him, baptized into Him, guided by His Spirit, heirs of His glory.

It seems strange to turn from this noble view of the Church, to read of anger, wrath, malice, blasphemy, which were still found in the members of Christ; and of the administration which might reform these things we get little hint. Nothing is said of the Jerusalem authorities, nothing of the presbyters. We do, however, find one individual named as if responsible[1] for the whole (*Philem.* 2; *Col.* iv. 17) good order of the community.

It is when we turn back from the consideration of the wonderful fervour with which S. Paul speaks of the body of Christ to the primary idea of the kingdom of God which appears in the Synoptics and the *Acts*, that we find how wonderfully the conception has developed,—when we contrast the appeal which is made to the Colossian Church with that which was uttered by S. Peter at Pentecost. Yet the steps in the development are clear; there is no sudden break: the links of the chain are all there. The *Acts* only carries out the ideas of the Synoptics; S. James only insists on the same idea with a hint, which the *Apocalypse* amplifies, which by S. Peter is carried one step further, and finds its noblest

---

[1] Possibly, however, he is responsible as apostle for the teaching, not as ruler for the order of the Church: *vide sub.* p. 123.

expression from S. Paul. We find great differences in the manner in which the institution is represented by S. James, in the *Hebrews*, by S. Paul; but there is one fundamental faith common to them all, one Lord, one baptism, one body, and one Spirit. There are no struggles of opposing tendencies; there are different—vague, and again fuller—conceptions of the life that was working in all.

§ 12. Still the change was a startling one: this doctrine, so elevated and so free, towering so far above the Messianic expectation of the Jews, was it after all the doctrine of Jesus? Might it not be a duty to oppose it in the name of Christ?[1] Was it a legitimate interpretation of the work of the one Lord? or did it not conflict with His habits, as far as it went beyond His teaching as worded in the written accounts of His life?—These were the questionings[2] which met their answer in the *Gospel of S. John.*

S. Paul never repudiates the old idea of the covenant and the kingdom of God; it was even a

---

[1] 1 *Corinthians* i. 13.

[2] We do not say that these questions gave the motive to this book, but only analyse it for the sake of showing how completely it offers an answer to them.

charge against him that he did not do so: he carries it up with him, just as this Gospel shows us Jesus ever in contact with the disciples' low ideas of His kingdom, and ever trying to raise them to the truer level. It is often said that this Gospel was written to supply a more complete narrative than that of the Synoptics, by giving us a number of incidents which were omitted. But this is not what the Gospel professes to do; it indignantly repudiates the idea of giving a complete account of the incidents of our Lord's life, or a full report of His teaching (xx. 30, xxi. 25); it professes to bring into prominence those sides of Christ's life which were not understood at first,[1] and which, just because they were not understood till the fuller conception of the Christian Society had dawned on the minds of men through the inspiration of the Holy Spirit, could not be recorded in the earliest writings.[2] A very hasty survey will sufficiently show how, both in the incidents and discourses, we find a picture of the earthly life of Christ as Head of the Church, not merely as the expected king of Israel.

[1] S. John vii. 39, xii. 16.
[2] The closest parallel, but still at an infinite distance, to the later conception of our Lord's relation to the Church is in S. Matt. xxv. 40.

The conversations with Nathanael and with the woman of Samaria furnish cases in point; both of them shared the Messianic expectation, but to both He speaks of a spiritual reality which would hardly have satisfied their hopes,—to Nathanael of Himself as the means of ever-continued communication between God and man; to the woman, of a spiritual worship which transcended all the religious jealousies of the day. So, too, to Nicodemus he does not speak of repentance as the condition of entering the kingdom; He had hoped that a master in Israel might rise above the gross popular conception to grasp the truth that regeneration was the condition of membership; but it was altogether beyond him.

So too in regard to the miracles: in the Synoptics they are the credentials of an earthly mission; in *S. John* they are the evidences of a living spiritual power. The quickening power which was shown in the case of the paralytic (chap. v.) is the symbol of the quickening power which will raise the dead to life; the miraculous feeding of the multitude is a symbol of the way in which He still feeds those who partake of His Body and Blood (chap. vi.). The water poured out on the last day of the feast was a symbol of the Spirit which His followers should receive.

Another striking difference lies in the tone in which the Jewish leaders are spoken of. In the Synoptics they are regarded as blind, and hardened like those who rejected the prophets through culpable ignorance; here they are open and avowed enemies—the synagogue of Satan; in none of the New Testament writings is there such bitterness shown towards the "Jews," who not only sought to catch Him in his talk, but sedulously plotted against Him. These few suggestions may suffice to show how in this last Gospel the misunderstood side of the life of Christ is brought into prominence; He is Himself represented as giving the exalted teaching for which at the end of the first century the minds of Christian men were prepared; the regal aspect of His work, as king of Israel, is never repudiated, but it is exalted to its true dignity.

There is only one wholly new illustration of this intimate union between Christ and the Church: in his *First Epistle to the Corinthians* S. Paul had spoken of Christ as being the Paschal Lamb; but such language was only allegorical, as long as the feast was actually kept up at Jerusalem. It was only when that had ceased, that men came to feel that Jesus was the true passover, the true God-given means, by participation in which men were delivered from bondage.[1] The most striking difference between the Synoptic and the Fourth Gospels has a close connexion with this new view, for the day which is given as the date of the crucifixion is strangely harmonious with the thought of Christ as being the true Paschal Lamb. But of that we shall have to say more when we come to consider the Quarto-deciman controversy (§ 38).

§ 13. We have tried to present the idea of the Christian Society which was current in the Asian Churches at the end of the first century; we have believed that this could be most fairly done by trying to present that conception in its genesis as it can be traced in the generally received writings.

We have a picture of a Society existing in the world, but not of it; which, like a kingdom, shall spread until it embraces and overcomes all existing societies; which, like a flock, is tended by Christ Himself; which, as a nation, inherits the traditions and shows the hopes of the people of God; which, like a priesthood, consists of consecrated members offering services to God; which, as a temple, is built

---

[1] Baur, *First Three Centuries*, i. 160.

upon the foundation of Jesus Christ; which is, indeed, the body of the Lord.

We find that admission to that kingdom is obtained not merely now by repentance from actual sin, but by that regeneration of which Baptism is the outward sign; we find that the life of the citizens lies in that faith by which they are not only devoted to their king, or enthusiastic for their traditions and hopes for the Unseen, but actual partakers in the life of Christ; and that this life found its fitting expression in sacrifices of praise and thanksgiving, and in deeds of piety: we find that many of the members of Christ failed terribly to live up to this profession, or to realise the life of Christ in their own sphere, and that teaching and discipline, fasting and prayer, were provided as the means of restoring the fallen.

So far we have no divergence: but when we come to speak of the organisation that is hinted at, we find that there are two conflicting views. In the writings relating to the earlier period of the Society, the kingdom is described as ruled from Jerusalem by James and the presbyters who surrounded him: his was a sort of viceregal position, in the temporary absence of the king; the distant Churches appealed to him for guidance, and took their directions from his messengers.

On the other hand, in the *Apocalypse* the supremacy of Jerusalem is ignored, and a message from the king is sent through another channel. The *Epistle of S. Peter* seems to imply, though not so distinctly, the independence of the Church in each city, as if possessing powers of self-government, while it bears witness to the inter-communication between these various Churches. As to the internal administration we can learn little: of presbyters we hear, but the authority seems to lie in the Church, and not by any means in its officers.

How far do subsequent writings, which can be fairly said to represent Asian Christianity, bear witness to the maintenance and effectiveness of this conception of the Church on earth?

(3.) *Current Conception as maintained in sub-apostolical writings.*

a. *Nature of the Christian Society.*

§ 14. The conception of the nature of the Church which we have found above received little further development; but we have abundant evidence of its living power, for the minds of sub-apostolical writers, in the new illustrations which are put forward in different treatises. Many of the old ones are repeated. The kingdom of God is still spoken of,[1] and the idea of an army[2] is hardly very different from that of a militant kingdom or a body of soldiers equipped with the armour of God (*Eph.* vi.). The body and its members occurs again,[3] but the most popular conception is one that had only been hinted at before: the Church consists of the regenerate, therefore it is a new creation,—the most perfect and last appearing of the works of God, and yet one which was designed from the first, and for which all the rest were but a preparation. These ideas are worked out most fully in the *Pastor of Hermas*,[4] especially in the earlier visions: they are rendered clearer by the figure of the Church as an old woman (not as the Bride of the *Apocalypse* and of *Colossians*): but we find hints of the same thought in the *Epistle of S. Barnabas*,[5] and in one of the fragments of Papias.[6]

Another favourite image in the *Pastor* is that of

---

[1] *S. Clement to the Corinthians*, i. 50, ii. 12.
[2] *Ibid.* i. 37; see Appendix, p. 222.
[3] *Ibid.* i. 37, 46.   [4] *Vis.* i. 3.   *Vis.* ii. 4.
[5] *Ep. Barn.* vi.   [6] Routh, *Rel. Sac.* i. 15.

a tower;[1] it differs from the Petrine illustration of the temple, inasmuch as it views the Church rather as a witness to the world than as a priesthood serving God: but the same belief in the organic unity between Christ and His people is preserved. The longest of the *Visions* and the longest of the *Similitudes* are entirely occupied with working out this specially popular conception of the Church: and one statement in this connexion is interesting, where the Church is spoken of as renewing the spirit,[2] and as the agency through which teaching came.[3]

The position of Justin Martyr, as an apologist, led him to expound the views already current, rather than to attempt to put them in a clearer light for the edification of the Church. In the *First Apology* (10) we find the assertion of the Christian's fellowship with God; and the nature of the kingdom is clearly delineated (11). As against Trypho, he claims that Christians are the true heirs of the covenant—the true spiritual Israel (11). Of these, too, it is true that their filthy garments have been taken away, so that they are purified to be the true high-priestly race of God (115, 116). And if we do not find any distinct assertion of the organic union

[1] *Vide sub.* p. 79 and Appendix, p. 234.
[2] *Vis.* iii. 8.   [3] *Vis.* iv. 1.

between Christ and the Church, we need not be surprised that a conception which rose so entirely above the views of heathen, and even of Jews, was not introduced either into the *Apology* or the *Dialogues*.

§ 15. If the sub-apostolical view of the nature of the Church is thus identical with that of the Pauline and Petrine epistles, we need not be surprised that the same apostolic view of Baptism is maintained. The more we feel the greatness of the privileges into which we are admitted in becoming members of Christ's visible Church, the more shall we be likely to value the rite in which that membership is conferred.[1] Hermas represents the tower as built upon the waters, and refers to the rite many times;[2] and while faith is never undervalued (*Sim.* ix. 12), we find that he held the Catholic doctrine that those children who, brought to the font in faith, are baptized in faith and nurtured among the faithful, are partakers of the kingdom of God (*Sim.* ix. 29). The question which interests the writer most is in regard to sin after Baptism, but to discuss that

---

[1] The implied undervaluing of the rite in the *Epistle of S. Barnabas* need not detain us here. *Vide sub.* p. 103.

[2] *Sim.* ix. 16; *Mand.* iv. 3; *Vis.* iii. 2.

question here would be to anticipate our treatment of a later controversy.

On this, as on many other similar points, Justin Martyr is very clear: if his philosophy of religion is wholly inadequate, his account of Christian doings is invaluable. His description of the performance of the rite, his explanation of its meaning, and assertion of its efficacy in the *First Apology* (61) are most interesting:[1] equally decisive are the two passages in the *Dialogues* where the purifying baptism is contrasted with the broken cisterns of the Jews (14), and where Noah is spoken of as a type of the Christ who has regenerated us (138).

§ 16. Many interesting questions come into prominence as soon as we consider the life of the Christian Society: we find many hints, but not the complete picture we might expect, in the *Pastor of Hermas*. There is here little reference to the devotional life, and none to common worship: the difficulties which the writer feels are those of subduing the lusts of the flesh, and thus practising God's commandments; and there is a singular silence on the means by which personal graces may be strengthened[2]

---

[1] See Appendix, p. 244.
[2] *Mand.* xii. 3, 4, 6. See, however, below, p. 179 note.

or communicated at first. The virtue on which stress is chiefly laid is that of charity to the poor: and from the frequent recurrence to the same subject, and from the denunciation of the rich as rounded stones, who could not be used in building the tower, we can gather that, in the Roman Church of this period, there were many rich members, and that the duties of benevolence were somewhat neglected. The parable of the vine and elm, where one by its strength supports the other, so that it can bear fruit in prayer and devotion (*Sim.* ii.), gives us a clear view of his ideas on this subject.

For a fuller picture of Christian life we are indebted to the writings of Justin Martyr, where we read how, by their civil obedience (*First Apology*, 17), by their continence (29), and by their deeds of piety to one another, the Christians carried out the commands of their Master (15). It is indeed almost the main argument of the *First Apology*. But this is a matter of common repute on which it is unnecessary to dwell: the ample evidence of the same which could be drawn from sub-apostolical writers need not detain us.

A more careful consideration must be given to the prevalent idea of the worship of the Church: it is from his references to this subject that we see that Justin did not fall below the Pauline conception, but believed that the Christian was a real partaker in the life of Christ, and that the Eucharist was the means by which he might thus partake[1] (*First Apol.* 65, 66). Most interesting in this respect, though it occurs in another connexion,[2] are the remarks on the blood of Christ in the *Dialogue* (54). But there is another aspect of Christian worship; it is not only the opportunity of receiving strength from God, it is the opportunity of sacrifice—of devoting ourselves to God. The faithful are priests, offering spiritual sacrifices; and thus, while Justin indignantly repudiates the supposition that God needs anything at our hands (*First Apology*, 10), he still holds that the Eucharist is a sacrifice of praise and thanksgiving, and that in offering the bread of the Eucharist and the cup of the Eucharist to God we glorify His name, at least as truly as was done by the leper who offered the oblation of fine flour (*Dialogue* 41). That this aspect of the Eucharist should not be put forward in an apology addressed to heathens, whose sacrifices were not—as in the case

---

[1] See Appendix, p. 246.
[2] The blood which washes the Christian priesthood.

of the Jews—a help, but a hindrance to the comprehension of it, need not surprise us. This passage from the *Dialogue* is most interesting, though not isolated evidence, that the sacrificial aspect of the Eucharist was explicitly maintained at that time, if any such evidence were needed; though there can of course be no doubt that those who recognised so clearly the priesthood of all Christians felt that all their worship, as all their life, was a sacrifice to God: and if a martyrdom was a special sacrifice of a life,[1] so was the highest act of Christian worship a commemoration of the one sacrifice for sin. The language of Irenæus, and also the phraseology of the shorter Greek recension of Ignatius, are other expressions of the same view.

In Justin also we find an account of the other objects of the Christian gatherings: there was a weekly meeting on Sundays for the reading of the writings of the apostles and prophets, after which instruction and exhortation were given by the president. The celebration of the Holy Communion is said to follow, and an opportunity is given for the rich and well-to-do to supply the needs of the poor—there was, in fact, a weekly offertory.

[1] *Martyrdom of Polycarp*, 14; see Appendix, p. 259.

This complete picture is hardly to be amplified by any of the scattered hints which occur in other writings; we may indeed contrast the state of things here delineated with the unruliness of which S. Paul had heard in the Corinthian Church. We may just call attention, however, to a very decided reference to the teaching of the apostolic doctrine, but one that is possibly interpolated, in a chapter in the *Epistle to Diognetus* (11), where we feel how much the author regarded the Church as the true centre of religious life. There seems too to be a suggestion of the weekly offertory in the *First Epistle of S. Clement* (40), though perhaps we may more rightly find in "the offerings" which are to be regularly presented, a reference to the Eucharist.[1] An interesting hint in regard to the administration of the common fund is to be found in the *Epistle of Ignatius to Polycarp* (Syriac), 4. Here we read of the widows, and the charge which the bishop has over them; while the use of the common funds for purchasing the freedom of slaves is deprecated. The whole recalls to one's mind the description of the voluntary communism of the Jerusalem Church: that that attempt was systematically carried out for

[1] Drake, *Priesthood and Sacrifice*, p. 11 seq.

any length of time we cannot suppose: certainly we feel that in the time of Ignatius and Justin the communistic principle occupies a very minor place in Christian life.

§ 17. We have so far found the sub-apostolical writings maintaining a complete accord with the canonical ones in regard to the idea of the Christian Society; but a difficulty now presents itself, for we must remember that in the canonical writings there are two different systems of organisation sketched out: on the one hand, that which we have described as the viceregal government of James at Jerusalem, while we have also language which implies the local self-government of the Civic Churches in Asia. In the sub-apostolical writings both of these systems are again implied.

The first of these demands but little consideration at our hands, as this view of the government of the Church is not found in writings that originated in, though it does occur in some addressed to, Asian Churches. In the short recension of the *Epistle of Ignatius to the Trallians*,[1] we find an explicit statement of this view; the bishop is to be thought of as

[1] See Appendix, p. 230.

in the place of God, and the presbytery are his council, a sort of Sanhedrin, to be honoured like the apostles (4), while the deacons have no place in ruling, but are to be esteemed like that Jesus who sojourned with His apostles as one who served. There is a hint of the same opinion in the *Epistle to the Magnesians* (6), where the bishop is spoken of as presiding in the place of God; and similar language occurs in the *Epistle to the Smyrnæans* (8). This comparison seems unintelligible—one might say blasphemous—unless we keep in view the conception of the Church as a kingdom, and of the first bishop of Jerusalem as ruling that kingdom, as vice-regent for the true king, and as, therefore, in a sense the representative of God. A similar train of thought occurs in the *Clementines;* the openings of the epistles of SS. Clement and Peter to James may be adduced in point, as may also the language in III. 60, 62, 66, 70;—the bishop "sitting in the chair of Christ;" "to follow some one as leader, honouring him as the image of God;" "honour therefore the throne of Christ." This view is not consistently maintained, for the accounts of the founding of bishoprics in Sidon, Tripolis, etc., seem to conflict with it; while the position given to S. James in the opening epistle is inconsistent with that which S. Peter has in the main body in the homilies; still we may here recognise a reminiscence of the form of Church government which is described in the earlier chapters of the *Acts*.

§ 18. Of much greater interest, in regard to the province in which we are specially concerned, are the hints which we get as to the other conception of Church government: that of the self-regulation of the Church in each city.

First of all we may notice, that it is the Church which regulates itself; we cannot but suppose that just as the whole body is thought of as a kingdom of priests, so does that body regulate itself through its officers; it is not represented to us as governed by them as lords over God's heritage, but as self-regulated through them. This is clearly brought out in the *First Epistle of S. Clement;* the supreme authority in the Corinthian Church lay with the "multitude" there (54): the consent of the whole Church is required for the setting apart of men to fill any office[1] (44), and the very argument, against dismissing the worthy presbyters whose case was

[1] See Appendix, p. 228.

under consideration, implies that the body of faithful men possessed this power, though it would be most wicked to exercise it at that time (47). The *Epistle of Polycarp* seems to show that this power had been rightly exercised by the Church in Philippi against an unworthy presbyter named Valens (11).

If the Church was thus supreme over itself in matters of discipline, it was equally clear that the officer was not appointed to conduct divine service, but to be the agency through which the Church conducted her common worship. So, for example, in Justin's description of Christian worship, he is careful to note the consensus of the whole assembly in the prayers and thanksgivings of the president [1] (*First Apology*, 65, 67).

We saw that in the *Apocalypse* and later epistles, the civic, self-disciplining Churches are represented as being in constant communication with one another. The *Epistle of S. Clement* (i. 9), the *Epistle of S. Polycarp* (13), allude to the practice, and the *Martyrdom of S. Polycarp* and *Ignatian Epistles* bear witness, by their very existence, to the common recognition of this as a habit of the times. If the Civic Churches are shown to us as self-

[1] See Appendix, p. 246.

disciplining, they are not represented as making any pretence to being "independent," but as always relying on each other for help and counsel. We may notice in connexion with this side of Church life, that though the communications are carried on through the bishops, it is, in some cases at least, the message and advice of the Church that he gives: there is a striking difference from the practice of the apostles, who spoke authoritatively in their own name, and, *e.g.* the opening of the *First Epistle of S. Clement*, which contains the salutation of the Church at Rome to the Church at Corinth. This is no longer the case with the epistles of Ignatius, but we must remember that they are the personal messages of a dying man who was separated from his flock, not regular despatches like the other letters; and though Polycarp addresses the Philippian Church, and writes to them about "your" letter, he writes in the name, not of the whole Church, but only of the presbytery.

The last word suggests a further question: We find in S. Paul's *Epistle to the Ephesians* a hint of a special responsibility on the part of one individual for the government of the Church: how far is this trait to be observed in the sub-apostolical pictures of Civic Church government? Is there an individual who is chief ruler? We find no trace of one in the *Epistle of S. Clement*,[1] though that is specially devoted to questions of Church administration; the misapplied quotation from Isaiah adds great force to the argument that the author only recognised two orders of ministers in the Church—the presbyters (whom he speaks of as bishops) and the deacons; this would be of the greatest importance if we were trying to unravel the tangled history of the early episcopal succession at Rome, but we must remember that a letter written from Rome and addressed to Corinth does not give us direct evidence as to the state of things in the province of Asia. There is reason to believe that the Church of Rome did not adopt the Catholic form of Church organisation, with a threefold ministry, so early as the Churches of Asia and some neighbouring districts. It is worth observing that while each of the other six Ignatian epistles[2] insists strongly on the respective duties and status of the three orders, that addressed to the Romans contains no allusions of the kind, as if the

---

[1] *S. Clement to Corinthians*, i. 42. See Appendix, p. 226.
[2] So far as it goes, this tells in favour of dating these epistles early—*e.g.* considerably before the *Pastor of Hermas*.

writer felt they were unsuitable when addressed to the Church in the capital of the world.

On the other hand, as already mentioned, the distinction is implied in the opening of the epistle of the Bishop of Smyrna, and is explicitly stated in the Syrian version of the letter addressed to him by S. Ignatius (6), as well as in the salutations and conclusions of the other Ignatian letters.

But, as it seems, the clearest light on the subject is to be found in the *Pastor of Hermas*.[1] There is a twice repeated allegory in which the Church is represented as a tower being built in a plain with strangely different mountains surrounding it: from these mountains various materials for the tower are fetched. The briefer form of the allegory will be found in the Appendix: but the long and elaborate description which forms the *Ninth Similitude* seems to have made a deep impression on the minds of the readers, for it has been noticed in three different instances as the subject of illustrations in catacombs: it occurs twice at Naples,[2] and once

---

[1] I must in fairness call attention to the entirely different interpretation given by Ritschl, *Entstehung* (ii. Auf.), 403. The passage in *Vis.* iii. 5, according to the Sinaitic reading, which Ritschl could not have seen, seems to me to affect the argument considerably.

[2] Bellermann, *Ueber die ältest. christ. Begräbniss.*, p. 77.

at Rome.[1] The frontispiece has been copied from the remains of one of the designs in the cemetery of S. Januarius, and reproduced from the great work of Garucci,[2] by whom it is carefully described. Twelve virgins, of whom only three are here shown, are engaged in building the tower: they are the heavenly powers—Faith, Continence, etc.—under whose influence men are fitted for a place in the Church. We read further in the *Similitude* that the tower rests on the rock, the eternal Son of God; that its base consists of two tiers of ten righteous men, then come thirty-five prophets, and then forty apostles and teachers: this helps to delineate the continuity of the old and newer dispensation (*Sim.* ix. 15). The place which the apostles and teachers take together is not a little remarkable. Still more curious are the three later chapters (25, 26, and 27) describing the persons who came from different mountains: from the eighth, come the apostles and teachers; from the ninth, the deacons who misuse their ministry; from the tenth, the bishops who exercise hospitality to all, and protect the weak, and lead holy lives. We have here three

---

[1] Dressel, *Patrum Apost.*, note on *Vis.* iii. 3.
[2] Garucci, *Storia della Arte cristiana*, pt. ii. p. 89, plate 91-2.

distinct functions, with apparently distinct officers to discharge them. A similar enumeration of apostles, bishops, teachers, and deacons occurs in *Vision* iii. 5, according to the Sinaitic and more important Latin versions.[1] Though it is not quite clear in which class we should place the presbyters who are spoken of in *Visions* ii. and iii., we are inclined to identify the presbyters with the teachers, as it was their duty to read the visions in the Church (*Vis.* ii. 4), and apparently the author was one of the number. The only other hint which we get in regard to the presbyters is the doubtful inference from *Vis.* iii. 1 that they were less worthy of honour than the confessors and martyrs. We should thus be inclined to say that Clement is represented as the bishop of Rome who was charged with the protecting of his own flock, and with keeping up communications with Churches at a distance.

This interpretation is more than confirmed by a passage in the *Apostolical Constitutions* (iii. 20), which delineates the duties of bishops, presbyters, and deacons.

Thus do we find in the sub-apostolical writings the same two conceptions of Church government

---

[1] See Appendix, p. 238.

lying side by side, as we noticed in the canonical books. In every particular we have found a complete correspondence between the pictures of Church life from the two sources, even when, as in the matter of organisation, there are two irreconcilable views portrayed in both. We have been treading on remarkably sure ground, in so far as we have succeeded in confining our attention to the discussion of the *Current Conception*. The early date and probable reception in Asia of the documents we have used is practically established beyond a doubt. Isolated incidents are difficult to group at this distance, but the reproduction of a Current Conception is not so hard to accomplish. But as we believe a great conception of this kind cannot lie dormant: it is a great social force, and is apparent in actual life, since it must express itself in the conduct of those who are influenced by it. We must now briefly review the ground we have already traversed, with the view of finding, not merely the Current Conception, but the development in space and time of the actual institution. We have depicted Christianity as then conceived in itself; we must now see it as related to its surroundings.

PART II.

THE CONFLICT WITH OTHER INFLUENCES.

Part II.

THE CONFLICT WITH OTHER INFLUENCES.

(1.) *Non-Christian Elements of Society.*

§ 19. Obviously the first question in passing from the study of the conception to the delineation of its effects in the world, is to try and portray the nature of the world into which it came. Our sources for information, regarding the actual state of each of the Asian towns at the time of the founding of the Church, are too slight to enable us to do this successfully; we can only indicate the elements which were present in all of them, without being able to state in what way these elements were actually combined in each town. Judging from the language of the *Apocalypse*, we should be inclined to say that the Greek element predominated in Pergamos, the Jewish in Philadelphia, and that both were markedly present in Ephesus; but we cannot get far beyond a vague suggestion of this kind.

The three aspects of society with which the new faith came into contact were—(1) Judaism; (2) Greek civic life; (3) Roman Imperialism. Its close connexion with Judaism has already been pointed out in considering the growth of the conception of a Christian Society; it is obvious that the practice of its precepts introduced a new element into the social life of Greek towns, while it was impossible for its professors to escape the omnipresent activity of the Roman administration. We may treat of each of these in turn.

It may be a matter of surprise that we have not thought it necessary to mention gnosticism as a phenomenon with which the faith came in contact, and by which it was considerably affected; but, according to our view of gnosticism, it would be a mere confusion to do so. Gnosticism was not by any means an organised sect, such as Montanism, or Novatianism, or Arianism became, or even such as Ebionitism aspired to be; it had no direct bearing on practical life, and the most opposite moral codes might be deduced from the teaching of different thinkers. Nor is gnosticism the name of a philosophical school that developed and maintained the same fundamental principles. If Marcion be included among the gnostic thinkers, there is, we believe, no one philosophical doctrine which can be traced as common to them all.[1] Gnosticism was a direction of thought, not a sect of believers nor a system of doctrines; a gnostic was a man whose habit of mind led him to speculate on the philosophy of religion—on the conditions of all possible revelations, like Fichte, or the doings of God in history, like Bunsen; sometimes the speculations of the gnostic led him into antagonism with the Christian Consciousness, as did those of Valentin and Marcion; at other times his speculations were welcome as a help to the Christian life, as were those contained in the *Gospel of S. John*, the *Epistle of S. Barnabas*, the writings of the Alexandrian Clement, the works of Henry More and George Berkeley in England, or of Boehme and Hegel in Germany. We have had many writings on the philosophy of religion that are full of earnest faith and deep devotion, and that have to some extent succeeded in the attempt which was made by heretical teachers in Syria and Alexandria, and in which they failed.

If then gnosticism is to be regarded as neither a

---

[1] Baur, *Die christliche Gnosis*, 105.

sect nor a system, it is impossible to treat it as a definite tendency, whose results can be traced when it is combined with other social elements. An analogy might be offered if we looked at the history of the Church in England during the last century. We might say that Clarke's justification of religion was a combination of Anglican status and rationalism, and that Priestley's teaching was a combination of Presbyterianism and rationalism; but that would give us no idea either of the growth and scope of the habit of mind which we call rationalism, or of the relation of Priestley and Clarke. It would be a far more intelligent statement if we said that Priestley was a Presbyterian who rationalised the gospel history, and Clarke an Anglican who rationalised the doctrines of the Church. So in the second century : we may have a Jew who speculates, or a heathen who speculates, or a Catholic Christian who speculates, or a heretic who speculates: the current philosophy of the day determined the mere form of their speculations,[1] just as the current

---

[1] And therefore any of these systems could be criticised from a purely philosophical standpoint without any religious interest, as was done by Plotinus ; or as the rationalistic form of the arguments of Priestley and Clarke would be from the standpoint of recent philosophy.

Aufklärung of the eighteenth century determined the tone of the writings of Clarke and Priestley; but in all cases the gnosticism of these men was dangerous, because the men who speculated were dangerous; it is a complete misunderstanding to regard the men as dangerous because they were gnostics. From our point of view their gnosticism is not to be regarded as a definite element, but as a phase of thought which showed itself alike among Jews and Greeks and catholics.

§ 20. We have already seen something of the various Jewish sects about the time of our Lord. We have seen how Christianity was a true development of their popular aspirations, and in describing the relation of Christianity to Judaism, we shall most easily depict it by considering to what extent various Jewish parties attained to, or fell short of, the new and fuller Messianic conception.

I. We found above (p. 36) that many of His followers were disappointed because Jesus did not go forth suddenly to a mighty triumph; and the belief which had such a hold on them, that a victorious leader would appear, conquering and to conquer, did not die out at once; even after the destruction of

Jerusalem it still held its own, and found vent for itself in the miserable insurrection of Bar Cochab. It is well known that the most cruel measures were taken by that fanatic against the Christians; their very existence was a protest against his own claims, and he persecuted them most bitterly; such Judaism as his had become definite in its hatred of Christianity; the grosser pre-Christian conceptions were consolidated in opposition to the more spiritual doctrine that had been preached. Jews of this type stirred up the people against S. Paul on his first missionary journey; the hatred which he then encountered was due to the doctrine he preached, not to the opinions he entertained in regard to the lax practice of the Gentile converts—for this question could not have then come to the surface. Nor can we doubt that a great deal of the persecution to which the Christians were exposed was due to the antagonism of these men. The amount of grievous injury which could be inflicted on Christians by malicious and secret foes will be most clearly seen when we come to consider the legal disabilities under which they were placed. The *Apocalypse* seems to imply the presence of this class of Jews at Ephesus.

II. The next class may be described as "pharisaic" Ebionites. So far as their whole tone of thought is considered, they are hardly to be distinguished from the class just described. The ordinary Jew expected a powerful but not a divine Messiah; some thought that he was yet to come, some thought he had come in the person of Jesus of Nazareth; but many of them, who accepted the divine mission of our Lord, had not risen to any very high conception of the nature of His kingdom, nor consequently to a true view of the nature of the king; professing their adherence to Him or to His vice-regent James, they had not really risen to the true Christian standpoint, and they refused— unlike their bishop—to have any fellowship with Gentiles who, while really taking Jesus for their leader, lived in disregard of the divine laws, and elaborate traditions that had been designed to regulate the kingdom which had existed long before, and which He came to resuscitate. This particular form of Jewish Christianity was exceedingly active in the time of S. Paul; the false brethren, the busy emissaries who stirred up dissension at Antioch, and destroyed the peace of the Church in Galatia, were pharisaic Ebionites, holding fast to the expectation of a realm ruled from Jerusalem, and to the perpetual obligation, in the resuscitated kingdom, of the Law that had been given for the former one. At the same time, the force of circumstances was against their opinions; the centre of Church government passed from Jerusalem even before the destruction of that city, and those who held the view we are discussing must have been driven into utter disbelief in Jesus, or to a nearer approach to the Catholic position. Not a few of them may have found refuge among the Nazarenes, a sect that seems to have preserved the true tradition of James the Just, and to have recorded it in the *Testaments of the Twelve Patriarchs;* they had attained to a more spiritual view of the kingdom, and did not desire to force the Law upon the Gentile converts, while they did not feel themselves justified in forsaking the practices in which they had been brought up. The Nazarenes were however so much of a local sect that they could have had little more influence on the Asian Churches than that pharisaic Ebionitism, which had, in all probability, been extinct for some time, even at the very dawn of the second century.

III. The above sects were derived from the popular and pharisaic Judaism: the last type which we shall have to discuss sprang from Alexandria rather than Jerusalem. Like the rest (excepting the Nazarenes), these Alexandrian Ebionites believed in the precise identity of the old kingdom and the new; but they reached this idea, not by reducing the new kingdom to the level of the old, but by spiritualising the old kingdom, till it did not differ from the new. They thus subjected the Law and the Prophets to the finest criticism, and repudiated every incident that seemed to them derogatory to God, as He was now revealed to them. Unlike the other forms of Ebionitism, this habit of thought continued to exert a powerful influence, during at least the second century; it therefore deserves fuller treatment at our hands. Not only was it long continued, but it was comparatively widely diffused, for it linked itself to the intellectual habits of the learned scholars of Alexandria, as well as to the pious beliefs of the Essenes who dwelt in the desert or were scattered among their dispersed brethren. The Alexandrian student rejected the anthropomorphism of the Old Testament, as unworthy of his conception of the nature of God: the Essene rejected the performance of sacrifices and the institution of marriage as incompatible with his own sense of what was pure and holy: very different as the scholar of

Alexandria and the dweller in the desert might be, they had this in common, that they had risen to a more spiritual conception of religion; and in their endeavours to find that spiritual religion in the Old Testament Scriptures, they were forced into rejecting much of the positive teaching they contain, or duties they enjoin.

§ 21. These Alexandrian or Essene Ebionites may be arranged in three classes according to their understanding of the positive enactments among the Jews.

(*a.*) Those who rejected Judaism as a positive religion altogether, and adhered only to the spiritual elements contained in the worthless shell. This train of thought is represented by the *Epistle of S. Barnabas*. The author of this epistle recognises Christ Jesus as the revealer of true religion which had been merely anticipated by the saints of old. It is thus quite compatible with an orthodox view of His person. On the other hand, there can be little doubt that this rejection of the positive side of the Old Testament Scriptures, when it was unaccompanied by this purifying faith in Jesus, was often an excuse for the gross licentiousness into which too many of the nation fell.

(β.) On the other hand, it might be said that some of the positive enactments ought to be continued, such, *e.g.* as circumcision, but that the supposed later additions to primitive and pure Judaism should be discarded. This is the standpoint of the *Clementine Homilies*. In this aspect Jesus was a mere reformer of Judaism, and as such a mere man.

(γ.) There is another view which serves to combine these two. It would commend itself to speculative minds, and may be briefly said to be this: That the positive enactments (or some of them) have a relative value for all time, as means of attaining to the true spirituality. This is of special interest for us, for it seems to have been the teaching of Cerinth,[1] and it certainly is the sort of doctrine into which a man would be led by trying to find a philosophic justification of the immediately preceding view. Cerinth seems to have been an Ebionite who speculated about his religious belief, and whose speculations gave his teaching a super-

[1] There is much difficulty in getting a clear view of the position of this heretic. Irenæus, Epiphanius, and Hippolytus were too far removed from the period of his teaching to give us much help, and they were not very careful in trying to understand the views of a heretic. The statements embodied by Eusebius in his *History* (iii. 28), especially those of the Presbyter Gaius, are of considerable importance.

ficial appearance of agreement with Christianity which it did not really possess.

While Valentinianism and some other systems claimed an affinity with Platonism, the teaching of Cerinth had more connexion with Oriental than with Greek thought. Like many other speculators, he seems to have regarded God as that empty abstraction, mere Being, which, just because it is only mere being and nothing more, stands out of all relation to the world of created things. But he does not attempt to think out the problem by endeavouring to display, in their mutual connexion, the necessary logical conditions of existence as we find it. He was content to rely on his imagination, and picture personal agencies as the instruments by means of which the world of matter, and life and spirit, came into existence. His philosophic standpoint is not advanced far beyond that of the Ionic teachers: he must have some physical existence by means of which to figure to himself the powers of which he writes,—*e.g.* Spirit is not thought of as Spirit, but rather as light.

But his philosophy was not only called on to explain how the world came to be, but rather to explain how the religious aspiration can be satisfied, and man rise into a spiritual realm above the fleshly burden which weighs on him here. He did believe in a spiritual kingdom into which man might introduce himself, and thus he believed in Christ, the true spiritual life which entered at His baptism into the man Jesus: the man Jesus was only a man as other men are, but He first tasted in its full measure of the spiritual life; but at the end of the world, the nation of purified men, who had while here attained to a measure of spirituality, should also be full partakers of that highest spiritual life, and fully redeemed from the flesh. This intimate union of the perfect Spirit with the nation of spiritual men was figured as a marriage-feast which should last for a thousand years.

Here then we have a philosophy of Ebionitism. With the *Epistle of S. Barnabas* Cerinth believed in a nation of spiritual men; he believed that the highest spiritual life, Christ, had appeared in the man Jesus; he believed that the spiritual nation would be partakers in the fulness of Christ at the end of the age; but his doctrines led him to agree with the Ebionites, that the partial observance of the Law was one means by which man might become more spiritual, and thus prepared for the intimate union with Christ: while the distinction which he drew, between Christ as the spiritual principle and the man in whom the Christ had for a time appeared, led him to agree with them as to the mere manhood of Jesus.

To try and point out the practical consequences of these teachings:—We have no belief in an actual partaking in the life of Christ here and now, but only a belief that a certain spiritual aristocracy would eventually do so; and it is by one's own efforts, by intellectual superiority or conformity to the purer law that one can enter into this spiritual aristocracy; the real attainment lies in one's own efforts, not in the God that is already working in us. By the undue exaltation of the true spirituality as something not fully attainable now, it reduces the measure of spirituality that is possible now to something that spiritual men attained for themselves.

This recognition of a spiritual aristocracy might lead to either of two different, but by no means incompatible, ethical habits; the pride of spiritual superiority might tempt men to pretend to absolute indifference to the flesh and its passions,—indifference as to whether they were gratified or not, and moral indifference is but one step from gross license; or the necessity of keeping one's place in the spiritual aristocracy might force men into a pharisaic exactness about the most trifling matters in the world.

There is some ground for believing that the followers of Cerinth fell into this double mistake of overvaluing some arbitrarily selected means of spirituality, and undervaluing those duties to which their high spirituality made them indifferent.

Having thus tried to piece together the fragmentary accounts of the teaching of Cerinth, we may notice how far it presents a superficial resemblance to the *Apocalypse;* there too we read of a spiritual kingdom of purified priests; among them those who had risen above the flesh ranked specially high. There too we read suggestions of a bride adorned for the marriage; there too we have suggestions of the continuance of Jewish society in the mention of the ancient tribes. Lastly, we have throughout, the idea of a kingdom that would come down from God hereafter, while the actual affairs of the Church on earth are controlled by angels. In its main drift and in many of its details there is a wonderful accord between the *Apocalypse* and the teaching of Cerinth, and we cannot wonder that some Churches long viewed with suspicion a book which was so little removed from what the heresiarch might have written. (Eusebius, *H.E.* vii. 25.)

All the more can we fancy the bitterness which S. John or his disciples may have felt towards the man who misread and misapplied his writings thus. We may well believe that the *Gospel of S. John* was written to correct these heresies; it was the noblest of all refutations, just because it never stoops to argument, but presents the Catholic Faith in its completeness. It never glosses over the incidents to which Cerinth attached most importance, for the baptism is described just as in the other Gospels; but it asserts that the Word became flesh, not merely appearing during the life of a man; and, as we have already noted, it brings into the strongest prominence the true Christian doctrine that we may be actual partakers in a divine life now.

We have dwelt thus at length on the teaching of Cerinth, because his conflict with S. John is such a striking incident in the history of the Church in the leading city in Asia. We have, moreover, evidence that the tone of thought, of which he is the typical representative, was largely present in Asia at an early date, and lasted for a considerable time.

The proof of the first position is to be found in S. Paul's *Epistle to the Colossians*,[1] that of the second in the canons of the Council of Laodicea.

In the *Epistle to the Colossians* we have a vigorous re-assertion in the strongest language of the two great truths which were embodied in the Gospel narrative of S. John; the fulness of the Godhead dwelt in Jesus Christ (i. 19; ii. 9), and men might be even now partakers in the life of Christ (i. 24, 27; ii. 6, 10; iii. 3). Not only so, we get not a few indications of the nature of the heresies which the apostle sought to oppose. We have a reference to a doctrine of emanations, similar to that of Cerinth, in ii. 15, 18; we have continual exhortations to the cultivation of a oneness which was incompatible with any recognition of a spiritual aristocracy (ii. 19; iii. 11); we have a protest against the petty observances of this aristocracy, and a warning against the fleshly indulgences to which they were, in this fancied superiority, indifferent (ii. 20; iii. 5).

This was not then, merely the personal teaching

---

[1] Here again the doubts which have been started as to the authenticity of the Epistle do not affect its value as evidence for the actual existence and diffusion of an early Asian heresy of this character.

of one man, it was an early and widely diffused way of thinking, which had serious results on the life of the Church; and, as such, it did not die with one man, but held its own way for long years. The Council of Laodicea[1] which assembled about the year 344 A.D. or later, found it necessary to condemn errors, which were at least cognate to the teaching of Cerinth; Sabbath observance and angel-worship were alike denounced by the bishops there.

§ 22. We may here pause to sum up the results which we have reached, and sketch the relation of Judaism to the Catholic Church. All that was best in the earlier religion had been absorbed into its successor: the Messianic hope had been more than fulfilled; the divine kingdom was understood more fully, and the kingdom would overcome all mankind by embracing them, not by destroying them; and so of the Law,—that too was not destroyed but fulfilled, since a nobler life could be lived in a nobler spirit: true Judaism had passed over into Christianity; it no longer existed as a real power in the world. Survivals of it there still were: the gross chiliasm of some Catholics; the angry spite of the

[1] Lightfoot, *Colossians*, p. 67.

synagogue of Satan, the narrow correctness of the Nazarene, the spiritual pride of the Ebionite disciple of Cerinth, these were important features of the age, but the stars in their courses fought against them, —they emphatically were for the age, and not for all time.

It is a strange thing to find ourselves thus in the presence of death—the death of a spiritual power— yet a death which is, after all, a resurrection to a higher life. This thought of a kingdom of God upon earth had cheered the hopes of God's people for a thousand years; it had inspired the victories of David as of Judas Maccabæus, the labours of Solomon as of Nehemiah, the psalms and songs of the prophets: and now it had passed for ever, passed into the belief in one Catholic and Apostolic Church, —the actual kingdom of God upon earth,—for it had done its work, and all that remained outside the Catholic Church was a barren sentiment[1] that has had no practical bearing on the development of Christendom, and a spiritual scorn that was only

[1] The belief that the Jews have yet a mission before them is, to some, an article of faith; but those who maintain that they have yet a part to play tacitly admit that they have contributed little to modern civilisation; and a faith which can show no influence on the history of the world may be described as a barren sentiment.

too spitefully avenged on the hated Jews of after days.

§ 23. When, in the province of Asia, Christianity extended beyond the confines of the synagogue and the cosmopolitan crowd in the streets, and began to take a hold upon the dwellers in the town, it came across a political tradition which was wholly unlike that of the Jews; perhaps the greatest difference lay in the fact that the Greeks inherited only the remembrance of their greatness, and not the expectation of its immediate restoration. Vague longings and sentimental hopes might be cherished here and there, but it was not an intense enthusiasm, and eager anticipation like that which burned in the hearts of the Jews. The Greek cities had submitted to the Roman yoke as the Jewish people would not do, and there was no one centre which could be a rallying point for resistance. Greek art and philosophy had sunk so low as to become the fashion at Rome, and the highest development of Greek life, their political liberty—in self-governing cities,—this was a thing of the past.

On the other hand there was but little in Christianity, as far as we have traced its leading doctrines, which could appeal to the Greek: the preaching of a new kingdom awakened no echoes in his heart, for the kingly office had long fallen into disuse; and the story of Jesus, the incidents which proved His power and His Messiahship, were to the Greek, foolishness. In the guise in which it appealed most strongly to the Jew, the new gospel presented no interest to the Greek, who despised the squabbles of the Jews, and the disputes about one Jesus who was dead, and whom Paul affirmed to be alive.

Nor does it appear that much success attended the preaching of the gospel to the heathen; it might cause excitement for a time, as at Lystra; but we gather that even if the unbelieving Jews were the chief centre of open opposition, the Christian congregations were formed for the most part of Jews and proselytes, and the synagogues continued to offer the best openings for missionary operations. We have no evidence of much permanent success among the heathen in any one town, until long months or years had been devoted by some patient labourer to Church organisation in that place. Such work had been done by S. Paul and S. Barnabas in Phrygia, as well as in Antioch, by S. Paul in Ephesus and Corinth, by Epaphras in Colossæ, by Titus in Crete; and thus

Christianity was presented to the Greek public, not as a doctrine or a kingdom, but as an actual living Society in their own city. A brotherhood in worship and deeds of piety was springing up in each town, and the epistles of SS. Peter, Paul, and John, addressed to these regions, are long-continued exhortations to the cultivation, not so much of personal holiness, as of true Church life.

If Greek opinion was thus awakened to the existence of a new social power, there can be little doubt that the Christian Society was, consciously or unconsciously, modelled in accordance with Greek ideas. We have already noticed the conception of Church government which is hinted at in the canonical and sub-apostolical writings connected with Asia, and we cannot fail to be struck with the analogy which it presents to a federation of free Greek cities. We see that the Christian Society did become, on Asian soil, that which the Greeks had striven to realise—a federation of free democracies; the Church in each city was self-disciplining, possessing authority over its officers, and worshipping and communicating with other Churches as an unit; yet the Church throughout the world was after all one, and it was well that each city should interest itself in, and care for the needs of all the federation. This democratic constitution has been preserved by the Church through all the middle ages, when the personal power of her ministers was so enhanced. In spite of the influence which has been concentrated in the hands of territorial magnates, the laity in each English diocese are consulted before any man can be admitted to deacons' orders; and again, both in their parish, and as assembled from the diocese, before he is ordained a priest; the consent of the laity is as much recognised as an element in the ordination service, as the imposition of the hands of the bishops and presbyters; other societies have intrusted the guardianship of the popular rights to selected representatives,—the Church, like the democracies of old, still demands the consent of the assembled people themselves.

So long as the free citizens in Greek cities were fired with an enthusiasm for the common weal and regardless of their private interests—so long did the State flourish. So soon as the private interests of the citizens overcame their care for their city, so soon as the pride or ambition of any city asserted itself as against its confederates, so soon did the political power of Greek States begin to wane. It is just because there is one Spirit in all the members of the Church in each city, one Spirit in all the branches of the Catholic Church, that the Christian Society has the assurance of a perpetuity to which the free States of Greece could not attain.

If we find in the Asian epistles no direct allusion to the political life of old, we can hardly believe that it had no place in the thoughts of the apostle of the Gentiles, who alluded so often to the body and its members—the favourite political illustration of earlier writers. And in the warnings and exhortations which we read, we feel how he is directing attention to the same causes of decay as had proved fatal to the political liberties, and exhorts his readers to unity of the spirit. If, as seems not impossible, at the date when these letters were written, the supremacy of Jerusalem and its bishop was partially recognised, S. Paul could scarcely go further than he did in applying to the Christian Society the political ideas of Greece.

If Christianity did not attract men by the doctrines it preached, and offered them a Society which, in spite of its real identity, had little superficial resemblance to their own traditional ideal, it came into positive conflict with their social habits by declaring the equality of all. This point has been so often discussed that it is unnecessary to do more than draw attention to it here. It may suffice to notice how prominent a place the duties of slaves occupy in the epistles to the Colossians and Ephesians, while that to Philemon has a more direct bearing on the subject. One may notice too, how even in asserting the equality of all as before God, S. Paul, like his Master, makes no aggressive attack on the institutions—evil though they might be—of ancient society; nor did he refrain from making use of this apt and well understood illustration, when he talks of the household of God and the slaves of Christ.

Besides this, there could be nothing but antagonism between the old religion and the new: the glorification of beauty and passionate enjoyment of the gifts of God had little in common with the spiritual aspirations which Christianity put forward, and the overcoming which it enjoined. Yet some of those who had wearied of this service, who had sought by hidden wisdom and unknown rites to attain perfection found what they sought by initiation (τελείωσις) through Baptism, and in partaking of the Body and Blood of Christ.

Our sketch of the relation between Christianity and Greece has shown, not how Christianity influenced Greece, for the kingdom of heaven did not come with observation, but how Greece influenced the Christian Society. And this she did, not by implanting new doctrines or higher morality or nobler thought, but by modelling the institution of the Church in the form which the wisdom of the nation had worked out long before. Just as the best of the Jewish kingdom survived in the *matter* of Christian faith, so did the best of the Greek States survive in the *form* which the Christian Society took. And thus while the art and philosophy of Greece had become the playthings of her tyrants, the noblest result of her wisdom found its undying realisation in the constitution of the Christian Church.

§ 24. If there was little affinity between Christianity and the life in Greek cities, there was next to none between Christianity and the Roman administration which existed in Asia: a great military despotism—the embodiment of brute force—it had no kinship with the spiritual power that was rising against it; only when all that was powerful in pagan Rome had been overthrown by barbarians did the Christian Society link itself to the traditions of that empire, on the ruins of which it rose. In that undivided Christian empire much of the Roman administrative system survived, and the Church appeared in its most splendid, if not in its noblest or final, form; but in the second century no prophet's eye could read any signs of this. Pagan Rome was a brutal force whose proud toleration of all religions was but a mere indifference to the truth or falsehood of any; the one standpoint from which she judged of the permissibility of a religion was that of political expediency; and the arguments of a Justin who pleaded for the truth or nobleness of the religion were irrelevant,—they did not prove its convenience.

Yet if pagan Rome was a mere opponent, it had done not a little in paving the way for the spread of Christianity; it cleared away not a few obstructions by shaking the foundations of old national faiths, and by opening freer and more constant channels of communication. This it did if nothing else, and this prepared the soil in which the seed was to be sown.

(2.) *Actual Growth of the Church.*

§ 25. We have already discussed the current conception of the Church as found in early writers. We must now consider the actual progress that was made by the adherents of the new Society in gaining a hold on the world.

We need not pause to ask whether the infant Society actually corresponded closely to the conception of it in the minds of its members, for we have no knowledge of the internal condition of the Church, of the nature of its worship, of the character of its service, of the means of admission within its pale, but from the descriptions of Christian writers. The pictures they painted of Church life were surely accepted as accurate by the contemporaries who valued their books; they have already served to help us in reaching their view of the nature of the Church, they may also serve as evidence of what the Church was. Of the inattention and carelessness which marked the services that Justin describes we know nothing; but the disorders that saddened S. Paul in the first century,[1] and that attracted the attention of Diocletian and of Julian, were not improbably present to some degree in the second

---

[1] 1 *Corinthians* xiv. 26.

century also. How far the letters of Hadrian[1] may be taken as evidence of this in Alexandria is a question of some little difficulty. There is at anyrate no sufficient additional evidence to enable us again to go over this branch of the subject; the current conception of Church life may serve as the best description we can get of what it really was.

But on one point we must inquire more closely as to the actual condition of the infant Society: we saw that two inconsistent delineations of Church organisation were alike current: the viceregal episcopacy of the *Acts*,[2] and Ignatius and the *Clementines*; the civic independence of the *Apocalypse*, the *Acts*, the Petrine and Pauline epistles, and of the *Epistle of Clement* and *Pastor of Hermas*; we must therefore seek for some means by which we may remove this inconsistency and give an intelligible account of the growth of the organisation of the Church.

---

[1] Lightfoot, *Philippians*, p. 223.
[2] If the *Acts* be a second-century composition in a mediating interest, its value as evidence for the actual condition of the earliest Church organisation is of course greatly lessened (see below, § 30); in the meantime we may notice that the actual existence at some time of a viceregal episcopacy, such as is described in the *Acts*, is confirmed by the facts adduced by later writers.

James the Just has become the subject of so many strange legends that we may be sure there was something striking about his personality: curiously fabricated as is the story of the ascents of James, there is little reason to doubt that he was held in considerable respect by all the dwellers in Jerusalem for his uprightness of life;[1] and we may picture him to ourselves as a firm, unbending character, particularly fitted to exercise an ascendency over others, and thus well able to preside over the whole Christian Church: but as to the amount of influence he exerted over distant communities, it is impossible to judge. While we learn that the decrees of the Jerusalem Council were published in Phrygia and Galatia (*Acts* xvi. 4), the apostolic delegates did not enter Asia; and it is possible that the claims of the mother Church were never acknowledged there, for we have no proof that any of the Churches of that province took part in the systematic "remembering of the poor" at Jerusalem, which had been enjoined by S. James (*Gal.* ii. 10), and which was frequently urged by S. Paul as obligatory on those whose spiritual benefits had originally flowed from the Church in Judea (*Rom.* xv. 27). The sense of this

---

[1] Lightfoot, *Galatians*, p. 365.

obligation must have been diffused by the weekly offertory (1 *Cor.* xvi. 2), while the bishop of Jerusalem would have a means of influencing distant Churches in the delegates who brought their bounty (1 *Cor.* xvi. 3; 2 *Cor.* ix. 4; *Acts* xi. 30, xxiv. 17). But even if this influence was considerable, it was not long continued; according to the interesting fragment of the work of Hegesippus preserved by Eusebius,[1] a change came over the Church immediately after the death of James the Just. Symeon —also a blood relation of our Lord's, and therefore best suited for the viceregal chair—met with some opposition even in his own congregation, and we have no evidence that he exercised any influence on distant communities, as his predecessors had done.

But though it was impossible that such authority could continue to be exercised over the widely extended Church, especially when it fell into feeble hands, its downfall was hastened by the destruction of Jerusalem. The bishop and presbyters of the mother of all Christian congregations removed to Pella before the dire calamities came; but they could not, as fugitives from their own city, expect to influence more prosperous communities; and the

[1] *H. E.* iv. 22.

judgments that had fallen seemed to be a divine voice declaring that Jerusalem was no longer a favoured city from which authoritative decisions might be expected; its already shaken prestige was destroyed; nor when Aelia was founded, and a Gentile bishop ruled in that city, was any pretence put forward to a special authority: only at a later date did the see attain to patriarchal dignity. Some attempts were indeed made to establish a similar wide ruling episcopate elsewhere. Sozomen remarks that in his day there were in Syria many cities with one bishop among them;[1] while in Scythia also, according to an ancient custom "which still prevails," all the Churches of the whole country are under the sway of one bishop.[2] On the other hand, we find traces of the same kind of episcopate in Alexandria; the adherence to the number twelve among the presbyters there, and the relation of the bishop to the twelve, is surely a survival of the relations which existed between James and the brethren.[3] In all these quarters we may find traces of the survival of the viceregal episcopate, though no claim could be set up to exercise the power which had been wielded

---

[1] Sozomen, *Ecclesiastical History*, vii. 19.
[2] *Ibid.* vi. 21.   [3] Lightfoot, *Philippians*, p. 195.

by the first bishop of Jerusalem: here and there the form lingered on; here and there the idea was recalled, and applied to the chief officer of each self-regulating Christian community; but the thing itself, as a practical, controlling power, had perished long before the destruction of Jerusalem, and had perhaps, though influential in more distant regions, never been effective in the province with which we are chiefly concerned.

§ 26. What substitute could be found to exercise a controlling influence over the Christian communities, when this viceregal episcopate had fallen into decay? To answer this question we must look specially at the Church administration in Asia and Greece, and at the various functions which were discharged by the officers in these cities: in the Church, as in other organisms, the development of organs can be best understood if we can trace the specialisation of functions.

And we find the three different functions, for the performance of which officers were needed in the Church, by no means hard to distinguish. We know that there was above all things a need of teaching: faith came by hearing, and the duty of spreading the gospel message among those who were without, or edifying and exhorting the members, was most essential to the growth of the Church. A still further duty was that of governing the Christian communities, of guiding the worship, in the earliest days of arranging which of various brethren should exercise their gifts so that everything might be done decently and in order, of administering discipline on unworthy members, of deciding about the distribution of alms. And further, there was need of active care in carrying out what the rulers determined, especially in visiting the poor so as to give them their apportioned share. The analogy of clerical duties to-day may help us to understand them: we talk of one priest as a good preacher, of another as a capital organiser, of another as diligent in visiting; one man excels in one, another in another, of these clerical functions, but there is need of all in edifying the body of Christ.

In the Church of Jerusalem we find at a very early period three different sets of officers who performed these different functions: the main duty of the apostles was that of teaching, they were to be witnesses of what they had seen and heard: at the time of the second persecution, the body of teachers was dispersed far and wide;[1] it was then that we first hear of the presbytery (*Acts* xi. 30), though we need not suppose that up to this time the Christian synagogue at Jerusalem had, unlike all other synagogues, been destitute of rulers; and we first hear of the presbyters as intrusted with the sums which had been collected from distant communities, and which it was still the duty of the deacons to distribute. The formation of the diaconate had taken place at an earlier date, and it does not seem necessary to suppose that it had, by this time, fallen into abeyance:[2] even, however, if this were the case, it was, when revived, the office to which these duties were again assigned. In the Church of Jerusalem the functions of teaching and visiting were performed by apostles and deacons, while that of organising or ruling was intrusted to the presbytery with James at its head.[3]

Much learning has been expended on the ques-

---

[1] Lightfoot, *Galatians*, p. 303.

[2] As Ritschl argues on what hardly seem sufficient grounds. *Entstehung*, p. 355. Cf. Lightfoot, *Phil.*, p. 185.

[3] The relation of the presbytery to James has been indicated above as that of a council to a regent. The matter is discussed, and the admitted reliance of the regent on his council brought out by Bishop Lightfoot, *Philippians*, p. 195. Cf. also *Acts* xii. 17; xv. 2, 3, 4; xvi. 4; xxi. 18.

tions as to the number of those who bore the name "apostles." Perhaps we shall regard these difficulties as hardly worth the pains that have been spent upon them, when we realise that "apostles" were simply the guardians and expounders of the Christian tradition. An apostle might be sent forth on a journey, as were SS. Barnabas and Paul, or located at one centre as Epaphroditus was at Philippi (*Phil.* ii. 25), and as tradition asserts that S. John was at Ephesus and S. Paul at Rome. The precise functions of an apostle are clearly brought out in S. Paul's Epistles. It was not his special work to admit new members to the Christian Society (1 *Cor.* i. 17)—that was the duty of the presbyters— but to proclaim the message with which he had been intrusted (1 *Tim.* ii. 7; 2 *Tim.* i. 11). In the third chapter of the same *First Epistle to Timothy* we find an equally clear delineation of the characteristics which would fit a presbyter (bishop) and a deacon for ruling, and for parish work respectively. About the latter order we hear comparatively little, but we have evidence of the existence of a presbytery in each Christian community; and we find that about the date 53 A.D., presbyters had been ordained all through Phrygia and Galatia to rule the Church in each city, but still in subordination to the central authority at Jerusalem (*Acts* xiv. 23; xvi. 4).

§ 27. When the death of James and subsequent destruction of Jerusalem caused the viceregal episcopate to decline and cease, the Christian communities in distant cities were left without any final court of appeal, and it became necessary to re-organise the system of ruling. Whether in imitation of the method which had been devised at Jerusalem, or from the mere sense of its convenience, the plan was generally, and as far as Asia is concerned universally, adopted, of giving a special prominence to one of the presbyters, who, as ruler in a special sense, came to be called, *par excellence*, the bishop.[1] In the disturbed state of many communities the influence of one man might be effective where great danger would have arisen from the possibility of divided counsel, while for the purpose of communicating with the Christian body in other

---

[1] We need not point out that a change, which, as we have reason to believe, took place during the lifetime of the last of the apostles, probably took place with their sanction. It is more important to note that a change, which met with general recognition at first, and with the ultimate approval of the universal Christian Consciousness, certainly took place under the guidance of the Divine Spirit, who rules the Church.

towns, either personally or by letter, it was well that a single authoritative representative should be used, while the experience which he thus gained in other places would justly increase his influence in his own city. Left more entirely to their own resources in regard to ruling, the independent Christian communities in each city found that internal discipline and common counsel were alike best discharged when they relied upon the care and wisdom of one man.[1] Doubtless the experience of one community was different from that of another, though in many the disturbances were probably due to Ebionites.[2] The disadvantages of presbyterial rule were not so early perceived at Rome as at Colosse, but as soon as dissension and unruliness had called out need for active authority, the work of ruling the Christian community was carried on in a new way.

Another change had occurred during the same period: the original college of Apostles had almost wholly disappeared; death and persecution had carried off one after another, till at length one only was left,

[1] Cf. S. Jerome, as quoted by Lightfoot, *Philippians*, p. 204.
[2] And also to Nicolaitans, who seem to have been Gentile Christians, who did not keep aloof from the contaminations of heathenism, thus letting liberty degenerate into license.

whose declining years were spent in the chief city of Asia. Here was a new difficulty to be faced. Just as the decay of the Jewish episcopate had caused some confusion in regard to ruling the Christian communities, so had the death of the original apostles created a difficulty about the preserving and continuing of the Christian tradition. The difficulty was keenly felt, but had scarcely been met at the time when S. John complained of the doings of those who claimed to be, but who were not, apostles. Apostolic authority was urged on behalf of the views of Cerinth,[1] and there was need for the committing of the Christian tradition to hands in which it might be carefully treasured. But who could be more fitted for this task than the presbyters of the Church in each city? It was to them that the function of the apostles was committed when they themselves were taken away. The *First Epistle to S. Timothy* gives us an indication of presbyters assuming the rôle of teachers, and we can well believe it was no unusual thing, if we are to judge by the analogy of the synagogue; but when the apostles passed away, the care of the

---

[1] Possibly, however, this was the authority not of a fellow apostle, but of S. John himself ; *vide supra*, p. 100.

Christian tradition was definitely committed to this body in each Church.[1]

We have thus found two different tendencies simultaneously at work, and producing considerable changes in the organisation of the Church: the apostolic doctrine is committed to the presbytery; while the increased need for administrative vigour and for formal intercourse with other communities led to the concentration in the hands of one individual of many of the duties of "ruling." Thus it was that the bishop came to be the organ by which each community administered internal discipline, and the organ by which each community communicated with all the rest.

Much confirmatory evidence may be adduced of the justness of this view, even without appealing to the opinions of S. Clement of Alexandria or Tertullian. It is evident from the language in the *Pastor of Hermas*, that the author regarded the presbytery, and not the bishop, as the successor to the apostolic function of teaching: the bishop, being

---

[1] Though S. Clement is speaking of the duty of ruling rather than that of teaching, it is clear that he regards the presbyters as successors of the apostles, not the bishop, whose office was not yet specialised at Rome. Cf. *Epistle to the Corinthians*, 44.

a presbyter, was himself a teacher, but he was a teacher because he was a presbyter, not because he was a bishop. We find exactly the same sort of phraseology in Hippolytus: he talks of a bishop as a presbyter, because he is, at the moment, thinking of him in his teaching capacity. Thus too in the Ignatian Epistles, the presbyters are uniformly regarded as holding the place of the apostles: so soon as the two offices came to be clearly distinguished, we find early writers unanimous in describing the presbyters, and not the bishops, as taking the place of the apostles.

On the other hand, the duties of a bishop were onerous and of ever-increasing importance: it was through him that the common services of the Church were arranged; and thus in separating from him, men were separating from the Church: the bishop was the "centre of unity in each community:"[1] this is especially the view that is taken in the Ignatian Epistles: still more, it was through the bishop's care that new presbyters were ordained, and the continuity of apostolic teaching in each place preserved: lastly, but most important of all, it was through the episcopate that the various

[1] Lightfoot, *Philippians*, p. 232.

Christian communities were kept from falling into isolation,—the episcopate was a living power that connected the scattered societies into one Catholic Church. This is the picture of the early episcopate which we gather from the letters which Ignatius and Polycarp wrote in the exercise of their own episcopal duties.

The whole subject may be rendered clearer by the analogy of the three orders in the English Church at present: the deacon is to read the Scriptures and to assist in the sacraments, and instruct the young in the formularies of the Faith; but it seems that his "teaching and preaching" are regarded as exceptional things, to be only done by special arrangement. It is the presbyter who is the inheritor of the apostolic commission to go into all the world and preach the gospel; and though the bishop cannot in his new sphere neglect his duty as a presbyter, his real function is to rule: it is as ruling *for* the Church—not *over* it—that he confers the apostolic commissions on new presbyters, and thus maintains the continuous spread of Christian truth,—it is as the mouthpiece of the Church in his own city that he confers with other bishops on the needs of the people of God.

§ 28. We have deduced the administration of the Church from considering the functions of its officers; we might easily show its appropriateness to the circumstances in which the Church was placed. Torn with rivalries as to the exercise of spiritual gifts, distracted by wranglings as to the essential duties of Christian life, a firm head was needed to preside at the weekly assemblies to check individual eccentricities, to receive the offerings which were brought by the rich, and to bless the bread and wine which was distributed to those present and sent to the absent. Still more was it necessary that when one brother held aloof from another because of days and meat, there should be a centre round which those might rally who longed to keep the fellowship of the Spirit in the bond of peace: it was the unruliness of gifted men that made a powerful president necessary in the weekly assemblies, it was the dissensions of Judaisers and Ebionites that made men come to regard communion with the bishop as the true mark of the member of the body of Christ who was willing to sacrifice his individual vagaries for the sake of maintaining Christian fellowship.

It was thus that the dissensions of Judaism

tended in favour of the individualising of the function of ruling. Nor was it only by its "quickening opposition" that Judaism affected the Church: it had supplied the organ by which the function of treasuring the Christian tradition was now to be carried on: the body of presbyters who now inherited the commission of the apostles had originated in the days when the Christian congregations were like other Jewish synagogues in all respects save one—that they cherished a living faith, while the others sickened under the blighting influence of a deferred hope.

We have called attention above to the substantial resemblance between Greek forms of government and the constitution of the Christian Church: we have only hinted at the possibility of an actual historic connexion between the two; but we may now examine how the case stands. For it is from Asia that we have the earliest evidence of the self-regulation of Civic Churches—in the *Apocalypse;* and it was in Asia alone that the Greek civic autonomy had at all survived. Greece proper had been too long and too effectively Romanised to maintain the same interest in political life as was still felt in the province of Asia, where Augustus had marked his displeasure by depriving some cities of their autonomous rights, and conferring special privileges on others.[1] Phrygia and the other provinces were under the direct control of the Emperor: Asia still looked to the Senate as its governor, and thus enjoyed a greater measure of freedom from military rule[2]—even though its chief magistrate held the rank of a proconsul. All this gave the dwellers in these towns a great aptitude for self-government, which could now be exercised in a nobler direction than in arranging details of police and rating.

If the duty of presiding within the Christian assembly was concentrated in one individual through the squabbles of Judaisers, another of the episcopal functions seems to have been modelled upon a feature in the political life of these autonomous cities; in constant communication with one another,[3] they frequently sent delegates to communicate their views to the Roman Senate;[4] and the people of Ephesus, the chief of all these autonomous cities,

---

[1] Merivale, *Romans under the Empire*, iv. 162.
[2] Le Bas and Waddington, *Asie Mineure*, iii. part i. 663.
[3] Compare the communications addressed to Teos in Le Bas and Waddington's *Asie Mineure*, iii. pt. i. 60-85.
[4] Merivale, *Romans under the Empire*, iv. 29.

must have been frequently accustomed to the arrival and departure of these delegates, who were the organs of communication between each city and their masters, just as the bishops were the organs of communication between one truly autonomous Christian community and another.

We have thus seen that the changes within the Church rendered it impossible that the functions of ruling and teaching should permanently continue to be discharged by the viceregal episcopate from Jerusalem, and by the original apostles respectively; but ruling and teaching were never more necessary for the maintenance of Christ's Church than in these distracted days; and the organs by which these necessary functions were performed had been most naturally developed in a society formed in the midst of Jewish synagogues and Greek autonomous cities; the presbytery, though now the guardian of the Christian tradition, was no new institution; the duties of the bishop as the organ by which the Church in each city ruled itself, were called forth by the disorders of the day; his duties as a delegate were analogous to those that were exercised by the selected *decuriones* of the autonomous Greek cities.

§ 29. We have now tried to describe the actual growth of the Church in the world; we have discovered the nature of its primary constitution, the causes which necessitated a change, the circumstances that helped to determine the direction of the change; and we have seen that there was no sudden revolution, but a gradual evolution of the old constitution out of the new, as circumstances called for the change in one town or another; especially in Syria and Alexandria did imitations of the original constitution survive, till a date when men were no longer aware that the civic episcopate was a later form of Church administration, but thought of these local usages as mere curiosities of Christian life. In so far as this has been successfully attempted, the history of the growth of the Church of Justin Martyr out of the Church of Pentecost has been rendered intelligible. But additional clearness may be given to the view here stated by contrasting it with other theories of the government of the Christian Church in apostolical and immediately succeeding times.

The one test which we desire to apply is that of *intelligibility;* wherever we come on the creation of a system that has no links with the past, or on a well-constituted government for the passing away of which no general cause can be assigned (but only the petty ambitions which exist under every rule), we there come on something which is unaccountable and unintelligible, and which has therefore no place in History; unless the irrefragable evidence by which it is vouched compels us to recognise it as a wholly exceptional and unaccountable fact. But in regard to most of the theories which we shall have to consider there is no important difference in regard to the nature or value of the evidence adduced. We have only to compare them with our own as regards their success in rendering a simple, intelligible account of the matter in hand.

It does not seem necessary to assume with Rothe a council called at the time when almost all, but not all, the apostles were dead, to settle the Church organisation of the future; from our point of view a council would have been impossible at the time. The first Council had consisted chiefly of the Jerusalem presbytery; that body could no longer rule, in fact the new difficulties had chiefly arisen as the prestige of that body decayed. Nor could there be any formal meetings of the delegates of Churches, until the self-ruling of each community was so advanced that they were able to elect, and to abide by the determinations of, qualified representatives. While the Church of Corinth was torn with schism, how could they select a qualified representative? The growth of internal discipline and of episcopal meetings for counsel must have gone on simultaneously, and no council could have enforced such a dictum as the theory supposes.

Neither can we suppose that the apostles originally united all these offices in their own persons, and divested themselves first of one and then of another. Such a view is incompatible with the constitution of the Church,—taught of God by her presbyters, but disciplining herself through her bishops, and ministering to human needs through her deacons. Rather would it be true to say that the apostles always kept to the same work—that of teaching, and refused to take the new duties which were required when new emergencies arose. These were provided for by the Church itself （*Acts* vi. 3) though the commission was sealed by apostolic prayers and apostolic hands (*Acts* vi. 6).

The puritan opinion that each Christian community was not only independent, in the sense of being self-disciplining, but isolated as well, hardly needs remark. Such a state of things may have existed for a time during the transition from the viceregal episcopate to the civic episcopate, but it was neither the primitive form of Church government, nor the final one, in all probability, that was reached during apostolic times.

It is not too much to say that while the whole view of the Christian Society attributed in the Bible to its Founder and His followers is in antagonism to this idea of a series of isolated communities, the growth of one episcopate from so many quarters before the middle of the second century is inexplicable, if this isolation of Christian communities had ever existed as a permanent state with which the Christian Consciousness was contented.

Still more unintelligible does the history become if we adopt the presbyterian theory, and regard the council of Jerusalem as the first General Assembly. What then is the meaning of the position given to James the Just both in *Acts* and in the *Galatians?* If the distinction between ministers and laymen turned, not on a divine commission to teach God's truth or work for His Church, but on the license of the presbytery to exercise individual gifts, how are we to account for the early and entire disappearance of all memory of presbyters who were not teachers? or for S. Paul's silence on the subject when discussing the question of spiritual gifts? We have ample evidence of the survival of other forms of government: the want of evidence of the existence of a presbyterian system is in itself a fact that demands explanation on the hypothesis we are considering. Once more, if the system ever existed, by what steps did it pass away? Those who point to the general tendency of things human to decay do not answer these questions, nor have they attempted to show any connexion between a presbyterian oligarchy and the forms of Jewish life, or the primitive synoptic Christian belief in, not a Church, but a kingdom. We have tried to trace, as a question of history, how the episcopate was developed: the theories of the congregationalist or presbyterian require him to show—1. That the system he advocates once existed; 2. How it failed, if not through its inherent weakness; 3. By what steps it gave place in all quarters at an early date to episcopacy.

On the other hand, we claim that according to

our delineation the course of the history becomes intelligible: we have sketched the controlling idea of the day, and have seen how the Christian Consciousness gradually attained to a fuller conception of the nature of the divine Society: we have now seen how there was a similar gradual development in the divine Society till it too appeared as a body politic organised everywhere on one system.

§ 30. So far we have considered various views which have all claimed the same evidence in their support, and it has been our endeavour to show that they in many cases conflict with the alleged evidence. It is, however, often asserted that the alleged evidence, especially that of the *Acts*, is untrustworthy, because that is said to be a book written with a purpose,—with the view of narrowing the breach between Jewish and Gentile Christianity, and that the facts it contains may therefore be coloured in this interest: a series of elaborate hypotheses have been started to explain the purpose of the author, which led him, consciously or unconsciously, to represent the apostle Paul in a different light from that in which he is represented in his epistles. Before considering these attempted explanations it is desirable to look at the "facts" that they are intended to explain.

It might be worth while to point out that S. Paul does not represent himself as a marvellously consistent character whose belief in the "universality" of the gospel was a barrier that cut him off from the Jews, just as truly as the latter were restrained from associating with the apostle of the Gentiles by a belief in the perpetuity of the Law. A lay figure moved by an abstract principle could never have done the work in the world that was brought about by the glorious inconsistency of S. Paul. The same apparent inconsistency which was a cause of offence to the Jews of old is a stumbling-block to the critics of to-day. While then we believe that there is no difficulty that requires to be explained by means of a confused web of unsupported hypotheses—even if any difficulty can be said to be explained that is only got over thus—we may still assert that the *Acts of the Apostles* was written by a Gentile Christian with the view of tracing the historic connexion between Gentile Christianity and the original apostles; but we contend that the Gentile Christianity he describes is of a very early type, and has not yet realised its full measure of freedom, not a Gentile Christianity which, born in freedom, has renounced that freedom for the old bondage. And this belief we base chiefly on the entire absence of any of the more spiritual ideas of the Church, and entire absence of any reference to the later form of organisation—a civic episcopate.

As has been noted above, there is in the *Acts* a constant reference to the Messianic hopes, and none to the Church as a spiritual Society; the difficulties in regard to the Law are of a very early type; the Gentile Christians are regarded as proselytes, and the question is as to *how far* the Law is binding on them; lastly, there is no hint of the civic independence of churches, but only of presbyteries in subordination to the centre of Church life at Jerusalem.

A history of this kind written at Ephesus in 117 A.D.[1] would have been a worthless anachronism, as much out of place as the publication of a book like S. Matthew's Gospel would have been at the date when the Fourth Gospel was written, carrying on its face a later date with its "advanced" views of Christ and the Church; so far as the Jews of the dispersion were concerned, the old Messianic hope was not a powerful incentive in 117 A.D.; Alex-

[1] The date assigned by Overbeck in De Wette's *Handbuch*.

andrian learning had weakened it, the destruction of Jerusalem had rendered it still feebler: why then is it the chief view put forward in the *Acts?* The Pharisaic Judaisers who had difficulties about keeping the Law, but few about understanding it, were not at the time an important party at Ephesus. The real question about the Law among the Essene Ebionites was rather, in what sense is it to be understood—literally or spiritually? So too the Gentile Churches had a civic self-government; the Ebionites admired the viceregal form of episcopacy, and the *Acts* takes no notice of the later form, far less attempts to justify it. It is admitted that the *Acts* could not effect a real mediation,[1] because it only pared down the differences instead of announcing a nobler truth which embraced the two opposed and partial views; but it is difficult to see what purpose it could have served if written so late as 117 A.D. in a centre like Ephesus;[2] for it neither seems to bring Gentile Christianity any nearer to the then dominant form of Judaising Christianity nor to explain the connexion between Gentile Christianity *as it then existed* (with its civic self-government) and the

[1] Overbeck, *op. cit.* p. 13.
[2] That Ephesus was the place of publication is probable from the local allusions.

Christianity of the original apostles. For the very reason that we believe the *Acts* was no meaningless work, but was written for a purpose, we are compelled to suppose that it was written at such an early date that its statements are to be trusted for all the details of Church organisation about which we have used it. And, if we accept this work, the connexion of the Christian Church with the synagogue system cannot be set aside as Baur[1] attempts to do. It may be that in many places Christianity found acceptance in households rather than in more public assemblies; but we have no reason to suppose that it attracted whole families any more than that it attracted whole sections of synagogues, or that the head of each family was a self-constituted bishop in his own house: family religion is only an offshoot and never the centre of true Church life.

§ 31. From two different sides there arose an antagonism between the Roman authorities and the Christian Church; the Christians were unpopular from their refusal to participate in much of the unhallowed social life of heathen cities, and they were apparently disloyal from their refusal to pay ido-

---

[1] *Ursprung des Episcopats*, pp. 85-89.

latrous respect to the Emperor; this was the social difficulty felt by individual members. But a much more terrible trial came upon the Church, when its widespread organisation had begun to excite apprehensions as to the possibility of this extended power being used for political purposes; then the Christian not only was called on to suffer for the eccentricities of his conduct and the riots they caused, but for having cast in his lot with a dangerous organisation.

We have ample descriptions of the earlier form of persecution in the *Acts*, where the apostles are invariably charged, not with disloyalty, but with causing sedition and uproar; the Jews made the uproar, it is true, but the Christian teacher was the exciting cause; and in spite of occasional refusals to condemn them, such as was made by Gallio, we cannot doubt that the Christian, as the innovator, generally got the punishment as well as the blame of the disturbance. But not only were the Christians a cause of riots among the Jewish population, but among the Gentiles as well. Demetrius and the craftsmen found that their trade was interfered with, and had personal motives for dislike; as had cattle-dealers and other traders as well, according to Pliny's letter.[1] But public opinion is always intensely conservative on social matters; the asceticism of the Christian made him an object of dislike, and the fact that Jewish sorcerers and others had found a place in the Society[2] made the whole body an object of suspicion, as possessed of diabolic powers of doing mischief. Nero, in blaming the Christians for the burning of Rome, was, in all probability, only giving vent to a popular dislike which had long been cherished, but seemed now to be more than confirmed.[3] The tradition which connects the martyrdom of Ignatius with popular excitement, caused by an earthquake, may be alluded to in the same connexion,—whether the earthquake was supposed to be due to Christian necromancy, or to the anger of the gods that such persons were permitted to live.

It is in the time of Trajan that we have the first hint of the recognition of Christianity as a dangerous political power, and this it only became when it appeared as an organised Society; to be a Christian was, in the province of Bithynia, a political crime, which was capitally punished. The eastern borders

---

[1] Pliny, *Ep.* x. 96.
[2] *Acts* xix. 19.
[3] Tacitus, *Ann.* xv. 41.

of the Empire were disturbed; there was a restless expectation of the return of Nero in many quarters; and the Jews were scattered everywhere, but seemed never to be amalgamated with their neighbours, or to have entirely discarded the idea of a revolt. The Christians thus came, not unnaturally, to be the objects of political suspicion, and to be condemned to capital punishment. But the answer which Trajan sent to Pliny's letter shows that the Emperor did not consider them as a real danger; if they confessed their guilt, they must of course be punished, but the men were to be practically protected from the suspicions of the mob, for informers were to receive no encouragement. At the same time, as Neander has pointed out,[1] the effect of an imperial condemnation of what had hitherto been ignored—the unlawfulness of Christianity—was to give an implied sanction to the popular hatred of the religion. In the time of Hadrian we have riotous attacks upon the members of the Church in Asia; but a rescript was issued which more carefully insisted on legal processes, and gave a check to mere personal outcry.[2]

The protection which Hadrian endeavoured to

[1] Neander, *Church History* (Bohn), i. 138.
[2] See this document as quoted by Justin Martyr; Appendix, p. 250.

afford lasted during the two succeeding reigns; but there is evidence that in the time of Marcus Aurelius the authorities were becoming embittered against the Christians. The miseries of the time were ascribed to the enemies of the gods,—the base informers who coveted the wealth of the Christians were not discouraged;[1] in fact, we can easily understand, from the story of our own Mary Tudor, how a gentle and pious nature may be conscientiously relentless in persecuting those who seemed to be bringing down divine anger on the realm: just because Marcus Aurelius was more than a mere politician, was he less just to the Christians than Hadrian had been. Christians were now sought out like other criminals, not merely punished when their existence was obtruded on the public tribunals; and their punishment of death was not awarded only if they continued contumacious, they were now to be examined under torture.

§ 32. We can have no doubt that these troublous times called for much care in the ruling of the Church. We hear of frequent councils of bishops being called for this purpose towards the end of

---

[1] Melito of Sardis, in Eusebius, *H. E.* iv. 26.

the century, and as soon as this practice began, we see the episcopate assuming a more weighty function: they had to settle the principles according to which the Church should be ruled; the diverse usages of different communities could be compared, the dangers which had attended a particular course in one congregation[1] could be guarded against elsewhere, and thus a body of canonical usages grew up—the combined experience of the Christian Church as formulated through the bishops. It was as the mouthpiece of the Church in his own city that the bishop spoke, and thus it was that through the councils of the bishops the religious experience of the whole Church was gathered and consolidated:[2] thus it was that at length a final decision was attained on the various books of the *Old and New Testaments*, and that at the last there came to be Canonical Scriptures.

Thus too were wise and to some extent uniform

[1] Polycrates (in Eusebius, *Hist. Eccl.* iv. 22) mentions that, in his time, some of the Christian communities had, along with their bishops, been terribly lax in keeping the Christian profession unsullied.

[2] The often asserted fact that the first councils were summoned in consequence of the teaching of the Montanists does not conflict with this view of the influence of persecution: for it was about persecution that the Montanists held the most startling tenets.

practices introduced in regard to worship, and on such difficult questions as to the treatment of those who fell from the faith in times of persecution.[1] This process of formulating Christian experience gave a new strength and a new unity to the Church: just as the teaching of the apostles, inherited by the presbyters, gave a standard by which to try and condemn false teachers, so did the consolidated experience of the Church give a standard by which to arraign and condemn the laxity of discipline which might find favour in any one city, or the over-severity which might be a danger in another.

This reacted also on the position of the bishops in their own community. They were no longer set to rule as the organ of the Christian opinion in their own city, they must now consider Christian opinion throughout the world. It was the access which they had to this, in the councils to which distant bishops came, that raised each of them to a more authoritative position in his own community. The bishop must still rule, not as a capricious lord, but as the instrument of the Christian Consciousness; but he had now ceased to be merely the organ of his own self-governing community, and become the organ

[1] See Appendix, pp. 261, 276.

by which the Christian experience of the Church throughout the world was applied to the difficulties that arose in each separate city. If the presbyter is called to instruct in the doctrine of the apostles, the bishop is called to rule—not as the caprice of his flock may determine, but in accordance with the inherited experience of the universal Church.

Thus the effect of persecution in creating a necessity for common counsel was to consolidate a body of Christian experience; and by so doing, to produce a marked difference in the position of the bishop. He is no longer the servant of his own community, the organ by which it governs itself, he is rather the organ by which the universal Church governs in that community.

The other effect of persecution in leading to a spreading of the Christian faith has been so often dwelt on that we need not enlarge on it here. Tacitus notices with scorn how the multitude pitied the victims of Nero, and the story of the impression created by the martyrdom of S. Polycarp has been often told; nor need we argue that these were solitary cases, nor doubt that when the body was thus lifted up as the Head had been, all men were drawn to it.

One more effect was produced by persecution: the faith was not only spread more extensively, but also held more intensely. But to consider this would lead us to the new epoch to which we must now definitely turn. Indeed, in the present division, we have not been careful to confine ourselves to effects that can be proved to have actually occurred during the first half of the century. The tendency which persecution had, in the early years, to consolidate the Christian experience may be fairly supposed, for we know of its actual tendency in this direction within a very short time later. Even if we have anticipated the date of these actual councils, and of the consequent increase of episcopal authority, the subject may be most suitably introduced at this point, so as to complete our view of the growth of the Christian Church as it was affected by the Jewish, Greek, and Roman elements, in the midst of which it grew up. Developed out of Judaism, it received its permanent form under Greek influence, and was consolidated by the necessity of resisting the suspicious vigour of the Roman administration.

PART III.

THE NATURE OF THE CHRISTIAN INSTITUTION AS REFLECTED IN EARLY CONTROVERSIES.

Part III.

THE NATURE OF THE CHRISTIAN INSTITUTION AS REFLECTED IN EARLY CONTROVERSIES.

(1.) *The Discipline of the Church.*

§ 33. We have endeavoured to show that about the middle of the second century the Church had been planted in many regions, and that the completest form of its constitution was being gradually introduced in all directions: so far we have seen that the history of the Church is the history of its contact with other social forms, a contact by which it absorbed the more valuable elements that they contained, or was consolidated by the necessity of definitely opposing them. But when we consider the middle of the second century, we see that the Church has attained to an organised life of its own; it is no longer so easily affected by influences outside itself: the growth of the Christian Society is now to be found in tracing the controversies that arose within its own pale. The opponents of the faith are no longer heathen or Jews, but heretics, who claim to set forward a better Christianity than that which was current in the Church: it is at this early date that we first find a desire expressed for a "return to primitive purity." Times of fiery trial are not always times of refinement: in so far as the effect of persecution had been to extend the Church rapidly, it had doubtless come to contain many impulsive natures, who were suddenly moved to cast in their lot with the Christians, but whose religion was somewhat emotional, and not a truly formed habit. In so far as the persecution had disorganised the government of the Church in any community, discipline must have been relaxed: and the Christian life of a Church which had thus come to be largely recruited with unworthy members, cannot have been an edifying spectacle. Contemporary Church life failed to satisfy men's ideas of what religion ought to be, and the question was forced on the minds of all thoughtful men—What is real religion, and how may it be mine? To this question three very different answers were given by Marcion, by the Montanists, and by the Catholic Church.

§ 34. There is a striking difference in the language which Christian writers use of other gnostics and of Marcion: the doctrines which other speculators propounded were theories which influenced the minds of a few disciples, but had little practical bearing: Marcion, on the other hand, was the founder of a religious sect, who endeavoured to provide his followers with a Christian literature, and who attempted, by his speculations, to find a philosophical justification for his religious position. Marcion is no mere speculative thinker, but a popular power,[1] who attempted to support his teaching by historical documents and learned arguments; and thus he attracted infinitely more attention than any of those gnostics who were mere speculative teachers: even if Irenæus never wrote his projected work, we find a considerable space in his *Refutation* devoted to this one heresy; and Hippolytus attacks it with a minuteness which he does not use in treating of other doctrines. Tertullian, too, has much to say of this heresy, for the Marcionites were a real power which his practical mind was forced to take into consideration. None of the other heresies met with so much refutation;

---

[1] Baur, *Die christliche Gnosis*, p. 240 seq.

of few was the influence so widely spread; and we cannot venture to suppose that the teaching which emanated from Pontus, before 147 A.D.,[1] and was temporarily welcomed at Rome, found no support in Asia.

The Marcionites revolted against the life of the Church, and found true spiritual life, each for himself, in the recesses of his own heart. The Spirit bears witness to our spirits, and all external aids but detract from the pure religion which dwells in the inmost soul: all external forms or outward expressions can only blemish this pure spiritual religion: such was the central principle of the religious movement which Marcion led. It is one which we may easily understand, for it has reappeared at different times: one might almost say that a similar exaggeration attended nearly all the attempts to purify the spiritual life of the Church that have been made: it is so easy to make the fatal transition from truth to error, to say that because true religion is a thing of the heart, which must have a hold on man's inmost being, that therefore true religion is a thing *in* the heart, which only dwells in his inmost being. That is assuredly no

---

[1] Justin Martyr, *First Apology*, 26, 58.

true religion which consists of acts of piety and duty, but does not reach the soul; but still less is that religion true which professes to have reached the heart, and is content to dwell there, rejoicing in subjective sentiments and glorying in subjective graces. Wherever we find men drawing a hard and fast line between "spiritual religion," on the one side, and "external worship" or "good dispositions" or "mere morality," on the other, we may fear lest they are tempted to think of "spiritual religion" as something which can exist apart from these things, and not as something which, just because it is spiritual, must embody itself in one or other, indeed in all of these ways. In the teaching of Marcion we only find this tendency, which is sufficiently familiar to us to-day, carried consistently to its logical issue:[1] his system is the philosophical expression of the belief that true religion is a spiritual thing which can be found in its purity only in the individual heart: a very brief résumé of his doctrines may render this clear.

---

[1] "So gewiss also im Bewusstsein ein Gegensatz ausspricht, so gewiss muss derselbe Gegensatz auch durch die ganze objective Welt hindurchgehen."—Baur, *Die christliche Gnosis*, p. 292.

If God be a pure spiritual being, who can only be truly revealed to the spirit, then there can be no true expression of God's will in nature: that is material, finite, sensible, how can it testify of the Eternal, Unknowable Spirit? Any hints the world may suggest of its Maker and Preserver do not tell us of the Spirit who is apart from Nature, and the religion of nature cannot be the true religion. As material nature is wholly unlike spirit, there can be no likeness or analogy such as Butler worked out between natural and revealed religion: the God of nature is not, and cannot be, the God of Grace; the Creator is only a Demiurgus, not the true God.

But all religions, pagan and Jewish alike, have professed to worship the Creator; they cannot then have been true religions, or opened the way of coming to the true God: indeed, not to dwell on the contents of pagan beliefs, there are signs of anthropomorphism in the Old Testament, and the Jews were only worshipping a Creator—ruling in nature and with some natural limitations,—not a spiritual, eternal God. So wholly false was their naturalistic faith, that it was rather a hindrance than a help to coming to the truth; and while Cain and the Sodomites who had rejected the naturalistic faith would gladly turn to Him who went and preached in the place of the dead, Abraham and Noah, and others who had lived by the false faith, would surely harden their hearts against the true.

Still more, if there be this gulf between matter and flesh, and spirit, it is impossible for the true God to take upon Him our flesh and dwell amongst us; He only appeared in the likeness of a man; unborn because not human, Christ appeared in the world as though He had been flesh, and the Jewish worshippers of the Creator conspired against and condemned this human appearance of the true God —as the flesh ever rebels against the spirit.

These doctrines appealed to a side of religious feeling that has asserted itself in nearly every age; and we cannot wonder that they attained a wide popularity; but they came into direct conflict with the statements of the Gospels and Epistles. But Marcion was ready with a way out of the difficulty: firmly convinced in his inmost soul of the truth of his doctrine, and possibly believing[1] that the Chris-

---

[1] We may give him the benefit of this supposition ; but in any case, none can dare to condemn him, whose preconceived opinions are so dear to them that they ignore—since they cannot

tian writings had been tampered with, he revised that Gospel which happened to present the greatest affinity to his views, and issued an edition of S. Luke, based, it would seem, on a specially accurate text,[1] but omitting all reference to the incarnation, and bringing the whole into accordance with his views; some of S. Paul's epistles were made to submit to a similar revision. The affinity between the Gospel as we have it, and the views expounded above, might be easily shown.

Such was the teaching of Marcion: we need not draw out any long statement of its inconsistency with the fundamental truths of Christianity; if Christ did not become flesh, the gulf between the Eternal Spirit and man as he is, is left unbridged. Nor need we repeat the sorrowful tale that such false spirituality tends to the forsaking of Christian fellowship and the neglect of mere "natural" duties; we have less need of the assertion of Hippolytus that it was so, because we know that in our own day it is so; yet it was by such teaching as this

---

erase—any scriptural teaching that conflicts with the doctrines they hold, or who fear that their faith may be shattered by textual criticism or more careful translation.

[1] Hilgenfeld, *Evangelien Justins*, iii. See also Sanday, *Gospels in the Second Century*, Appendix.

that Marcion pretended to restore the faith and purify the Church.

Nor must we yield to the temptation to pause to trace an analogy between the current religious philosophy of to-day and that of Marcion. Doctrines which relegate God to the region of the Infinite, and the Absolute, and the Unconditioned, have, like the heretic of Pontus, set an impassable gulf between God and man. The abstract Dualism of Hamilton and Mansel cannot escape the trenchant criticism which has been urged against the abstract Dualism of Marcion; nor can Belief accept on historical evidence what has been pronounced irrational on logical grounds. But it is not uninteresting to remark that, just as we find among us to-day a survival of the Marcionite hankering after "merely spiritual religion," so too do we find a survival of the system by which Marcion endeavoured to support it.

§ 35. Although the Marcionites and the Montanists found the same objection to the life of the Catholic Church, the remedies which they recommended were of the most strangely opposite character. Marcion sought for a spiritual life which was uncontaminated by all external things; Montanus and his followers believed in a divine Spirit which was patently manifested in the words and conduct of living men and women. For Marcion, God is a Spirit, and just because He is a Spirit, He cannot be revealed except in the Spirit; He cannot be revealed in nature, nor in human form. For Montanus, God is a Spirit who not only has revealed Himself, but is revealing Himself still.

The opposition comes out most strongly in noticing the views of the two sects on the history of Religion. To the mind of Marcion, all non-Christian religions had natural elements, and were therefore merely and wholly false: to the mind of a Montanist, God had manifested Himself, truly but incompletely, to Adam, to Noah, to the prophets, in Christ; but now He had at length revealed Himself fully through the Spirit. There is a doctrine of four stages of manifestation as opposed to Marcion's view of the sudden introduction of the truth, or the Ebionite doctrine in the *Clementines*, that false doctrine must necessarily precede the true.[1]

Yet, when we consider the form of the last and highest manifestation, it does not at once commend

---

[1] *Clementine Homilies*, ii. 15.

itself as better: the whole conscious life of Christ was an embodiment of the Spirit, while in the new prophets it produced a kind of ecstasy in which they were unconscious of what passed. It would be of great interest to us if either the treatises of Tertullian *On Ecstasy*, or of Melito *On Prophecy*, had come down to us, as we might expect to have great light thrown on the whole subject; the difficulty of finding a test by which true and false prophets had been distinguished is referred to in *Deuteronomy*, and had been felt in the time of Elijah, as well as of Jeremiah: it had pressed upon the minds of men in the time of our Lord (*S. Matt.* vii. 15), and in the days of the early Church; and we cannot but doubt that, while the Marcionites—not to mention the heathen—claimed their prophets, a very clear test was sought for in the second century.[1]

So far as we can judge, it seems that Tertullian claimed that the *manner* of these new prophets was identical with the *manner* of the inspiration of apostles and prophets,—that the ecstasy was in itself a proof of inspiration; and that the *matter* of the prophecy afforded the best evidence whether the inspiration was from above or from a demon: if

---

[1] Ritschl, *Enstehung*, p. 470.

there was ecstasy there was inspiration, if the utterances harmonised with apostolical teaching, then the Spirit was of God (1 *S. John* iv. 1).

Whether the manner of prophesying was, though undoubtedly similar, exactly identical with that of apostolic times, and with the current conception of inspiration, is a question which cannot be easily settled. In their desire to assert the effectiveness of the divine Spirit, Justin Martyr and Irenæus use language which seems to imply the entire passivity of the prophet: as also does Athenagoras. At the same time, passivity—the want of human volition in the matter—is a different thing from unconsciousness—the want of knowledge of what is going on. A swimmer may be carried away by a current—he is powerless to resist, and passive, but he is not therefore unconscious: and there may be the same passivity in the presence of a moral force, which is still not unconsciousness. This distinction does not appear to have been drawn by Justin or Athenagoras, and their teaching on the subject does not distinctly differ from that of Tertullian, though the latter seems to imply a belief in the Divine Consciousness as taking the place of the human intelligence, rather than as using it: on the other hand, S. Paul speaks slightingly of an ecstasy which does not appeal to the understanding (1 *Cor.* xiv. 9), and it seems as if he regarded the truest spiritual gifts as accompanied by understanding. This we may certainly say, however, even if the statements of Justin and Athenagoras do not contradict the later opinions of the Church, these writers are vague and uncertain in treating of a point on which the mind of the Church afterwards became decided: while not denying that the inspired man was overwhelmed by the message he had to deliver, the Councils and Fathers denied that the prophet was non-conscious: passive under the power of the divine Spirit, he was yet an intelligent man, not devoid of his own faculties because he was straining them in God's service. Were we to accept any other doctrine of prophecy than this, Biblical criticism would have no function to discharge, for the personality of all inspired writers would be necessarily ignored. Till the time of Montanus, the question of the relations of the divine Spirit to the human consciousness of the prophet had been spoken of vaguely: the effect of the excesses of Montanus was, that this relationship was now considered, and to some extent defined: but it is surely an exaggeration to say with Mr. de

Soyres[1] that the Councils, in asserting that prophets were conscious, branded the teaching of Justin, that prophets were passive, as heretical. The teaching of Justin is less definite, but it is quite consistent with the later view.

There was, therefore, nothing in the manner of prophesying that startled contemporaries, nor called for any immediate interference; nor was there anything in the doctrines maintained that differed from the ordinary teaching of the Church. Even if we had not the admission of Epiphanius,[2] we might remember that the orthodoxy of their teaching is put forward by Tertullian as the principal note of the reality of the prophet's mission: if further demonstration were needed, it would be found in the careful analysis of Montanist teaching which occurs in the essay referred to above.[3] Nor was there anything wholly new in the practical teaching of the prophets: it chiefly consisted of the re-assertion of duties that had been enjoined long before, and which were afterwards recognised, as excellencies at least, by the Church.[4] In these circumstances there is some difficulty in understanding why this teaching,

---

[1] *Montanism*, p. 65.
[2] *Hæres.* xlviii. 1.
[3] J. de Soyres, *Montanism*, Book II.
[4] *Ibid.* p. 116.

if it was new neither in its manner nor its matter, caused all the ferment it did. The secret was this, that Montanus and his followers attached a wholly new importance to the prophetic power which had till now occupied a subordinate place in the life of the Church.

The prophets gave a new and stricter rule of life. Up to this time the ultimate appeal had lain in the custom of the Church as carried out by the bishops; but it seemed to the Montanists that this custom was too lax, as doubtless in some cases it was (*vide supra*, p. 145). They regarded the Spirit, speaking through the prophets, as the source of a purer rule of life—*Paracletus, novae disciplinae institutor*.[1] Just as Christ forbade what the law of Moses permitted, so did the Paraclete forbid indulgences which S. Paul allowed. Just as Christ spoke against the degenerate customs of the Pharisees, so did the Paraclete witness against the too lax customs of the Church.[2] Against this opinion no sound objection can be urged; but the Montanists went further when they desired to make their new code binding upon all the Church, and thus the acceptance of these revelations was spoken of as essential

[1] Tertullian, *De Monog.* 11.   [2] Ritschl, *Entstehung*, 492.

to true Christian life. The precise nature of the excellencies which the Montanists regarded as duties will be described below. In the meantime we may note that the value which the Montanists attached to these revelations was equivalent to the introduction, not only of a higher ideal of life, but of a new code to be imposed upon all.

This at once led to a separation in the Christian community between those who accepted the new code and those who did not. Had the Montanists put forward these duties as an ideal to which Christians might have grace given them to attain, there need have been no such schism. But circumstances made it inevitable. The spiritual men experienced ecstasies or accepted the message of the Spirit thus revealed. The other Christians were faithful, it is true, but only with a psychic (*animalis*) not a spiritual faith; indeed, inasmuch as they refused credence to the new prophets and their revelation, they were fighting against the Spirit of God.[1] By a strangely different road we have reached a conclusion which is not very unlike that of Marcion. Once more we find a spiritual aristocracy and a practical denial of the truth that the Spirit of

---

[1] Ritschl, *op. cit.* p. 521.

God is truly present working in the hearts of all the members of the Church. The claims of the Montanists were incompatible with loyalty to the Christian Consciousness, while the pretensions of the new aristocracy were wholly alien to the democratic spirit of the constitution of the Church.

There is reason to believe that in some quarters the claims of the new prophets received episcopal sanction, and that the new code was, as far as possible, enforced by the ordinary rulers of the Church. Schwegler suggests, on insufficient grounds however, that Melito of Sardis was one of these Montanist bishops; but there can be no doubt that in most cases the bishops were opposed to the innovations. The prophets professed to proclaim a higher rule than the Custom of the Church, but the bishops were the administrators and guardians of the Custom of the Church. As such their office was attacked by the prophets, who claimed, not merely to announce a divine code—not merely to gather round themselves a spiritual aristocracy—but to take into their own hands the ruling of the Church. If they really were the mouthpiece of the Holy Ghost, how could any mere administrative official dare to uphold his decisions against their own?

As stated above, the greater part of the duties set forward by Montanus were subsequently regarded by the Church—probably were regarded by the Church all along—as excellencies. But the peculiarity of the new teaching was that it would bear nothing indeterminate, but set forth a code for all the trivial incidents of life. While others claimed full liberty for their own conscience, where the Bible gave no express command, the Montanist asserted that *what was not explicitly permitted was implicitly forbidden.*

In their eagerness to enforce a higher standard than that of the Custom of the Church, the Montanist framed a code which left no scope for the conscience of the Christian man. Partaking of meats offered to idols, wearing of crowns, veiling of virgins, these were matters on which men demanded definite direction as much as on the sins which the apostles had condemned. The clearest instance of this tendency is the care which they bestowed upon the subject of fasting. The Wednesday and Friday fasts were customs of which no clear account could be given; but now the observance of these Stations in a stricter form was enjoined, and two additional weeks of fasting, in June[1] and December, were

[1] See Appendix, p. 258.

instituted. The duty was no longer to be done as before, but it was enforced as strictly as the Jewish fasts of old.

Not only did the new code attend to these details, it required the highest virtues from all alike. This is particularly plain in the treatment of the question of martyrdom. In the *Martyrdom of Polycarp* we read of the sad failure of one who rushed self-confidently into the terrible trial.[1] Perhaps the Montanist might not have urged such foolhardiness, but he condemned in the strongest terms the weakness of trying to escape from persecution. The advice of our Lord (*S. Matt.* x. 32), was interpreted as a mere temporary permission to the apostles,—not as a rule for all time. While Montanism was particularly urgent against the weakness of those who tried to escape, it was terribly relentless against those whose strength failed them in the time of temptation. The public denial of Christ was a sin for which no penitence could atone. Never again might the faithless one join in the company of the faithful or the life of the Church; only from a distance in humiliating garb could he behold the blessings which he had forfeited. Pardon there might be, but the declaration that such sin is pardoned could not be fitly made for

[1] See Appendix, p. 261.

fear of blinding the eyes of Christian men as to the heinousness of such guilt.[1] This may open our eyes to the danger of such a code. It accentuates external doings, example to others becomes paramount; the inner disposition of penitence, how sincere soever it be, is ignored. Duties are definitely described, but they are to be done as external duties, not from the prompting of a devoted heart.

A somewhat similar attempt to enforce a code of external duty to the neglect of the inner spirit is to be found in the treatment of marriage—as a necessary evil. Virginity was of course the highest state, but in the face of the direct command of the Creator, Montanism was forced, for once, to admit a distinction in regard to duties, and to look on marriage as a necessary institution; it failed to solve the inconsistency by apprehending the doctrine which regards continence in the married state as a true chastity, because this teaching rises above the possible application of any petty code. Looking for a mere external test in this matter, as in all others, it drew an arbitrary line at second marriages,—a principle which was probably copied from the Jewish ordinances for the priests.

[1] J. de Soyres, *Montanism*, 89, 90.

The intense religious spirit which announced this rigorous code, and the earnest men who tried to live up to it, were just those whose minds would be most likely to kindle at the hope of a speedy coming of the Lord. When the prophets reiterated the assurances that had sounded before, their words fell on willing ears, and this vivid expectation served as an additional motive for seeking to conform to the duties thus laid down.

Such, then, was a second effort to revive the earnestness and purify the discipline of the Church; and of it, what shall we say? Shall we not thank God, who saved His Church from this new danger, of a spasmodic ecstasy which claimed to over-ride the truth that was treasured in the consciences of Christian men; from the danger of a haughty aristocracy that condemned all other Christians as psychical; from the danger of rulers who claimed to pronounce judgments by their personal inspiration, not as the mere administrators of the Custom of the Church; from the danger of a code that left no place for the consciences of God's children, and had no pity for weakness, nor declaration of forgiveness for penitence; from a system which, beginning by a claim to special inspiration, led only to petty regulations of external conduct? It was from this threatening danger that God saved His Church, through the firm attitude of the episcopate as a body.[1]

But such a specious form of error is not easily destroyed; in every age of the Church has there been a need to mourn over the terrible differences between the ideal and the reality of Christian life; and ever and anon men have sought to purify the community by enforcing a strict religious code of duty: the attempt has been self-condemned where it has been most successful. Let us by all means cultivate a high ideal of the life to which we are called, let us by all means provoke one another to good works of piety and devotion, but woe to the Holy Office, or Prophets, or Presbyteries, that dare to impose an authoritative law, be it as prescribed in the Bible, or revealed by a prophet, if that law has not the sanction of the current Christian Consciousness in its favour.

§ 36. Thus have we seen the failure of two attempts to purify the internal life of the Church:

---

[1] There were of course some exceptions: Melito of Sardis has been spoken of as a bishop who was perhaps carried away by the new enthusiasm.

it could neither be done by teaching the pure subjectivity of religion with Marcion, nor by enforcing a strict code with Montanus; both of these efforts could only result in a real schism in the body of Christ by cutting off a spiritual aristocracy from the rest of the faithful; but another effort was made to work the necessary reform, *by insisting on greater care in the administration of the common means of grace.* The Montanist set up a positive test, and only included the worthy. The Church provided a system of negative tests, and only excluded the obviously unworthy; the sacraments were means of grace for Christian men, not mere seals of Christian perfection; and if it was before all things necessary to exclude the unworthy from them, it was not less necessary that none but the unworthy should be prevented from receiving the strength God gave through them. The history of the contact of Christianity with other elements of life has shown us to some extent how its external form and constitution were actually determined, the present is a good opportunity for endeavouring to trace the history of the internal life of the Christian Society. Its constitution was determined by its contact with those that were without, its institutions by the influence of internal disputes; how far the general delineation which we give of the life of the Christian Society can be proved to be true for the special communities in which we are particularly interested, will be considered below.

In the earliest days of the preaching of Christianity, while it was proclaimed principally to Jews and Proselytes, there was little need for providing for the special training of those who desired to join the new Society. They were already accustomed to follow a strict rule of life; they had already a large measure of knowledge about God and His will: the one condition which seemed necessary for admission was that of faith in Jesus as the Messiah. This is clearly the case all through the earlier part of the *Acts of the Apostles*, but especially in the story of S. Philip and the Eunuch.

So soon as the Church began to attract the heathen, however, a change was necessary, and it became needful to prepare those who wished to join, for the life of the new community: it was not merely instruction in theological doctrines, or in the history of Jesus, that was needed, but an actual preparation for living a Christian life: and this could be best done by introducing them to Christian homes. Such adherents were spoken of as Christians, for they had shown a desire to enter on the new life; but they were not, in the earliest stage of their profession, taken to the actual gatherings of the baptized members of the Church. Of the actual existence of this state of things we have ample evidence from Origen, and in the *Clementines*:[1] the former distinguishes three classes of catechumens, one of which, the earliest, lived under these restrictions, and we can have little doubt that it was to households of this sort, as distinguished from the Church in the city, that the apostle sent his special greetings.

But if preparation for leading a Christian life was the essential for entering the Christian community, it was also necessary that there should be instruction in Christian doctrine, and this was to be best obtained by bringing the catechumen to the Christian assemblies. It is true that they did not mingle freely with the rest of the brethren, but occupied the room of the unlearned; but they had the same opportunities for Christian instruction as were offered to the baptized members of the Church: only after they had undergone a period of instruc-

---

[1] Quoted by Rothe, *De disciplina arcani*, p. 12.

tion, as well as one of preparation, were they admitted to the full privileges of the Christian Society.

We have some evidence of constantly increasing stringency in the regulations with regard to catechumens; and we are justified in believing that the practice of a party like the Marcionites, who professed to be introducing primitive Christian habits that were uncorrupted by later inventions, offers the best possible evidence of what primitive, if not purer, Christianity arranged. We find that one of the charges which Tertullian brings against them is one of very great laxity in this very matter of catechumens. Whether they made no distinction among different class of catechumens, or, as seems more likely, did not separate the catechumens who were under instruction from the baptized, in their assemblies, we cannot certainly say: in either case they preserved a tradition of laxity in regard to the external ordinances of Christianity which was quite harmonious with their overvaluing of mere subjective spirituality. A further evidence of this increasing strictness might be drawn from the practice of a threefold classification which appears in *Origen*, but we cannot tell how far this is only an Alexandrian, not a Catholic use.

This state of things, when a considerable portion of the Christian congregations consisted of adherents who were not yet members of the Church, had a double effect on worship: the sacraments of the Church came to be spoken of and thought of as mysteries, to which only the initiated were admitted: the analogy with the heathen mysteries was too striking to be missed, though we have every reason to believe, from the tone of Justin's writing, that in his time the sacraments were still publicly celebrated, and were not by any means really mysteries confined to a few participators; still the language and thought of Christians were affected by the habitual consorting with them of so many of the uninitiated who had no real part in the sacred rite.

There can be no doubt too that the seclusion of many of the congregation from the mystery of the body and blood of Christ tended to produce a more exalted view of the Sacrament itself, and of the office of the minister by whom the worship was conducted: just as the Sacrament was spoken of as a mystery, so did the force of analogy lead men to think of the celebrant as being, in a spiritual sense of the word, a priest—the definite organ through whom the Christian community drew nearer to

God; through his lips the baptized confessed their sins, through his lips the Church prayed for forgiveness, from his hands His members received Christ's strength for the Christian life; at his direction they offered sacrifices to God; he was the organ of all the worship of the Church.

Such is the nature of Christian worship in the time of Justin Martyr: but it was to undergo a very important change; with the progress of the persecution greater strictness became necessary on many grounds: not only was it necessary that the purity of the Church should be preserved, but it was also a matter of the first importance that the members should be protected from the presence of spies and informers; partaking in the Holy Communion was the one undoubted mark of a Christian, and thus it became necessary to separate the great mass (if not all) of the adherents from being present at the celebration of the Christian mysteries: so soon as this was done, they not only were called, but actually became "mysteries" for the initiated alone.

They became "mysteries" in a double sense: they were no longer semi-publicly celebrated, and no longer currently spoken of or described: the first change gave rise to misapprehensions in regard to Christian worship. It was when the semi-public celebration of Christian worship ceased, that suspicions of unhallowed feasts and rites came to be current.[1] And it was because the Christian rites were now secret, that the later apologists were unable to bring forward the strongest defence against these allegations by declaring fully what was the nature of the worship in the Christian Church: from the use of this line of argument they were excluded: teaching in regard to the nature of the highest act of Christian worship had already become a *disciplina arcani*.

We have thus the best possible evidence for fixing the date when this change took place.[2] In the days of Justin Martyr the Holy Communion is spoken of as if it were a mystery; in the times of Athenagoras it has actually become such: the one describes it, the other does not.[3] The one has no misunderstandings to repel, the other finds that the gravest charges are urged against his brethren. This,

---

[1] See Appendix, p. 276.

[2] Rothe, *De disciplina arcani*, § 13.

[3] This, too, may perhaps account for the otherwise unaccountable silence of the *Pastor of Hermas*, though there is a difficulty about the date.

too, is the case with Tertullian, Minucius Felix, and Origen: all have to meet the same misunderstanding, and yet all preserve the same reticence. We may say with almost absolute certainty that the general change from the sacraments having only the form, to being really mysteries took place between 150 and 180 A.D.

We have hardly any direct evidence which specially connects either Marcionitism or Montanism or the new internal developments of Church life with Asia: we only know that these tendencies were practically universally extended; for the evidence comes from widely different centres of Christian life. We know, too, of great ecclesiastical ferments in Asia during this period, and we can have no doubt that Marcionitism and Montanism were the causes of these troubles, and none that the stricter discipline was enforced by the councils of the bishops of Asia; if indeed it did not emanate from the quarter where the most important steps had been taken in framing the constitution of the Church.

§ 37. Such an important step in the development of the internal life of the Church could hardly take place without a corresponding change in its organisation. We have seen different functions which the ruler was called on to discharge: ruling in the individual congregation to preserve decency and order; consulting for the common weal, and thus formulating the Custom of the Church; there now came to be another,—deciding who should, and who should not, be admitted to participation in the full Christian life.

It is necessary to put the matter in this way to avoid all fear of misapprehension. There never can be a question as to the power of forgiving sins—that rests with God alone. How far He may extend His grace to the ignorant in this world we cannot say; how far He may extend His mercy to the hardened in the next we can but speculate; but whatever opinion we may hold in regard to the universality of God's redeeming love, we cannot argue that because God's love is extended to all, that therefore the enjoyment of Christian privileges should be open to all. The "power of the keys" is the power of admission to membership in Christ's Church on earth, to the participation in Christian fellowship, and to the blessings of Christian worship. It has reference not to the final decision of the last judgment, but to the actual state of salvation—participation in the life of Christ here upon earth.

The question which has again and again distracted the Church has been this: How far moral guilt ought to exclude men from the enjoyment of Christian privileges. Discipline at Corinth was exercised on an incestuous offender by the assembled Church. There was a great controversy between Pope Zephyrinus and Tertullian as to the advisability of admitting to full Christian communion those who had thus fallen after being received into the Church: the latter, while fully admitting the power of God's grace to restore such sinners, yet protested strongly against the inexpediency of re-admitting the sinner to Christian fellowship, however penitent he might be. A large part of the business of the Courts Christian in England, and of the Kirk Sessions in Scotland, was devoted to difficulties of the same kind.

It was felt that the heinousness of such fleshly lust was aggravated by the fact that the Christian had given way to it after his probation was complete, and when he had been admitted to the full enjoyment of Christian privileges by Baptism. The gross sins of a heathen were altogether on a different footing, but the gross sin of a baptized member of the Church showed a defiance of the promptings of the indwelling Spirit, and brought discredit on the Christian fellowship. It was on this account that its guilt seemed so terrible; not because such guilt was beyond the reach of God's grace, but because such guilt was incompatible with true sympathy in the life of God's people. But there was a still graver crime: the man who, under the pressure of temptation, denied the Faith[1] and blasphemed, might indeed be forgiven, as S. Peter had been, but could never be confidently restored to his place among God's people. Such, at least, was the opinion of Tertullian, and of no inconsiderable section of the early Church, not merely of the Montanists, though they maintained it firmly.

As we have seen, in the earliest days the Christian community itself pronounced these decisions, the bishop (or presbyter) being the organ by which the decree was announced. But the decree of Zephyrinus

[1] All this may be rendered most familiar to us by a consideration of the Athanasian Creed, where these distinctions are clear. The final judgment is distinguished from the present condemnation. The men who are pronounced to be condemned already are those who, having failed to keep the Catholic Faith whole and undefiled, have proved unworthy to continue to participate in Christian fellowship—the state of salvation.

was indicative of a claim on the part of the bishops to pronounce these decisions of their own authority, and to decide themselves, and without any consultation, who should and who should not be admitted to the Christian fellowship. We have already indicated circumstances which tended to render the bishops independent of the opinion in their own Churches,[1] but as far as we know, the action of Zephyrinus was the first case when the power was used in such a manner as to provoke a protest. Tertullian[2] inveighs bitterly against this new claim, and carefully distinguishes between the succession to apostolical teaching and a succession to apostolical authority; but from our point of view Tertullian made a mistake in referring to apostolic authority at all. We have found no evidence of apostolic ruling, only of apostles' teaching and treasuring the gospel tradition: the power of ruling in apostolic days lay with James and the presbyters, or with the self-regulating civic Christian communities. And while the bishops—like other presbyters—were successors to the apostolic commission to teach, they had also succeeded to be the sole organs of ruling: Tertullian would have found a remedy in committing the power

---

[1] *Vide supra*, § 32.   [2] *De Poenitentiâ*, 21.

of ruling to the prophets—men who, as inspired, might have true insight, such as the apostles possessed, *e.g.* in the case of Ananias; but this was not a real return to the primitive order—it was only the dangerous exalting of ecstatic individuals to personal power, instead of trying to limit the undue personal power of the bishops by insisting on their acting as administrators, and after consultation, not of their own authority. Tertullian preferred to submit the ultimate decision to one set of individuals rather than to another; and the failure of the party who based the claim to individual power on personal gifts, strengthened the position of those who rested their claim to individual power on the fact of their holding a particular office.

Thus the more careful exercise of discipline led to the exalting of the office of the ruler: a corresponding change took place in the liturgical services. In older days the congregation had joined together in prayer to God to forgive the offender: there was no real usurping of God's place when it became customary for the bishop to declare that, believing as they did in God's forgiving love, this penitent, whose remorse seemed sincere, should be re-admitted into the Christian fellowship. The office may have been prostituted in after days to private ends, and the language misunderstood of the personal power of a man; our work is neither to approve nor condemn, but only to trace the causes which affected the growth of the Church and its institutions: few of these have been more important in their effects than that need for stricter discipline which tended to change the public worship into the celebration of mysteries, and to exalt the personal power of the officers of the Church.

(2.) *The annual commemoration of the Passion and Resurrection.*

§ 38. The first great controversy that convulsed the Church had reference to discipline: the next, not a subsequent, but a somewhat later struggle, was a controversy in regard, so far as we can see, to no dogma of faith, but to a matter of opinion—the keeping of the 14th Nisan as a solemn day. The orthodoxy of the Quarto-decimans on all other points is asserted by Hippolytus (viii. 11): indeed the real difficulty of understanding the controversy is entirely due to the fact that we can detect no great principle which was involved in the dispute. The whole matter may become a little clearer if we begin by attempting to show to what extent the disputing parties were agreed.

They apparently agreed as to the days of the week on which the crucifixion and resurrection took place: in every week there was a Friday commemoration of the crucifixion and a Sunday commemoration of the resurrection: there was no difference of opinion as to the occurrences which they kept in mind, nor yet as to the manner in which they might be most fitly commemorated: it was by fasting that they kept in mind the suffering of our Lord, and His rising from the dead was fitly marked by a festival. The early and general recognition of the weekly fasts and festival hardly requires proof: their existence gives evidence of general agreement as to the days of the week on which these crowning events of Christ's life took place, and as to the fittest mode of commemorating each. There was no difference of opinion on these points.

But besides the weekly, there was from very early times an annual commemoration of Christ's death and resurrection; in regard to this there were two entirely distinct grounds of difference, which can be best understood if they are kept entirely apart.

There was, first of all, a divergence of opinion as to a *matter of fact*—the precise day of the month on which the crucifixion took place: but there was in addition a difference as to the *mode of calculation,* for Christians were not everywhere agreed as to the best means of identifying the recurrence of the days of the crucifixion and resurrection.

We can have no difficulty in comprehending the precise point in dispute in regard to the date of the crucifixion, for each of the conflicting traditions has been preserved for us: according to the Synoptic Gospels, Christ partook of the Passover with His disciples on the 14th of Nisan,[1] and was crucified on the first day of the Feast of Unleavened Bread; but, on the other hand, the Fourth Gospel is very clear in describing a meal with His disciples, which, however, could not have been the Passover, as He, the true Paschal Lamb, was slain on the 14th of Nisan, and lay in the tomb on the first day of the Feast of Unleavened Bread. The point is so interesting that we may look at it more closely, as we can do by following the precise chronology of the Fourth Gospel.

[1] I throughout speak of the days according to modern use, as lasting from midnight till midnight, not after the Jewish practice, as lasting from evening till evening.

With the Jews, the preparation for the Passover began on the tenth day of the month, when the lamb was selected: it is hardly fanciful to point out that the "anointing of Jesus for his burial," which marked Him out as one that was to be slain, and which led to the decision of the rulers, took place on that very day.[1] But without pressing this, we may notice that this Gospel distinctly states that the Last Supper took place before the Passover (xiii. 1 and 29). Again, the conduct of the Jewish rulers and of the governor is explained by the fact that the Feast was still in view (xviii. 28, 39). But besides all this, the account of Pilate's conduct is interrupted by the definite statement, "it was the preparation of the Passover, and about the sixth hour."

On the other hand, the Synoptics undoubtedly seem to represent our Lord as actually eating the Passover with the disciples, in which case the crucifixion took place on the Great Sabbath, as the first day of the Feast of Unleavened Bread was sometimes called. The whole may be rendered clear by a glance at the accompanying table:—

[1] If the πρὸ ἓξ ἡμερῶν τοῦ πάσχα be counted after the Roman method. *S. John* xii. 1.

Synoptics.	Jewish Rites.	Fourth Gospel.
S.	10 Lamb chosen.	M. Anointing at Bethany.
M.	11	T.
T. Decision of Rulers.[1]	12	W.
W.	13	Th. Last Supper.
Th. Last Supper or Passover.	14 Day of Preparation for Feast. Passover slain.	F. Crucifixion.
F. Crucifixion.	15 First day of Unleavened Bread. Great Sabbath.	S.
S.	16 Second day of Unleavened Bread.	Su. Resurrection.
Su. Resurrection.	17 Third day of Unleavened Bread.	

The inconsistency of the two accounts is obvious; it would be going altogether beyond our sphere to attempt to discuss fully the intricate question as to which of these conflicting traditions is the more accurate. It may suffice to say that there has never been a sufficient answer to the arguments by which the Alexandrian and Roman fathers demonstrated the improbability of the High Priest and Pharisees committing so many breaches of the Law as were

[1] In this particular this tradition conflicts with the Catholic use, which commemorates the betrayal on Wednesday.

involved in a condemnation and crucifixion on the Great Sabbath. Nor are there wanting inconsistencies in the account given by the Synoptics, so that on examination they appear by a few particulars to confirm the date given in the Fourth Gospel:[1] we need not lightly discard the more precise account, even though it was composed at a later period than the others.

Be this as it may, there can be no doubt that the Synoptic tradition was very widely current, and more especially that it was the more popular one in Asia, or at all events in Smyrna. Reference has been already made to the epistle of the Church at Smyrna,[2] relating the martyrdom of its aged bishop, and it affords most interesting evidence on the question before us,—evidence which is all the more important, because it is excluded from the abstract of the early portions of the *Martyrdom of Polycarp* that is given by Eusebius (iv. 15). The whole is regarded as a visible repetition of the events of our Lord's Passion; the events occurred and are reported "in order that the Lord might show forth

---

[1] This latter line of argument has been followed with great clearness by Dr. Westcott in his *Introduction to the Study of the Gospels*, p. 339.

[2] See Appendix, p. 259.

among us the martyrdom according to the Gospel." The very names of the betrayer and of the judge coincide in the two cases (*Martyrium* v.), and though we have no reason to believe that the account is consciously coloured, it is evident that every little incident which could heighten the resemblance is made the most of. The authors evidently regard the martyrdom of Polycarp as having been precisely analogous to the death of our Lord, and they distinctly assert that he was betrayed late, after supper, on the "day of preparation," and was tried, condemned, and put to death on a "Great Sabbath" (*Martyrium*, vii. viii.). Even if, as Zahn[1] contends, this could not be, in Polycarp's case, the first day of the Feast of Unleavened Bread, but another Sabbath that was called great for some unknown reason, it need not be denied that the author is working out an analogy between the bishop's martyrdom and the passion of our Lord as related by the Synoptics; even if there was a mere similarity between, and not an identity of the days on which the two events happened, that similarity seemed to the author worthy of notice as helping to shew forth the martyrdom according to the Synoptic

[1] *Patrum Apost.*, *Martyrium Polycarpi*, viii. note.

tradition. Hilgenfeld argues that the same tradition was preserved at Smyrna till the period of the Decian persecution, for the presbyter Pionius, who suffered there at that time, was represented as being, in just the same way, a partaker in the sufferings of Christ; and the analogy is again worked out so as to show that, according to the current belief, Christ suffered, not on the day of the Passover, but on the Great Sabbath.[1] Whatever may have been the general opinion elsewhere, we can have no doubt as to the fact that the Synoptic tradition was the one which was accepted in this leading Asian town, and not improbably in the neighbouring Churches to which the encyclical epistles would in the first place be sent.

§ 39. We can easily see that there would be differences in the commemoration of Christ's death and resurrection, according as one or other of these traditions was followed. When the Christians in any one town agreed to fix the recurrence of the

---

[1] Hilgenfeld's *Paschastreit*, p. 247. This book contains a most complete discussion of the whole controversy in all its bearings, and to it I must acknowledge great obligations, even though I am compelled to dissent from many of the conclusions.

date by the Passover of the Jews, there would be serious variances of practice in their ways of observing the season, if they differed through not accepting the same tradition.¹ On the 14th of the month, the day on which the Johannine believers were fasting in remembrance of Christ's death, their neighbours would be recalling the institution of the Holy Communion. On the following day, the 15th, both parties would alike fast—but the one in commemoration of the rest in the tomb, the other in remembrance of the crucifixion. The day after, the 16th, would be the Easter of the Johannine disciples, while the others would be fasting still, and preparing to keep their Easter feast on the succeeding morning. A glance at the table on p. 190 will render all this clear.

Now it is obvious that the crucial difference between the two uses would be in the manner of keeping the 14th day. If every Friday in the year was

¹ The two uses are thus set side by side for the sake of clearness of argument, not as a piece of actual history; for we do not know that they ever came into actual conflict exactly thus: we have no record of any of the followers of the Johannine use who identified the recurrence of the Passion in the same way that was adopted by the followers of the Synoptic use. Steitz, in *Herzog's Realcyklopädia*, argues, on very insufficient grounds, that the conflict in Laodicea, about which Melito wrote, was between Synoptic and Johannine Quarto-decimans.

a solemn fast, much more so was the very day of the actual Passion; to make that day in any sense a festival was surely indecorous.[1] But, on the other hand, it was not unseemly for those who regarded the 14th as the day of the institution of the Holy Communion to meet together to do as Jesus had done at that very time. While the followers of the Synoptic tradition "kept" the 14th day by doing as our Lord had done, the Johannine disciples did not thus keep the day, but fasted strictly. Thus it was that those who followed the Synoptic tradition in their annual commemoration of the Passion were called Quarto-decimans; as we have already seen, the Synoptic tradition was currently accepted in the Asian Churches, and there too we find a stronghold of Quarto-decimanism.

A further confirmation of the fact that Quarto-decimanism was allied to the Synoptic tradition, is to be found in the *Apostolical Constitutions*, a work

---

[1] Steitz (*Herzog's Realcyklopädia*) supposes that the earlier portion of the day was kept as a fast in commemoration of Christ's death, and that in the evening there was a solemn communion in commemoration of the victory won; but the previous fasting was for the guilt of the Jews (Appendix, p. 253), and there is not a tittle of evidence that any section of the Church regarded the time of His descent into Hell, rather than that of the Resurrection, as the true moment of Christ's victory over Death.

which, according to Bunsen, probably emanated from Asia. Though in the interpolated form in which it has come down to us frequent use is made of the Fourth Gospel, the writer's chronology is certainly that of the Synoptics. He writes, "On their very feast-day they apprehended the Lord;" that is, not on the day of preparation, but on the Great Sabbath (v. 15), and an equally clear statement occurs in a later chapter.[1] Now it is here that we find an account of the practice of the Quarto-decimans, as distinguished from that of the Jews. Christians were to fast on the first two days of the feast of the Jews, but to hold their feast, commemorative of the Last Supper, while the Jews ate the Passover meal. The work has undoubtedly been interpolated in the interest of the opposite party, and this makes it impossible to know how far the details, with the very strict fasting that is enjoined, can be regarded as the use of either party, or of both; perhaps we may say that these have no special bearing on the controversy, while both in the strictness of the regulations, and in the Old Testament warnings by which they are enforced, we find a trace of the mode of thought which characterised the Montanists. In

[1] V. 17, according to Epiphanius. See Appendix, p. 254.

any case we may conclude, from the fact that there was a temptation thus to tamper with the work, that in its original shape it was consistently Quarto-deciman in its teaching.

The argument which establishes the connexion of Quarto-decimanism with the Synoptic tradition is so conclusive that it would probably have passed unquestioned had it not led to a curious dilemma. The Quarto-decimans of Asia alleged the example of the apostle John for their use: for this statement there was excellent authority, and no reasonable man would attempt to set it aside. But it would thus appear that S. John, as a man, pursued a practice which was in accordance with Synoptic tradition, but which was inconsistent with the account in his own Gospel. In the face of this inconsistency can we ascribe that Gospel to that apostle?

But after all there is a wider difficulty than any merely personal problem: that there should be two different uses in the commemoration of the Passion, and two different accounts of the date of Christ's death, is surely a fact that demands an attentive consideration, and, if possible, an explanation.

We have already seen reasons for preferring the date given in the Fourth Gospel to that in the Synoptics; we may proceed to ask whether on the assumption that it is historically correct we can at all explain the growth of the other use and tradition.

We must remember that during the first twenty or thirty years of the Christian Church, when its usages were being formed, a very large proportion of its members, at any rate in some quarters, were Jews. These Jews did not, generally speaking, lose their interest in the prospects of the covenant people, nor cease to feel the obligation of the Mosaic institutions, even if they did not insist on imposing them on Gentile Christians; and thus there can be no doubt that a considerable number of Christians would continue—as born Jews—to eat the Passover on the 14th Nisan. But to them the rite would have additional associations besides those which filled the mind of their brethren who were still blinded. To the Christian Jew that rite would be chiefly interesting because it reminded him of what the Lord had done in instituting the Supper. He would partake of the Passover on the 14th, but in so doing he would be in his heart commemorating the events which had happened on the 13th. As he naturally recalled the Christian events of the 13th, while participating in the Jewish rites of the 14th, so would the two following days be naturally kept in commemoration of the crucifixion, the rest in the tomb, and the resurrection respectively; that is to say, they would be commemorated on the 15th, 16th, and 17th, though they had happened on the 14th, 15th, and 16th. We may thus see that it was perfectly natural for Jewish Christians who continued to partake of the Passover on the 14th, to throw the whole commemoration of Christ's Passion one day late. We can thus account for the origin of the Quarto-deciman use, on the supposition that the Johannine date is strictly accurate.

Nor does it seem strange that this Quarto-deciman use, which would from the first prevail in Jewish Churches, should have affected the current accounts of the crucifixion: an oral gospel which was repeated in communities where the 14th was kept as the day of the Last Supper would be likely to derive a colour from its surroundings: there might still be hints of the true date which a close study could detect, but the belief that Jesus did partake of the Passover with His disciples would be extremely likely to impress the narrative. If we may thus derive the Quarto-deciman use from the practice of the Jewish Christians in continuing to partake of the Passover on the 14th, we may say that the apparent improbabilities in the Synoptic account are explained if we believe that they give us a tradition which had been modified by the actual existence of the Quarto-deciman use.

A certain confirmation may arise from the *reductio ad impossibile* of the other view. If we make the opposite assumption, and take for granted the accuracy of the Synoptic date, can we frame an hypothesis that will at all account for the origin of the mistaken date in the Fourth Gospel? or for the Catholic use which was defended by appealing to it? Hilgenfeld has devoted a considerable portion of his book to this attempt, and with very imperfect success. He takes the Quarto-deciman use as an accurate commemoration of the Passion. He then maintains that the Pauline converts were actively opposed to keeping the 14th, as it was a survival of Judaism. He next adduces the influence of the idea that Christ was the true Paschal Lamb, an idea which was embodied in and chiefly diffused by the

Fourth Gospel. The next step is the supposed desire to institute an annual commemoration of the true Passover, in opposition to the worn-out ceremony of the Jews. These changes, felt chiefly at Rome, were gradually introduced by Roman influence throughout the world. Each step in this argument seems to involve very serious difficulties. There is the difficulty of accepting the Synoptic account as accurate; there is difficulty of proving any more active antagonism to Jewish rites than that of S. Paul himself; there are few signs of any popular apprehension of the thought of Christ as the Paschal Lamb; it is difficult to see how an allegory like this would be effective in forming an annual institution like Easter; it is still stranger that the Fourth Gospel should have so readily met with approval when it definitely opposed the universal tradition on the very doctrine which it is said to have diffused; nor, even if there were some sufficient evidence that these changes had actually taken place at Rome, can we believe that that Church had attained to such influence as to be able to overbear the universal Christian tradition, and an honoured Christian practice. When this accumulation of difficulties is fairly weighed, we may surely say that it seems quite impossible that the Roman use should have superseded the true method of commemoration, and should have done so through the influence of a false account of the Passion written to impress the public with a favourite allegory.

Just as we have seen in the preceding section that the Johannine date is more probable than the Synoptic, so we may say that the growth of an erroneous Quarto-deciman use and Synoptic tradition is perfectly explicable; while we cannot explain the origin of the Johannine date and Catholic use, unless it be correct.

We may now return from this long train of hypothetical reasoning to consider whether the conclusion that has been reached throws any light on the dilemma, as to the practice of S. John and the narrative in the Fourth Gospel, and we shall find that it does. The apostles John and Philip were Jews, and as such would probably continue to keep the Passover, at any rate till the destruction of Jerusalem. They would thus give their sanction to the Quarto-deciman use as to the commemoration of the Last Supper. But the practice which had thus grown up, and to which the Church continued to adhere, was not inconsistent with the knowledge that each actual event had occurred on the day preceding that on which it was commemorated. Only, as it became obvious that the Quarto-deciman use was gradually introducing a mistaken tradition, the apostle might well wish to put on record the actual date with the special precision which has been used by the author of the Fourth Gospel.

§ 40. Thus far for the divergence of opinion on a matter of fact. It is now necessary to consider briefly the difference as to the best method of identifying the recurrence of the event.

The first point that demands attention is as to the precise day in the Passion-week whose recurrence was noted. We have already seen that the Jewish Christians were led to date the commemoration by the day of the full moon on which they partook of the Passover in remembrance of the Last Supper, but the Gentile Christians would not be inclined to join in this rite. The Mosaic law, or long custom which weighed with their brethren, were rather repellent to them, while there was an obvious fitness in making a special festivity of the Sunday after the Paschal full moon. The Sunday after the Paschal full moon was the day on which Jesus rose from the dead, and thus they determined the recurrence of the event, not by noting the day of the full moon as the beginning[1] of the commemoration, but by keeping Easter Sunday as the festival with which it closed. We have thus the further difference that while the Quarto-decimans identified the recurrence of the season by the day of the full moon, the Catholics made use of the Sunday after the full moon for the same purpose.

This latter method had the advantage of great practical convenience. It was sometimes so difficult for the Jews of the dispersion to determine on which of two days the moon was full, and the Passover kept, at Jerusalem, that they were obliged to keep the rite on two succeeding days, so as to be sure that they had not missed the day their brethren were observing. This difficulty was immensely diminished by keeping not the day of the full moon, but the Sunday thereafter.

But a further advantage was that the adherents of the two different traditions could join in a commemoration which was determined by a day of the

[1] Or middle, if we count the preceding fast.

week. About these there was no dispute: all parties agreed that the crucifixion took place on a Friday and the resurrection on a Sunday: thus while the Quarto-deciman use was in contradiction to the Fourth Gospel, the Catholic use was equally acceptable to both parties.

There was another difficulty which was common to both parties: the annual recurrence of Passion-tide was identified by a full moon: the whole problem of the adjustment of the lunar and solar year lay open: which lunar month was to be kept in any year as that of the Paschal full moon? Had astronomical science been more popularised this need have led to no difference of opinion; but it does not appear that the Jews made use of any cycle for determining the Passover, and the earliest known Christian cycles for determining Easter date from the third century.[1] Some at all events of the Quarto-decimans simply adopted the Jewish computations, but the calendar according to which this reckoning was made was not in general use, and was so incorrect as to lead at times to the fixing of a day inconsistent with the Mosaic ordinances. Those who calculated for themselves appear to have

[1] Hippolytus at Rome, Anatolius bishop of Laodicea.

gone by the simple system of watching for the first full moon that fell after the vernal equinox and keeping the succeeding Sunday as Easter. This could of course be easily determined anywhere, and as the Julian Calendar came into vogue, it was defined as the Sunday next succeeding the full moon that followed the 21st of March; but of course it was a great improvement when the cycle was introduced, and it was known beforehand when Easter would fall—if for no other reason, for the due observance of Lent.

§ 41. Having thus distinguished the different issues which were mingled in the one dispute, we may briefly sketch the history of this controversy in connexion with the Asian Churches.

We first hear of a difference of opinion on the occasion of the visit of Polycarp to Rome. Anicetus the Roman bishop, and Polycarp, did not allow this slight difference to interrupt the complete harmony of their intercourse, but " neither could Anicetus persuade Polycarp not to observe it, because he had always observed it with John the disciple of our Lord and the rest of the apostles with whom he associated; and neither did Polycarp persuade

Anicetus to observe it, who said he was bound to maintain the practice of the presbyters before him."[1] The "it" may without doubt be interpreted as the commemoration of the Last Supper, which the Quarto-decimans kept on the 14th, or day of the full moon. Supposing that both bishops were agreed as to the month of the Passover that year, the practice of Polycarp would conflict with the Catholic use. If the full moon fell on a Thursday, the two uses would coincide for the rest of the week, but even then it would be contrary to the Catholic use to " break the fast" that preceded Easter by this sacred festival; but this would be the least possible amount of disagreement. If the full moon fell on any other day, say Wednesday, then Polycarp's Easter would fall on the Saturday in Holy Week: supposing, that is to say, he kept to the Quarto-deciman method of reckoning. The passage seems to imply, however, that there was no such difference as to Easter; for it continues, " in the Church Anicetus yielded to Polycarp, no doubt out of respect, the office of consecrating," thus showing their complete agreement, in spite of the difference of use about commemorating the Last Supper on the 14th.

[1] Irenæus, quoted by Eusebius, *H. E.* v. 24.

The next controversy of which we need take note occurred in Asia itself. Melito, the bishop of Sardis, wrote a treatise on the subject, beginning with these words: "When Sergilius Paulus was proconsul of Asia, at which time Sagaris suffered martyrdom, there was much discussion in Laodicea respecting the Passover, which occurred at that time in its proper season, and in which also these words were written." What the precise point in this controversy may have been it is impossible to guess; at any rate, it appears that Melito's work was the occasion of another treatise by Clement of Alexandria. This last book urged the Johannine date of the crucifixion as quite inconsistent with the Quarto-deciman use: it would be a not unfair inference that Melito was an upholder of Quarto-decimanism, if indeed we did not know it from Polycrates' statement at a later date. But it appears that the bishops of Asia were not by any means unanimous, as about the same time Apollinaris of Hierapolis wrote a book on the same line of argument as Clement's.[1] As we have thus evidence of the existence of some leaders in Asia who were opposed to the Quarto-deciman use, we may readily believe that the dispute at Laodicea

[1] *Chronicon Paschale.*

was due to some such difference as that which had arisen between Polycarp and Anicetus, while yet it led to no rupture between them.

Last of all, we have an attempt to put an end to all these disputes by publishing an ecclesiastical decree, to which it was hoped that the Synods of all Churches would agree: it insisted on keeping Easter on a Sunday, and distinctly disclaimed the Quarto-deciman usage of "breaking the fast" before the day of the resurrection. Against this decree the Asian bishops, with Polycrates at their head, firmly protested: Victor, bishop of Rome, endeavoured, in a high-handed manner, to coerce them into agreement, and called on himself more than one deserved rebuke for his imperiousness. But if little excuse can be made for his manner of maintaining it, the cause he had at heart was proving itself a good one by its success: Palestine and Alexandria testified to their agreement with Rome in adopting and maintaining the Catholic use. That way of keeping the commemoration which agreed with the most accurate narration of the events of the Passion, and which had some important advantages in respect of practical convenience in calculating the date, did finally, and justly, carry the day, and attain to universal adoption.

§ 42. Nothing can be more striking than the truth which Irenæus asserts in connexion with this very matter, that these differences of opinion evidenced fundamental unity in the faith as held throughout the world. It was a small difference in opinion which caused an inconvenient conflict in practice, but the letters and councils which were called into being to help to remove the difficulty leave us ample evidence of the state of the Catholic Church. There was one Faith, one Lord, one Baptism: a similar celebration of holy mysteries that called forth in different places the same gross accusations: a similar commemoration of the sacrifice of Christ in weekly fasts and services. There was one organisation, with deacons appointed to visit and help, presbyters who treasured the apostolical traditions and conducted the worship of the Church, and bishops who ruled, each in his own city, and who, taking counsel together, became the repositories of the Custom of the Church: at this very time they were everywhere defending the free constitution of the Church against the tyranny of "gifted" men, and thus obtaining a more personal voice in the duty of enforcing the discipline of the Church. Even in minute details, in the manner of keeping the days of the crucifixion, and of the rest in the tomb, and of the resurrection, the Church was at one: men differed as to the means of identifying these days, and as to the historical tradition which they tried to show forth in their Paschal week.

But if there was a difference of opinion on this one point, there is evidence of a deep agreement among Christians on more important subjects: the language which was coming into current use shows that one most important controversy was practically settled, and that the evil influence of Judaism was extinct. When the Christian system was once formed, men came to find an analogy between the ancient and the newly planted kingdom of God: they applied the ordinances and practices that were recommended of old to their own times: the ordinances for the priests of old were binding on the people in these last days when all the Lord's people were priests of God: yet the special arrangements of the new system, with its bishop, presbyters, and deacons, had an analogy in the High Priest and priests and Levites of the old. The mere fact that this language could come into use, and be understood far and wide, is an evidence of the practical identity of the Christian system everywhere, since men could detect its likeness to the institutions of the Old Covenant. The teachers who had speculated on the relation of previous religions to Christianity were now out of date; the Consciousness of the Church had decided that the same God who had established an earthly rule for a time, had now planted an eternal kingdom upon earth; it drew no crude distinctions between a moral and ceremonial law, holding to one and discarding the other; it held to the Law and the prophets as revealing God's will for the people of the Jews of old, and as therefore being a guide by which the Christian Consciousness may be aided in coming to its decision as to what is right for the citizens of the eternal kingdom: the Old Testament was no longer regarded as a binding authority, but as a storehouse which contained many things helpful for attaining to, and continuing in, the state of salvation.

The language which rests on a recognised likeness between the new kingdom and the former nation is none the less interesting because the analogy on which it depended is entirely false. We have seen how the three orders of ministers developed from the necessity of exercising three different functions, how the bishops attained to greater power as their functions came to be of greater and greater importance; we have seen how the constitution of the Church was borrowed from Greece, how the Custom of the Church grew up within the new society; the memory of the Jewish hierarchy had no influence on this : the actual priests had been the vigorous opponents of Christianity while it was only a sect of Judaism, and with the destruction of the temple it shook itself free from the remaining ties that bound it to the traditions of the Jews. Still more clearly were the ministers, ordained from among each congregation, wholly unlike the hierarchical caste of the Sons of Levi: the commemorative sacrifice of the Church was in every particular unlike the sacrifices of the Jews: that section of Christians who held most strongly to a code, like the Law of old, were yet most pronounced in their antagonism to the hardened Jews. Only by shutting one's eyes to these facts is it possible to pretend that the institutions of a Christian sacrifice and a Christian priesthood grew up under the corrupting influence of Judaism.

§ 41. With the close of the second century our task is concluded; yet it may be well to review in a few lines the course we have travelled.

We saw first of all a noble idea of a new kingdom, and found that it was an effective idea, which was forced to make itself felt in the world: we saw the nature of the world in which it appeared, and how in these circumstances its constitution and institutions were shaped. We have found at length a great organisation, with a strict system for the training of new members, with the secret celebration of Christian mysteries, with weekly fasts and services, and one great annual feast; with three orders of officers duly set apart for ruling, teaching, and ministering; with powers for the due expulsion of unworthy and re-admission of repentant members. As we think of these things, and recall the idea of the kingdom of Jesus, which was preached at Pentecost, we seem to have travelled a wonderful distance: there is no superficial resemblance between the two; as, indeed, how should there be any such likeness? The Christianity of 200 A.D. is no longer the Christianity of 33 A.D.; no longer the same, not because it is less pure and earnest, but because it is more extended and more influential:

Christ founded a Church that should grow, and that, as it grew, became more highly organised, as well as of larger bulk. To pine for the resuscitation of the Christianity of 33 A.D. is to pine for the seed instead of rejoicing in the fruit: change is a necessary condition, not only of decay, but of progress.

We have not only treated Christianity as growing, but we have regarded it as a *self-developing principle.* Its power of growth lay within; external elements might be assimilated and modify its character, or external obstacles call forth a special exertion of its energies, but the active life lay within, in the faith of the members, not in any environment. Only thus does the history of Christianity come to be intelligible to us. To call forth a long series of mechanical actions and reactions is to explain nothing: it is easy to describe an abstract Judaism and an abstract Paulism and an abstract gnosticism, and still more easy to produce imaginary compounds of these elementary "isms" in Ebionitism and Marcionitism and Montanism; but this is mere playing with words, it is not studying history. Christianity was a life which had its roots in the life of God: it was not swayed hither and thither by abstract tendencies. We have tried to see what this life was, how it was related to other modes of life, how it was distorted in some of its phases; but neither in the hands of S. Paul nor of Montanus did it become a mere series of corollaries from some abstract principle; their doctrines were the intellectual expression, not the basis of their faith.

And this self-developing growth of Christianity we have treated as a matter of history; we have sought to understand the past, not to dogmatise about the present. Analogies with later religious phenomena we have not discarded, where these seemed likely to render the past struggles more comprehensible; but we have no hope of understanding the course of History so long as we look on its records as a confused store of weapons for contemporary controversy. One fatal anachronism has blinded too many writers: they have sought for anticipations of protestantism, and inasmuch as that word implies only a negation, there has been little difficulty in finding individuals to whom it can be applied. Marcion protested against any objective revelation, Montanus protested against the rights of the Christian Conscience as upheld by the episcopate: they were protestants, of a sort; but they were not protestants in the sense in which we claim that name to-day. The Reformation of the sixteenth century was a protest against the mere externality of faith and worship which was as widely current in the time of Leo as it was unknown in the times of Clement or Victor; that Reformation was not a mere negative protest, but a protest in favour of the neglected truth that men are made righteous by a divine principle working within, not merely by external participation, authoritatively demanded, in divine rites. In this modern self-conscious era we must assuredly all be protestant, and make religion our own, by recognising the worth of the Faith for ourselves, not merely accepting it at the lips of prophets, or receiving it on the authority of the Church;—we need not therefore pretend to make our own religion, or try to construct our own faith out of our own fancies. If the Faith be thus accepted on its own authority, as witnessed to by the conscience, so too is the rule of life to be enforced, not by any code or ruler, but by the conscience of each;—we need not therefore make our liberty an excuse for license. Rather shall we find the fullest measure of spiritual life in seeking to enter into the experience of the Church; by seeking in the doctrine of the Church the expression of our own faith, by taking the Custom of the Church for our own rule of life, and the worship of the Church for our own ideal of devotion.

APPENDIX.

Appendix.

A.

PASSAGES FROM CONTEMPORARY AUTHORITIES ILLUSTRATIVE OF CHRISTIAN LIFE IN THE SECOND CENTURY.

THE works from which the following extracts are taken are, with one exception, the undoubted productions of the second century. That exception is the *Apostolical Constitutions*, regarding the date of which the most various opinions have been expressed; we have however the authority of Baron Bunsen for regarding it as, in its original, not its present form, a collection of earlier fragments, made during the second or third centuries in some part of Asia Minor.

The translations are those of Whiston, Crusé, and the collaborateurs in the Ante-Nicene Library; but all have been revised after a careful comparison with lately corrected texts. While some passages have been transcribed with only trifling alterations, others have required considerable modification to make them faithful renderings of texts which contain the results of modern scholarship and of recent discoveries.

I.—Church Organisation.

1. *The (First) Epistle of S. Clement to the Corinthians*,[1] 37-44.

37. Let us then, men and brethren, with all energy act the part of soldiers, in His holy commandments. Let us consider those who serve under our generals, with what order, obedience, and submissiveness they perform the things which are commanded them. All are not prefects, nor commanders of a thousand, nor of a hundred, nor of fifty, nor the like, but each one in his own rank performs the things commanded by the king and the generals. The great cannot exist without the small, nor the small without the great. There is an intermixture in all things, and thence arises mutual profit. Let us take our body for an example. The head is nothing without the feet, and the feet nothing without the head; yea, the very smallest members of our body are necessary and profitable to the whole body. But all work harmoniously together, and are under one common rule for the preservation of the whole body.

[1] For this and the two following passages use has been made of the text of Gebhardt, Harnack, and Zahn.

38. Let our whole body, then, be preserved in Christ Jesus; and let every one be subject to his neighbour, according to the special gift bestowed upon him. Let the strong not neglect the weak, and let the weak show respect unto the strong. Let the rich man provide for the wants of the poor; and let the poor man bless God, because He hath given him one by whom his need may be supplied. Let the wise man display his wisdom, not by words, but through good deeds. Let the humble not bear testimony to himself, but leave witness to be borne to him by another. Let him that is pure in the flesh be pure still, and not boast, knowing that it was another who bestowed on him the gift of continence. Let us consider, then, brethren, of what matter we were made, who and what manner of men we came into the world; as it were out of the grave and out of darkness. He who made us and fashioned us, brought us into His world, having prepared His bountiful gifts for us before we were born. Since therefore we receive all things from Him, we ought in everything to give Him thanks; to whom be glory for ever and ever. Amen.

39. Foolish and inconsiderate men, who have neither wisdom nor instruction, mock and deride us, being eager to exalt themselves in their own conceits. For what can a mortal man do? or what strength is there in one made out of the dust? For

it is written, "There was no shape before mine eyes, only I heard a sound, and a voice saying, What then? shall a man be pure before the Lord? or shall such a one be without fault in his deeds, seeing He does not confide in His servants, and has charged even His angels with perversity? Heaven is not clean in His sight; how much less they that dwell in houses of clay, of which also we ourselves were made! He smote them as a moth, and from morning even until evening they endure not. Because they could furnish no assistance to themselves, they perished. He breathed upon them, and they died, because they had no wisdom. But call now, if any will answer thee, or if so be thou shalt see any of the holy angels; for wrath destroys the foolish man, and envy killeth him that is in error. I have seen the foolish taking root, but their habitation was presently consumed. Let their sons be far from safety; let them be despised before the gates of those less than themselves, and there shall be none to deliver. For what was prepared for them shall the righteous eat; and they themselves shall not be delivered from evil."

40. These things therefore being manifest to us, and since we look into the depths of the divine knowledge, it behoves us to do in order all things which the Lord has commanded us to perform at stated times. He has enjoined offerings and service

to be rendered, and that not thoughtlessly or irregularly, but at the appointed times and hours. Where and by whom He desires these things to be done, He Himself has fixed by His own supreme will, in order that all things, being piously done, according to His good pleasure, may be acceptable to His will. Those, therefore, who present their offerings at the appointed time are acceptable and blessed; for inasmuch as they follow the laws of the Lord, they sin not. For his own peculiar services are assigned to the High Priest, and their own proper place is prescribed to the priests, and their own special ministrations devolve on the Levites. The layman is bound by the laws that pertain to laymen.

41. Let every one of you, brethren, give thanks to God in his own order, living in all good conscience, with becoming gravity, and not going beyond the defined rule of service. Not in every place, brethren, are the daily sacrifices offered, or the freewill-offerings, or the sin-offerings, and the trespass-offerings, but in Jerusalem only. And even there they are not offered in every place, but only at the altar before the temple, that which is offered being first carefully examined by the High Priest and the ministers already mentioned. Those, therefore, who do anything beyond that which is agreeable to His will, are punished with death. Consider, brethren; the greater the knowledge that has been vouchsafed

to us, the greater also is the danger to which we are exposed.

42. The apostles preached the gospel to us by command of the Lord; Jesus Christ was sent forth by God. So as Christ was sent forth by God, so were the apostles by Christ. Both these appointments, then, were made in an orderly way, according to the will of God. Having therefore received their commands, and being fully assured by the resurrection of our Lord Jesus Christ, and established in the word of God, with full assurance of the Holy Ghost, they went forth proclaiming that the kingdom of God was at hand. And thus preaching through countries and cities, they appointed their first-fruits, first approving them by the Spirit, to be bishops and deacons of those who should afterwards believe. Nor was this any new thing, since indeed many ages before it was written concerning bishops and deacons. For thus saith the Scripture in a certain place, "I will appoint their bishops in righteousness, and their deacons in faith" (Is. lx. 17).

43. And what wonder is it if those in Christ who were intrusted with such a duty by God, appointed those ministers before mentioned, when the blessed Moses also, "a faithful servant in all His house," signified in the sacred books all the injunctions which were given him, and when the other prophets also followed him, bearing witness with

one consent to the ordinances which he had appointed? For when rivalry arose concerning the priesthood, and the tribes were contending among themselves as to which should be adorned with that glorious office, he commanded the twelve princes of the tribes to bring unto him rods, each one being inscribed with the name of the tribe. And he took and bound them and sealed them with the rings of the princes of the tribes, and laid them up in the tabernacle of witness on the table of God. And when he had shut the tabernacle, he sealed the keys, as he had done the rods, and said to them, "Men and brethren, the tribe whose rod shall blossom has God chosen to fulfil the office of the priesthood, and to serve Him." And when the morning was come, he assembled all Israel, six hundred thousand men, and showed the seals to the princes of the tribes, and opened the tabernacle of witness and brought forth the rods. And the rod of Aaron was found not only to have blossomed, but to have fruit on it. What think ye, beloved? Did not Moses know beforehand that this would happen? Undoubtedly he knew; but he acted thus that there might be no sedition in Israel, and that the name of the true and only God might be glorified; to whom be glory for ever and ever. Amen.

44. Our apostles also knew, through our Lord Jesus Christ, that there would be strife about the

office of the episcopate. For this reason, therefore, since they had obtained a perfect foreknowledge, they appointed those whom we have already mentioned, and have afterwards given permanence [1] to the office, that if these should fall asleep, other approved men should succeed to their ministry. Those therefore who were appointed by them, or afterwards by other eminent men, with the consent of the whole Church, and who have blamelessly served the flock of Christ with humility, quietly and unassumingly, with the witness of all for a long time,—such men, we are of opinion, cannot be justly dismissed from their ministry. For our sin will not be small if we eject from the episcopate those who have blamelessly and holily proffered the gifts. Blessed are those presbyters who, having already finished their course, have obtained a fruitful and perfect release; for they have no fear of any one depriving them of the place provided for them. For we see that you have removed some men of excellent behaviour from the ministry which they blamelessly fulfilled.

2. *The Epistle of S. Ignatius, Bishop of Antioch, to the Trallians, according to the short Greek Recension.*

Ignatius, who is also called Theophorus, to the holy Church which is at Tralles in Asia, beloved of God, the Father of Jesus Christ, elect and God-

---

[1] Read ἐπιμονήν.—Lightfoot.

worthy, at peace in body and spirit through the passion of Jesus Christ, who is our hope in rising again to Him; which also I salute in the fulness, in the style of an apostle, and pray that ye may joy abundantly.

1. I knew that you patiently keep a blameless and sincere mind, not from habit, but by nature, as Polybius, your bishop, has shown me, who was with me at Smyrna by the will of God and of Jesus Christ, and so rejoiced with me who am bound in Jesus Christ that I beheld the whole multitude of you in him. When therefore I had received, by God's favour, your good-will through him, I gave glory when I found that you were, as I knew, followers of God.

2. For since ye are subject to your bishop, as to Jesus Christ, ye seem to me to live not according to men, but according to Jesus Christ, who died on our account, that ye having faith in His death, may escape from dying. It is therefore necessary (as ye indeed do) that ye, without your bishop, should do nothing; but be subject also to the presbytery as to the apostles of Jesus Christ, our hope, in whom we shall be found continuing. It is also needful that those who are deacons of the mysteries of Jesus Christ should conciliate all in every way, for they are not ministers [deacons] of meat and drink, but servants of the Church of God: it is fitting therefore that they should guard against complaints as against fire.

3. Similarly, let all reverence the deacons as Jesus Christ, as also the bishop, who is a type of the Father, and the presbyters as a Sanhedrin of God and as a band of apostles: without these there is no Church. Touching this I am persuaded that you are going on thus; for I have received and keep by me the sample of your love in your bishop, whose very mien is a great lesson, and his gentleness a power, whom I believe even the godless reverence. Since I love you, I refrain from writing more strongly, although I am able. I do not think [of myself] so highly that, when under sentence, I should lay my commands on you like an apostle.

4. I aspire greatly, in God; but I take my own measure lest I should perish through boasting. For it is now needful for me to fear greatly, and to give no heed to those who puff me up; for they that speak to me scourge me. For I long to suffer, but I do not know if I am worthy. For this longing is not apparent to many, but me it assails all the more; therefore I need meekness, with which the prince of this world is overthrown.

5. Am I not able to write to you of heavenly things? But I fear lest I should offend you who are babes: and bear with me, lest not having been able to receive it, ye should be choked. For though I am bound, and though I am able to understand heavenly things, and the stations of the angels and

the gatherings of powers, things visible and invisible, I am not on that account already a [finished] scholar: for many things are lacking to us in order that we may not lack God.

6. I beseech you therefore, yet not I, but the love of Jesus Christ, to use the Christian nourishment only, and keep from all food of another sort, which is heresy. They, with baneful plausibility, interweave Jesus Christ with themselves, as if they gave a deadly drug with sweet wine, which the ignorant man takes readily, with sorry pleasure—to his death.

7. Be on your guard therefore against such persons: and this will be the case with you, if you are not puffed up, and are inseparate from [our] God Jesus Christ, and from your bishop, and from the ordinances of the apostles. He who is within the altar is pure: that is to say, he who does anything apart from bishop and presbytery and deacon,— such an one is not pure in his conscience.

8. Not that I have known of anything of this sort among you, but I warn you, who are my beloved ones, beforehand, since I foresee the snares of the devil. Wherefore taking to you the spirit of meekness, renew yourselves with faith, which is the Lord's flesh, and with love, which is the blood of Jesus Christ. Let none of you have a grudge against his neighbour. Give no occasions to the heathen,

lest the multitude in God should be evil spoken of through a few foolish men. "Woe to him by whose vanity my name is blasphemed among any."

9. Stop your ears therefore whenever any one speaks to you at variance with Jesus Christ, who was of the seed of David, the son of Mary, who was truly born, and did eat and drink, was of a truth persecuted under Pontius Pilate, and of a truth crucified and died in the sight of those in heaven, and those on earth, and those under the earth. Who was also of a truth raised from the dead, His Father having raised Him up, according to whose likeness, too, His Father will in Christ Jesus raise up us who have faith in Him, without whom we have no true life.

10. But if, as some that are godless, that is without faith, say, that He only seemed to suffer, who are themselves mere seeming, why am I bound? and why am I eager to fight with beasts? In vain then do I die; and I am then guilty of falsehood about my Lord.

11. Flee then those evil off-shoots which bear deadly fruit, whereof, if any one tastes, he instantly dies: for these are not the planting of the Father. For if they were, they would appear to be branches of the cross, and their fruit would be incorruptible. By it He calls through His passion to you who are His members, for the head cannot be born without

the limbs since God has proclaimed their oneness, and that He is Himself.

12. I salute you from Smyrna, along with the churches of God which are with me, who have refreshed me in all things, both in body and soul. My bonds exhort you, which I bear for the sake of Jesus Christ, praying that I may attain to God. Continue in your unity of mind, and in prayer with each other, for it becomes every one of you, and especially your presbyters, to refresh your bishop to the honour of the Father of Jesus Christ and of the apostles. I beseech you to hear me in love, so that I may not, by having written, be a testimony against you. And do ye also pray for me, who have need of your love, along with the mercy of God, that I may be worthy of the lot for which I am destined, and that I may not be found reprobate.

13. The love of the Smyrnaeans and Ephesians salutes you. Remember in your prayers the Church which is in Syria, from which also I am not worthy to be called, being the last of them. Fare ye well in Jesus Christ, being subject to your bishop as to the commandment, and similarly to the presbytery; and do ye, every man, love each other in sincerity of heart. My spirit is offered for you, not only now, but also when I attain to God, for I am as yet exposed to danger, but the Father is faithful in Christ Jesus to fulfil my petition and yours, in whom may ye be found without blame.

3. *The Pastor of Hermas.*

(Part of Vision III.)

2. ... Saying this, she wished to go away. But falling down at her feet, I begged her by the Lord that she would show me the vision which she had promised. And then she again took hold of me by the hand, and raised me, and made me sit on the seat to the left, and she sat on the right; and lifting up a shining rod, she said to me, "Do you see something great?"

And I said, "Lady, I see nothing."

She said to me, "Lo! do you not see opposite to you a great tower, built upon the waters, of shining square stones?"

Now the tower was built square by those six young men who had come with her. But tens of thousands of men were carrying stones to it; some dragging them from the depths, others removing them from the land, and they handed them to these six young men. They were taking them and building; and those of the stones that were dragged out of the depths they placed in the building just as they were, for they were polished and fitted exactly into the other stones, and became so united one with another that the lines of juncture could not be perceived. And the building of the tower looked as if it were builded out of one stone. The young men rejected some of the other stones which were brought from the dry land, some they fitted into the building, and some they cut down, and cast far away from the tower. Many other stones, however, lay around the tower, and they did not use them in building; for some of them were mouldering, others had cracks in them, others had been made too short, and others were white and round, but did not fit into the building of the tower. Moreover, I saw other stones thrown far away from the tower, and falling into the public road; yet they did not remain on the road, but were rolled into a pathless place. And I saw others falling into the fire and burning, others falling close to the water, and yet not capable of being rolled into the water, though they wished to be rolled down, and to enter the water.

3. On showing me these visions she wished to retire. I said to her, "Lady, what is the use of my having seen all this while I do not know what it means?"

She said to me, "You are a clever fellow, wishing to know everything that relates to the tower."

"Even so, Lady," said I, "that I may tell it to my brethren, and that they may be made merry, and, hearing this, they may know the Lord in much glory."

And she said, "Many indeed shall hear, and hearing, some shall be glad, and some shall weep. But even these, if they hear and repent, shall also rejoice. Hear, then, the parables of the tower; for I will reveal all to you, and give me no more trouble in regard to revelation, for these revelations have an end, for they have been completed. But you will not cease praying for revelations, for you are shameless. The tower which you see building is myself, the Church, who have appeared to you now and on the former occasion. Ask, then, whatever you like in regard to the tower, and I will reveal it to you, that you may rejoice with the saints."

I said unto her, "Lady, since you have vouchsafed to reveal all to me this once, reveal it."

She said to me, "Whatsoever may be revealed will be revealed; only let your heart be with God, and doubt not whatsoever you shall see."

I asked her, "Why was the tower built upon the waters, Lady?"

She answered, "I told you before, and you still inquire carefully, therefore inquiring you shall find the truth. Hear then why the tower is built upon the waters. It is because your life has been, and will be, saved through water. For the tower was founded on the word of the almighty and glorious Name, and it is ruled by the invisible power of the Lord."

4. In reply I said to her, "Lady, this is great and marvellous. But who are the six young men who are engaged in building, Lady?"

"These are the holy angels of God, who were first created, and to whom the Lord handed over His whole creation, that they might increase and build up and rule over the whole creation. By these will the building of the tower be finished."

"But who are the others who are engaged in carrying the stones?"

"These also are holy angels of the Lord, but the former six are more excellent than these. The building of the tower will be finished, and all will rejoice together around the tower, and they will glorify God, because the building of the tower is finished."

I asked her, saying, "Lady, I should like to know what became of the stones, and their nature of what sort it is?"

In reply she said to me, "Not because you are more deserving than all others that this revelation should be made to you—for there are others before you, and better than you, to whom these visions should have been revealed—but that the name of God may be glorified has the revelation been made to you; and it will be made on account of the doubtful who ponder in their hearts whether these things are or not. Tell them that all these things are true, and that none of them is beyond the truth, but all are firm and sure, and established on a strong foundation.

5. "Hear now with regard to the stones which are in the building. Those square white stones which fitted exactly into each other are apostles, bishops, teachers, and deacons, who have lived in godly reverence, and have acted as bishops and teachers and deacons chastely and reverently to the elect of God. Some of them have fallen asleep, and some still remain alive. And they have always agreed with each other, and been at peace among themselves, and listened to each other. On account of this, their fittings join exactly into the building of the tower."

"But who are the stones that were dragged from the depths, and which were laid into the building and fitted in with the rest of the stones previously placed in the tower?"

"They are those who suffered for the Lord's name's sake."

"But I wish to know, Lady, who are the other stones which were carried from the land?"

"Those," she said, "which go into the building without being polished, are those whom the Lord has approved, for they walked in the straight ways of the Lord, and practised His commandments."

"But who are those who are in the act of being brought and placed in the building?"

"They are those who are young in faith, and are faithful. But they are admonished by the angels to do good, for iniquity was found in them."

"Who then are those whom they rejected and cast away?"

"These are they who have sinned and wished to repent. On this account they have not been thrown far from the tower, because they will yet be useful in the building, if they repent. Those then who are to repent, if they do repent, will be strong in faith, if they now repent while the tower is building. But if the building be finished, they no longer find a place, but will be rejected. Yet this privilege only have they, to lie beside the tower.

6. "As to those who were cut down and thrown far away from the tower, do you wish to know who they are? They are the sons of iniquity, and they believed in hypocrisy, and wickedness did not depart from them. For this reason they are not saved, since they cannot be used in the building on account of their iniquities. Wherefore they have been cut off and cast far away on account of the anger of the Lord, for they have roused Him to anger. But I shall explain to you the other stones which you saw lying in great numbers, and not going into the building. Those which are mouldering are those who have known the truth and not remained

in it, nor have they been joined to the saints. On this account are they unfit for use."

"Who are those that have cracks?"

"These are they who are at discord in their hearts one with another, and are not at peace amongst themselves; they indeed keep peace before each other, but when they separate one from the other, their wicked thoughts remain in their hearts. These, then, are the cracks which are in the stones. But those which are shortened are those who have indeed believed, and have the larger share of righteousness; yet they have also a considerable share of iniquity, and therefore they are shortened and not whole."

"But who are these, Lady, that are white and round, and yet do not fit into the building of the tower?"

She answered and said, "How long will you be foolish and stupid, and continue to put every kind of question and understand nothing? These are those who have faith indeed, but they have also the riches of this world. When, therefore, tribulation comes, on account of their riches and business they deny their Lord."

I answered and said to her, "When, then, will they be useful for the building, Lady?"

"When the riches that now seduce them have been circumscribed, then will they be of use to God.

For as a round stone cannot become square unless portions be cut off and cast away, so also those who are rich in this world cannot be useful to the Lord unless their riches be cut down. Learn this first from your own case. When you were rich, you were useless; but now you are useful and fit for life. Be ye useful to God; for you also will be used as one of these stones."

7. "Now the other stones which you saw cast far away from the tower, and falling upon the public road, and rolling from it into pathless places, are those who have indeed believed, but through doubt abandon their true road. Thinking then that they could find a better, they wander and become wretched, and enter upon pathless places. But those which fell into the fire and were burned, are those who have departed for ever from the living God; nor does the thought of repentance ever come into their hearts on account of their devotion to their lusts and to the crimes which they committed. Do you wish to know who are the others which fell near the waters, but could not be rolled into them? These are they who have heard the word, and wish to be baptized in the name of the Lord; but when the chastity demanded by the truth comes into their recollection, they change their mind, and again walk after their own wicked desires."

She finished her exposition of the tower. But I,

shameless as I yet was, asked her, "Is repentance possible for all those stones which have been cast away and did not fit into the building of the tower, and will they yet have a place in this tower?"

"Repentance," said she, "is yet possible, but in this tower they cannot find a suitable place. But in another and much inferior place they will be laid, and that, too, only when they have been tortured and completed the days of their sins. And on this account will they be transferred, because they have partaken of the righteous word. And then only will they be removed from their tortures if the evil deeds which they have done come into their hearts. But if these do not come into their hearts they will not be saved on account of the hardness of their heart."

8. When then I ceased asking in regard to all these matters, she said to me, "Do you wish to see anything else?"

And as I was extremely eager to see something more my countenance beamed with joy. She looked towards me with a smile and said, "Do you see seven women around the tower?"

"I do, Lady," said I.

"This tower," said she, "is supported by them according to the precept of the Lord. Listen now to their functions. The first of them, who is clasping her hands, is called Faith. Through her the elect of God are saved; but that other, who is girded and acts with vigour, is called Self-restraint, she is the daughter of Faith. Whoever then follows her becomes happy in his life, because he will restrain himself from all evil works, believing that, if he restrain himself from all evil desire, he will inherit eternal life."

"But the others, Lady, who are they?"

"They are daughters of each other. One of them is called Simplicity, another Knowledge, another Guilelessness, another Reverence, another Love. When then you do all the works of their mother, you will be able to live."

"I should like to know," said I, "Lady, what power each one of them possesses."

"Hear," she said, "what power they have. Their powers are regulated by each other, and follow each other in the order of their birth. For from Faith arises Self-restraint; from Self-restraint, Simplicity; from Simplicity, Guilelessness; from Guilelessness, Reverence; from Reverence, Knowledge; and from Knowledge, Love. The deeds, then, of these are pure, and reverent, and divine. Whoever devotes himself to these, and is able to hold fast by their works, shall have his dwelling in the tower with the saints of God."

Then I asked her in regard to the seasons, if now there is an end. She cried out with a loud voice, saying, "Foolish man! do you not see the tower yet building? When the tower is finished and built, then comes the end, and it will be soon finished. Ask me no more questions. Let you and all the saints be content with what I have called to your remembrance, and with my renewal of your spirits. But it is not for your own sake only that these revelations have been made to you, but that you may show them to all. For after three days—this you will take care to remember—I command you, Hermas, to speak all the words which I am to say to you into the ears of the saints, that hearing them and doing them, they may be cleansed from their iniquities, and you along with them."

II.—CHRISTIAN RITES.

4. *The Conclusion of the First Apology of Justin Martyr.*[1]

61. And we shall also describe the manner in which we who have been renewed through Christ, dedicated ourselves to God, lest if we omitted this we might seem to be at fault in our narration. As many as are persuaded and believe that what is taught and declared by us is true, and engage that they are able to live accordingly, are taught to fast and pray and entreat God for the remission of their

---

[1] From the text edited by Dr. Otto of Jena.

past sins, while we fast and pray along with them. Then they are led by us where there is water, and are regenerated in the manner of regeneration in which we also were ourselves regenerated: for they then receive the washing of water in the name of God the Father and Lord of all, and of our Saviour Jesus Christ, and of the Holy Ghost.

For Christ also said: "Except ye be regenerated ye shall not enter into the kingdom of heaven." For it is clear to all that those who have once been born cannot enter their mothers' wombs. How those who though they have sinned are penitent may escape their sins is, as we have written above, declared by Isaiah the prophet. He has spoken thus: "Wash ye, be clean, put away your iniquities from your souls, learn to do well, judge the fatherless and plead for the widow, and come and let us reason together, saith the Lord, for even though your sins be as scarlet, I will make them as white as wool, and though they be as crimson, I will make them white like snow. But if ye will not hearken, the sword shall devour you; for the mouth of the Lord hath spoken it."

For this, we have also learned from the apostles this reason: as in our first birth we were generated without our knowledge or choice by the intercourse of our parents, and have been reared in depraved habits and evil training; so, that we should not remain the children of compulsion and ignorance, but of choice and knowledge, and should obtain in the water remission of the sins we have committed in times past, the name of "God the Father and Lord of all" is pronounced over him who wishes to be regenerated and repents of his sins: he who leads the person that is to be washed to the laver pronounces only this, for no one can utter a name for the God whom none can name, and if any shall dare to say he can, he raves with incurable madness; this washing is termed illumination, since they who learn these things have their understanding enlightened. Also in the name of Jesus Christ, who was crucified under Pontius Pilate, and in the name of the Holy Ghost, who foretold through the prophets all things about Jesus, is he washed who is enlightened.

65. But when we have thus washed him who is convinced and assents, we lead him to those who are called brethren, where they are gathered together, and make, in common, earnest petitions for ourselves and for him who has been enlightened, and for all men everywhere, [praying] that we who have learned the truth may be counted worthy, and that we may be found by our works to be good citizens and guardians of that which is enjoined on us, so that we may be saved with an eternal salvation. When we end the prayers we greet each other with a kiss.

Then bread is brought to the president of the

brethren, and a cup of water and wine mingled; and when he has taken them, he renders praise and glory to the Father of all, through the name of the Son and of the Holy Ghost, and makes a giving of thanks (εὐχαριστία) at some length for our being deemed worthy of these things at his hands. But when he has finished the prayers and the giving of thanks, every one of the people who are present respond by saying Amen: and Amen in the Hebrew tongue signifies, So be it. And when the president has ended the giving of thanks, and all the people have responded, those whom we call deacons give to each of those present to partake of the bread and wine and water, over which the thanksgiving was pronounced (τοῦ εὐχαριστηθέντος ἄρτου), and to those who are not present they carry away a portion.

66. This food is called among us the Eucharist, of which no one is allowed to partake but the man who believes that the things we teach are true, and who has been washed with the washing that is for the remission of sins and unto regeneration, and who is so living as Christ has enjoined. For not as common bread or common drink do we receive these: but like as Jesus Christ our Saviour, being incarnate by the word of God, bore about Him both flesh and blood for our salvation, so are we taught that this food—by which, as it is changed, our blood and flesh are nourished,—when it is blessed by prayer

($εὐχαριστηθεῖσαν$) in His words, is the flesh and blood of the incarnate Jesus. For the apostles, in the memoirs composed by them, which are called Gospels, have thus delivered unto us what was enjoined upon them; that Jesus took bread, and when He had given thanks said, "This do in remembrance of me; this is my body;" and likewise, after He had taken the cup and given thanks, He said, "This is my blood," and gave it to them only.

The evil demons have, in imitation, ordered this to be done in the mysteries of Mithras; for that bread and a cup of water are placed, with certain incantations, in the mystic rites of one who is being initiated, you either know or are able to learn.

.67. And we afterwards continually remind one another of these things: and the wealthy succour all who are needy, and we always associate together; and for all things with which we are supplied we bless the Maker of all, through His Son Jesus Christ, and through the Holy Ghost, and on the day called Sunday there is a gathering to one place of all who dwell in the towns or country, and the memoirs of the apostles or the writings of the prophets are read aloud, as long as time permits: then when the reader has ceased, the president gives oral exhortation and invitation to imitate these excellencies: then we all rise together and offer prayer; and, as is related above, when we have ceased praying, bread is brought, and wine and water, and the president likewise offers the most fervent prayers and thanksgiving he can, and the people respond and say Amen. And there is a distribution to each, and a participation in that over which thanks had been pronounced, and to those who are absent a portion is sent by the deacons. And they who are well-to-do, and willing, give voluntarily what each thinks fit, and what is collected is deposited with the president, who succours the orphans and widows, and those who are in want through illness or any other cause, and those who are in prison, and those who are strangers sojourning in a strange place, and in a word, takes care of all who are in need. But Sunday is the day on which we all assemble together, because it is the first day, on which God changed darkness and matter and made the world: and on the same day our Saviour Jesus Christ rose from the dead, for He was crucified on the day before Saturday, and on the day after Saturday, which is Sunday, He showed Himself to His apostles and disciples, and taught those things which we have submitted to you also for consideration.

68. And if these things seem to you to be reasonable and true, honour them; but if they seem foolishness, despise them as folly, and do not decree death against those who do no wrong, as you would against enemies. For we forewarn you that you

shall not escape the coming judgment of God if you continue in your injustice; and we ourselves will invite you to do that which is pleasing to God. And though from the letter of the greatest and most illustrious Emperor Hadrian, your father, we could demand that you order judgment to be given as we have desired, yet we have made this appeal and explanation, not on the grounds of Hadrian's decision, but because we know that what we ask is just. And we have subjoined the copy of Hadrian's epistle, that you may know that we are speaking truly about this. And the following is the copy:—

Epistle of Hadrian to Minucius Fundanus, Proconsul of Asia.—I have received the letter addressed to me by your most illustrious predecessor Serenius Granianus; and this communication I am unwilling to pass over in silence, lest innocent persons be disturbed, and occasion be given to the informers for practising villany. Accordingly, if the inhabitants of your province can so far sustain this petition of theirs as to accuse the Christians in some court of law, I do not prohibit them from doing so. But I will not suffer them to make use of mere entreaties and outcries. For it is far more just, if any one desires to make an accusation, that you give judgment upon it. If, therefore, any one makes the accusation, and furnishes proof that the said men do anything contrary to the laws, you shall adjudge punishments in proportion to the offences. And to this you must give special heed, that if any man shall, through mere calumny, bring an accusation against any of these persons, you shall award to him more severe punishment in proportion to his wickedness.

III.—THE CHRISTIAN YEAR.

5. *Extracts from the Apostolical Constitutions,* v. 13-20.[1]

13. Brethren, observe the festival days; and first of all, the Birthday, which you are to celebrate on the twenty-fifth of the ninth month: after which let the Epiphany be very much honoured by you, on which the Lord made to you a display of His own Godhead; and let it take place on the sixth of the tenth month. After which the fast of Lent is to be observed by you as containing a memorial of our Lord's rule of life and legislation. But let this fast be completed before the fast of the Passover, beginning after the second day of the week and ending on the day of preparation. After this, break off your fast, and begin the holy week of the Passover, and keep it as a fast with fear and trembling, praying on these days for those that are perishing.

14. For they began to take counsel against the

[1] Edited by Ueltzen.

Lord on the second day of the week in the first month which is Xanticus; and the deliberation continued on the third day of the week; but on the fourth day they determined to take away His life by crucifixion. . . .[1] And on the fifth day of the week, when we had eaten the Passover with Him, and when Judas had dipped his hand into the dish and received the sop, and was gone out by night, the Lord said unto us, The hour is come that ye shall be scattered and shall leave me alone; and every one vehemently affirming that they would not forsake Him, I, Peter, adding this promise that I would even die with Him, He said, Verily I say unto thee, Before the cock crow thou shalt thrice deny that thou knowest me. And when He had delivered to us the antitypal mysteries of His precious body and blood, Judas not being present with us, He went out to the Mount of Olives near the brook Cedron, where there was a garden; but we were with Him, and sang an hymn according to the custom. . . .[2] But when the first day of the week dawned He arose from the dead, and fulfilled those things which He foretold to us before

[1] The omitted passage gives an account of the Last Supper, similar to what follows, but based on the account in *S. John*, and introduced by the words: "Once when we were feasting with Him."

[2] The omitted passage contains a long account of the crucifixion, based principally on the narration in *S. Luke*.

His passion, saying,—The Son of Man must be doing in the heart of the earth three days and three nights. And when He was risen from the dead, He appeared first to Mary Magdalene, and Mary the mother of James, then to Cleopas in the way, and after that to us His disciples, who had fled away for fear of the Jews, but in secret occupied ourselves about Him. But these things also are written in the Gospel.

15. He therefore charged us Himself to fast those six days on account of the impiety and transgression of the Jews, commanding us withal to bewail over them, and lament for their perdition. For even He Himself wept over them because they knew not the time of their visitation. [But He commanded us to fast on the fourth day and day of preparation, the former on account of His being betrayed, and the latter on account of His passion.[1]] But He appointed us to break off our fast on the seventh day[2] at the cock-crowing, *but to fast on the Sabbath-day. Not that the Sabbath-day is a day of fasting, being the rest from the creation, but that we ought to fast on this one Sabbath-day only, because on this day the Creator was still under the earth.*

---

[1] This sentence, referring to the weekly fasts on Wednesday and Friday—the Jewish day of preparation for their Sabbath—interrupts the account of Holy Week.

[2] Or on the first day of the week, *i.e.* the seventh day, counting from the second day on which the six days' fast began.

For on their very feast-day they apprehended the Lord, that that oracle might be fulfilled which says, They placed their signs in the middle of their feast and knew them not. Ye ought therefore to bewail over them, because when the Lord came they did not believe on Him, but rejected His doctrine, judging themselves unworthy of salvation. . . . [1]

17. It is therefore your duty, brethren, who have been redeemed by the blood of Christ, to observe the days of the Passover exactly, with all care, after the vernal equinox; lest ye keep the memorial of the one passion twice in a year. Keep it once only in a year for Him that died but once; *but no longer keep the feast along with the Jews. For we have not now any communion with them, for they have been led astray in regard to the calculation itself, which they think they accomplish perfectly, so as to be led astray on every hand, and fenced off from the truth. But do you observe carefully the vernal equinox, which occurs on the twenty-second of the twelfth month, which is Dystros, observing carefully until the twenty-first [2] of the moon, lest the fourteenth of the moon shall fall in another week, and having committed an

---

[1] The omitted passage insists at length that the converted Gentiles have become the true covenant people, and that the Jews have forfeited their privileges.

[2] That is the latest day on which Easter could fall: if the 14th of the new moon were a Sunday, then Easter would be on the 21st of the moon.

error, we should, through ignorance, keep the Passover twice in the year, or celebrate the day of our Lord Jesus' resurrection on any other than the Lord's day only.*[1]

18. Do you therefore fast on the days of the Passover, beginning from the second day of the week until the preparation and the Sabbath, six days, making use of only bread and salt and herbs, and water for your drink; but abstain on these days from wine and flesh, for they are days of mourning and not of feasting. Do ye, who are able, fast the day of preparation and the Sabbath-day entirely, tasting nothing till the cock-crowing

---

[1] The passage between the asterisks is usually marked as an interpolation : it insists on the Catholic use, but in this it harmonises with the eighteenth chapter, in which definite days of the week are mentioned as connected with the commemoration of special events. The passage in asterisks in the fifteenth chapter takes the same view; while the rest of that chapter would harmonise with the Quarto-deciman use, of keeping a Paschal week according to the time of the full moon, without regard to the day of the week on which it fell. This is also the view maintained in the following extract which has been preserved by Epiphanius, and is supposed by all editors to have formed part of chapter 17, in place of the passage marked as an interpolation :—

"Do not yourselves compute, but keep it when your brethren of the circumcision do so : keep it together with them, and if they err in their computation, be not you concerned. Keep your nights of watching in the middle of the days of unleavened bread. And when they are feasting, do you fast and wail over them, because on the day of their feast they crucified Christ : and while they are lamenting and eating unleavened bread in bitterness, do you feast."

of the night; but if any one is not able to join them both, at least let him observe the Sabbath-day, for the Lord says somewhere, speaking of Himself: When the Bridegroom shall be taken away from them, in those days shall they fast. In these days therefore He was taken from us by the Jews, falsely so named, and fastened to the cross, and "was numbered among the transgressors."

19. Wherefore we exhort you also to fast on these days as we also fasted, when He was taken away from us, until the evening; but on the rest of the days, before the day of preparation, let every one eat at the ninth hour, or at the evening, or as every one is able, but on the Sabbath-day prolong it till the cock-crowing, and break off your fast at the dawning of the first day of the week, which is the Lord's day. From the evening till cock-crowing keep awake, and assemble together in the church, watching and praying, and beseeching God in your night-long vigil, read the Law, the Prophets, and the Psalms till the sound of cock-crowing; and baptize your catechumens, and reading the Gospel in fear and trembling, and speaking to the people such things as tend to their salvation, put an end to your sorrow, and beseech God that Israel may be converted, and obtain a place for repentance and the remission of sins. . . .[1] And since He was

---

[1] A few sentences about Pilate and the Jews have been omitted here.

crucified on the day of preparation, and rose again at break of day on the Lord's day, the scripture was fulfilled which says, "Arise, O God, judge the earth, for thou shalt have an inheritance in all the nations" (Ps. lxxxii. 8); and again, "I will arise, saith the Lord, I will put him in safety" (Ps. xii. 6); and, "But Thou, Lord, have mercy upon me, and raise me up again, and I shall requite them" (Ps. xli. 10). For this reason do you also, now the Lord is risen, offer your sacrifice, concerning which He made an ordinance for you, through us, and said, "This do in remembrance of me." And thenceforward leave off your fasting and rejoice, and keep a festival because Jesus Christ, the pledge of your resurrection, is risen from the dead; and let this be an everlasting ordinance unto you till the consummation of the world, until the Lord come. For to the Jews the Lord is still dead, but to Christians He is risen. To the former by their unbelief, to the latter by the full assurance that their hope in Him is immortal and eternal life.

Eight days after let there be again a notable feast, the eighth day itself, on which He fully assured me, Thomas, who was hard of belief, of His resurrection by showing me the prints of the nails and the wound of the spear in His side.

And again, from the first Lord's day count forty days, and from the Lord's day till the fifth day of the week celebrate the feast of the Ascension of the Lord, on which having fulfilled all the charge and command He ascended to God the Father that sent Him, and sat down on the right hand of power, and there remains till His enemies are put under His feet. . . .[1]

20. . . . And ten days after the Ascension, which makes the fiftieth day from the first Lord's day, let there be a great festival for you; for on that day at the third hour the Lord Jesus sent us the gift of the Holy Spirit, and we were filled with His power, and spake with new tongues as the Spirit spake in us; and we preached both to Jews and Gentiles that He is the Christ of God who is appointed by Him to be judge of the quick and dead. Of this Moses bore witness and said, "The Lord received fire from the Lord and rained it down" (Gen. xix. 24). . . .[2]

Therefore after ye have celebrated the feast of Pentecost keep one week as a festival, and after that keep one as a fast, for it is right to rejoice over that gift of God, and to fast after your relaxation. . . .[3] Do you also fast and ask your petitions from God. And after this week of fasting, we enjoin

---

[1] Here follow some sentences on the guilt and lamentations of the Jews.

[2] Several alleged Old Testament predictions of Whitsunday are omitted here.

[3] Several Old Testament examples of fasting are omitted.

you to fast every fourth day of the week, and every day of preparation, and the surplusage of your fast bestow upon the needy; every Sabbath-day except the one, and every Lord's day, hold your assemblies and rejoice, for he will be guilty of sin who fasts on the Lord's day, being the day of the resurrection, or during the time of Pentecost, or in general, who is sad on a day of festival to the Lord; for on them we ought to rejoice and not to mourn.

IV.—CHRISTIAN SUFFERINGS.

6. *The Martyrdom of S. Polycarp.*[1]

The Church of God which sojourns at Smyrna, to the Church of God which sojourns at Philomelium, and to all the sees of the Holy and Catholic Church in every place: mercy, peace, and love from God the Father and from our Lord Jesus Christ be multiplied.

1. We have written to you, brethren, with respect to the martyrs, and the blessed Polycarp, who, as if sealing it with his martyrdom, has put a stop to the persecution. For almost all the events that happened previously took place in order that the Lord might show us from above the martyrdom according to the gospel. For he waited to be delivered up, as also the Lord had done, in order

[1] Text of Gebhardt, Harnack, and Zahn.

that we should be his followers, in not "looking only on our own things, but also on those of others:" for it is a mark of a true and steadfast love to wish not only to be saved one's-self, but all the brethren as well.

2. Blessed and noble have all the martyrdoms been which took place according to God's will: for it is needful that we, who profess greater piety than others, should ascribe the authority over all things to God. For who would not admire their nobleness and humility and devotion?—who, when they were so torn with scourging that the frame of their bodies, to the very veins and arteries, was exposed, endured it, while those who looked on, pitied and bewailed. But they also attained to such nobleness, that not one of them sighed or groaned, and showed to all of us that at the very time they were tormented, the martyrs of Christ were absent from the body, or rather that the Lord was present with them, and kept them company. And holding to the grace of Christ, they despised the torments of this world, and by a single hour, redeemed themselves from eternal destruction: to them the fire of their inhuman tormentors was cool; for they kept before their view escape from the eternal and unquenchable fire, and with the eyes of their heart they looked for the good things which are laid up for those that endure, "which ear hath not heard, nor eye seen,

nor hath entered into the heart of man," but were revealed by the Lord to them, since they were no longer men but angels. In the same way too, those who were condemned to be thrown to the wild beasts endured dreadful tortures; they were stretched on spikes, and punished with other forms of varied torment, in order that, if it were possible, the tyrant might, by their continual tortures, bring them to a denial.

3. For the devil planned many wiles against them; but thanks be to God, he could not prevail over all, for the most noble Germanicus strengthened the timidity of others by his own endurance, and heroically fought the wild beasts. For when the proconsul wished to over-persuade him, and said he should take pity on his youth, in his eagerness he sought out the wild beast for himself, that he might the sooner be freed from this unjust and lawless generation. On this, the whole multitude, marvelling at the nobleness of the God-loving and God-fearing race of Christians, cried out, "Away with the atheists!" "Let Polycarp be sought."

4. (But one named Quintus, a Phrygian who had lately come out of Phrygia, became afraid when he saw the wild beasts; this was the man who had forced himself, with some others, to deliver themselves up of their own accord; him the proconsul persuaded after many entreaties to swear and to

sacrifice. On this account, brethren, we do not commend those who give themselves up of their own accord, since the gospel does not teach us so to do.)

5. When the most admirable Polycarp first heard of it, he continued unmoved, but wished to remain in the city. But many persuaded him to go away, and he went away to a little farm not far from the city. There he stayed with a few friends, night and day engaged in nothing but constant prayer for all, and for the Churches throughout the world; for this was always his practice. And three days before he was taken, while he was praying, in a vision, he saw his pillow consumed by fire; and he turned to those who were with him, and said, "I must be burned alive."

6. When those who sought him were at hand, he departed to another farm, and his pursuers came after him immediately. And when they did not find him, they seized two boys, one of whom, when he was put to torture, confessed. For it was impossible that he should be concealed, since those who betrayed him were of his own household. And the Irenarch, who was chosen by lot, and his name was Herod, hastened to bring him into the stadium so that he might fulfil his peculiar lot and be a partaker of Christ, and that they who betrayed him might undergo the same punishment as Judas.

7. Then taking the boy with them, the pursuers

and horsemen went out on the day of preparation, about the hour of supper, with their usual armour, "as if they were going against a robber." Entering upon him at a late hour of the day, they found him lying in an upper room; whence, though he might easily have escaped to another room, he would not, saying, The will of the Lord be done. And when he heard they were near, he went down and spoke with them, all those who were present wondering at his age and constancy, and that they used so much diligence to capture such an old man; immediately then, at that very hour, he ordered that food and drink should be set before them, as much as they wished, and he asked them to give him time for undisturbed prayer. And when they gave him leave, he stood and prayed, being full of the grace of God, so that he could not cease for two hours to the astonishment of all that heard him, and that many repented of coming against such a godly old man.

8. But after he had ended praying, and had therein remembered all that had ever been connected with him, small and great, noble and obscure, and the whole Catholic Church throughout the world, when the hour came for him to go, they placed him upon an ass and conducted him to the city, it being a Great Sabbath-day. He was met by Herod, who was the Irenarch, and his father Nicetes; who, taking him into their vehicle, persuaded him to take a seat

with them, and said, "For what harm is there in saying, Lord Cæsar, and in sacrificing with the other accustomed ceremonies, and thus saving your life?" He, however, did not at first make any reply; but as they persevered, he said, "I shall not do what you advise me." Failing, therefore, to persuade him, they uttered dreadful language, and thrust him down from the car with great vehemence, so that as he descended from the car he sprained his thigh. But not at all moved from his purpose, as if nothing had happened, he eagerly went on, and was conducted to the stadium. But there was so great an uproar in the place that not many could hear.

9. And a voice came from heaven to Polycarp as he entered the stadium: "Be strong, Polycarp, and contend manfully." No one saw who it was that spoke; but the voice itself was heard by those of us who were present. When he was led forward, however, a great tumult arose among those that heard Polycarp was taken. As he advanced, the proconsul asked him whether he was Polycarp, and he answering that he was, he advised him to renounce Christ, saying, "Have a regard for your age;" and adding similar expressions, such as is usual for them to say, he said, "Swear by the genius of Cæsar; repent; say, Away with those that deny the gods!" But Polycarp, with a countenance grave and serious, and contemplating the

whole multitude of lawless heathen in the stadium, beckoned with his hand to them, and with a sigh he looked up to heaven, and said: "Away with the godless!" As the governor, however, continued to urge him, and said, "Swear, and I will dismiss you—revile Christ," Polycarp replied, "Eighty and six years have I served him, and He never did me wrong; and how can I now blaspheme my king that has saved me?"

10. He still continuing to urge him, and saying, "Swear by the genius of Cæsar," said Polycarp, "If you are so vain as to think that I should swear by the genius of Cæsar, as you say, pretending not to know who I am, hear my free confession. I am a Christian. But if you wish to learn what the doctrine of Christianity is, grant me a day and listen to me." The proconsul said, "Persuade the people." Polycarp replied, "I have thought proper to give you a reason, for we have been taught to give magistrates and powers appointed by God the honour that is due to them, as far as it does not injure us; but I do not consider those the proper ones before whom I should deliver my defence."

11. The proconsul said, "I have wild beasts at hand, I will cast you to these unless you change your mind." He answered, "Call them, for we have no reason to repent from the better to the worse, but it is good to change from wickedness to virtue."

He again urged him,—" I will cause you to be consumed by fire should you despise the beasts and not change your mind." Polycarp answered, "You threaten fire that burns for a moment, and is soon extinguished, for you know nothing of the judgment to come, and the fire of eternal punishment reserved for the wicked. But why do you delay? Bring what you wish."

12. Saying this, and much that was similar, he was filled with confidence and joy, and his countenance was brightened with grace, so that he not only continued undismayed at what was said to him, but on the contrary, the governor, astonished, sent the herald to proclaim in the middle of the stadium, "Polycarp confesses that he is a Christian." When this was declared by the herald, all the multitude, Gentiles and Jews dwelling at Smyrna, cried out, "This is that teacher of Asia, the father of the Christians, the destroyer of our gods; he that teaches multitudes not to sacrifice, not to worship." Saying this, they cried out, and asked Philip the Asiarch, to let loose a lion upon Polycarp. But he replied that he was not permitted, as he had already completed the exhibition of the chase in the amphitheatre. Then all cried out together that Polycarp should be burnt alive, for it seemed necessary that the vision which he saw about his pillow should be fulfilled, when, seeing it on fire whilst he prayed,

he turned to those few faithful friends with him, and said prophetically, "I must be burnt alive."

13. This was executed, however, with such haste that it was no sooner said than done. The crowd, however, forthwith collected wood and straw from the shops and baths; especially the Jews, as usual, freely offered their services for this purpose. But when the pile was prepared, laying aside all his clothes, and loosing his girdle, he attempted also to take off his shoes, which he had not been in the habit of doing before, as he had always had some one of his brethren, that were soon at his side, and rivalled each other in their service to him; for he had always been treated with great respect on account of his exemplary life even before his martyrdom. Presently the instruments prepared for the funeral pile were applied to him. As they were also on the point of securing him with spikes, he said, "Let me be thus, for He that gives me strength to bear the fire will also give me power, without being secured by you with these spikes, to remain unmoved on the pile."

14. They did not nail him, but merely bound him to the stake. But he, closing his hands behind him, and bound to the stake as a noble victim selected from the great flock, an acceptable sacrifice to Almighty God, said: " Father of thy well-beloved and blessed Son Jesus Christ, through whom we

have received the knowledge of Thee, the God of angels and powers, and all creation, and of all the family of the righteous that live before Thee, I bless Thee that Thou hast thought me worthy of the present day and hour, to have a share in the number of the martyrs and in the cup of thy Christ, unto the resurrection of eternal life, both of the soul and body, in the incorruptible felicity of the Holy Spirit: among whom may I be received in thy sight this day as a rich and acceptable sacrifice, as Thou, the faithful and true God, hast prepared, hast revealed, and fulfilled. Wherefore, on this account, and for all things I praise Thee, I bless Thee, I glorify Thee through the eternal and heavenly High Priest, Jesus Christ, thy well-beloved Son. Through whom glory be to Thee with Him and the Holy Ghost, both now and for ever. Amen."

15. After he had repeated Amen, and had finished his prayer, the executioners kindled the fire. And when it arose in great flames, we saw a miracle, those of us who were privileged to see it, and who, therefore, were preserved to declare the facts to others, for the flames presented an appearance like an oven, as when the sail of a vessel is filled with the wind, and thus formed a wall around the body of the martyr. And he was in the midst, not like burning flesh, but as bread that is baked, or like gold and silver purified in the furnace. We also

perceived a fragrant odour, like the fumes of incense, or some other precious aromatic drugs.

16. At length the wicked men, seeing that the body could not be consumed by fire, commanded the executioner to draw near to him and to plunge his sword into him; and when he had done this, such a quantity of blood gushed forth round the spear-point, that the fire was extinguished. So that the whole' multitude were astonished that such a difference should be made between the unbelievers and the elect. One of whom was this wonderful martyr Polycarp, bishop of the Catholic Church in Smyrna, who was in our times an apostolical teacher and a prophet. For every word that he uttered from his mouth has been fulfilled or will be fulfilled.

17. But the envious and malignant adversary, the wicked enemy of all the righteous, seeing the lustre of his martyrdom, and his uniform walk and conversation, and him now crowned with the crown of immortality, and bearing off the indisputable prize, had provided that not even his corpse should be obtained by us, though many of us eagerly wished it, so as to have communion with the sacred body. Some, therefore, secretly engaged Nicetas, the father of Herod and brother of Alce, to go to the governor, so as not to give the body, lest, said they, abandoning Him that was crucified, they should begin to worship this one. And this they said on the

suggestion and urging of the Jews, who were also looking out while we were preparing to take him from the fire. Not knowing, however, that we can never abandon Christ, who, blameless as He was for the sake of sinners suffered for the salvation of those that are being saved from all the world, nor even worship any other. For Him we worship as the Son of God; but the martyrs we deservedly love as the disciples and imitators of our Lord, on account of their exceeding love to their King and Master, of whom may we only become true associates and fellow-disciples.

18. The centurion then, seeing the obstinacy of the Jews, placed him in the middle, and burnt it according to the custom of the Gentiles. Thus, at last, taking up his bones, more valuable than precious stones, and more tried than gold, we deposited them where it was proper they should be. There also, as far as we can, the Lord will grant us to gather and to celebrate the natal day of His martyrdom in joy and gladness, both in commemoration of those who have already finished their contest, and to exercise and prepare those who shall hereafter.

19. This, then, is the account of the blessed Polycarp, who, reckoning those from Philadelphia, was the twelfth who was martyred in Smyrna; yet he alone is specially commemorated of all, insomuch that he is everywhere spoken of among the heathen. He was not merely an illustrious teacher, but also a

pre-eminent martyr, whose martyrdom all desire to imitate, since it was according to the gospel of Christ. By patience he overcame the unjust judge, and thus obtained the crown of immortality; and rejoicing with the Apostles and all the righteous, he glorifies God the Father almighty, and blesses the Lord Jesus Christ, the saviour of our souls, and governor of our bodies, and shepherd of the Catholic Church throughout the world.

20. You indeed requested that we would make you acquainted, at some length, with what took place. We have for the present given a summary report by the hand of our brother Marcion. When ye have read this, do ye send the letter to the brethren at a greater distance, that they also may glorify the Lord, who makes choice of His own servants. To Him who is able to bring us all, by His grace and goodness, to His eternal kingdom, through His only begotten Son Jesus Christ, be glory, honour, power, and majesty for ever and ever. Salute all the saints: they that are with us salute you, and Evarestus, who wrote this epistle, with all his house.

21. And[1] the blessed Polycarp suffered martyrdom on the second day of the present month Xanticus, the seventh day before the Kalends of

---

[1] What follows is a later addition.

March. At the eighth hour on the Great Sabbath he was seized by Herod, when Philip the Trallian was High Priest, and Statius Quadratus proconsul, but Jesus Christ being King for ever and ever, to whom be glory, honour, majesty, and an eternal throne from generation to generation. Amen.

We wish you all happiness, brethren, while ye walk in the doctrine of Jesus Christ, according to the gospel: with whom be glory to God, even the Father and the Holy Spirit, for the salvation of all the elect saints: just as the blessed Polycarp suffered, so may we be found following his steps in the kingdom of Jesus Christ.

This Gaius transcribed from the copy of Irenæus, a disciple of Polycarp, who was also intimate with Irenæus. And I, Socrates, have transcribed the copy of Gaius at Corinth. Grace be with you all.

And I again, Pionius, have written from the previous copy, having carefully searched into the matter, and the blessed Polycarp having manifested it to me through a revelation, even as I shall show in what follows.[1] I have collected these, when they had almost faded away through the lapse of time, that the Lord Jesus Christ may also gather me along with His elect into His heavenly kingdom, to whom, with the Father and the Holy Spirit, be glory for ever and ever. Amen.

[1] The writing referred to is lost.

7. *The Encyclical Letter addressed to the Churches of Asia and Phrygia by the Churches of Lyons and Vienne.*—EUSEBIUS, *History of the Church,* v. 1.[1]

Gaul was the place where the arena was prepared for the above-mentioned conflict: her two distinguished capitals, Lyons and Vienne, are celebrated as surpassing all the rest. Through both of these the river Rhone passes, traversing the whole region with a mighty stream. The account, however, of the martyrs, was sent by the most illustrious Churches there to those of Asia and Phrygia, by whom the events that took place among them are related in the following manner. I will subjoin their own declarations: "The servants of Christ dwelling at Lyons and Vienne, in Gaul, to the brethren in Asia and Phrygia, having the same faith and hope with us, peace and grace and glory from God the Father and Christ Jesus our Lord." Then, premising some other matters, they commence their subject in the following words:—

"The greatness, indeed, of the tribulation, and the extent of the rage exhibited by the heathen against the saints, and the sufferings which the martyrs endured in this country, we are not able fully to declare, nor is it, indeed, possible to describe them. For the adversary assailed us with his whole

[1] Dr. Heinichen's edition.

strength, giving us already a prelude, how unbridled his future movements among us would be. And indeed he resorted to every means to accustom and exercise his own servants against those of God, so that we should not only be excluded from houses, and baths, and markets, but everything belonging to us was prohibited from appearing in any place whatever. But the grace of God contended for us, and rescued the weak, and prepared those who, like firm pillars, were able, through patience, to sustain the whole weight of the enemy's violence against them. These coming in close conflict, endured every species of reproach and torture. Esteeming what was deemed great but little, they hastened to Christ, showing in reality, 'that the sufferings of this time are not worthy to be compared with the glory that shall be revealed in us.' And first, they nobly sustained all the evils that were heaped upon them by the populace, clamours and blows, plundering and robberies, stonings and imprisonments, and whatsoever a savage people delight to inflict upon enemies and foes.

"After this they were led to the forum, and when interrogated by the tribune, and the authorities of the city, they confessed in the presence of the multitude, and were shut up in prison until the arrival of the governor. Afterwards, they were led away to be judged by him, from whom we endured all manner of cruelty. Vettius Epagathus, one of the brethren, who abounded in the fulness of the love of God and man, and whose walk and conversation had been so unexceptionable though he was only young, shared in the same testimony with the presbyter Zacharias. He had indeed walked in all the commandments and righteousness of the Lord blameless, and been untiring in kind offices to man, abounding in zeal for God, and fervent in spirit. As he was of this high character, he could not bear to see a judgment so unjustly passed against us, but gave vent to his indignation, and requested also that he should be heard in defence of his brethren, whilst he ventured to assert that there was nothing either godless or impious among us. At this, those around the tribunal cried out against him, for he was a man of eminent standing. Nor did the governor allow a request so just and so properly made, but only asked whether he also were a Christian? He confessed in as clear a voice as possible, and he, too, was transferred to the number of martyrs, being publicly called the advocate ($\pi\alpha\rho\acute{\alpha}\kappa\lambda\eta\tau$ο$\varsigma$) of the Christians. But he had the Paraclete within him more abundantly than Zacharias, which, indeed, he displayed by the fulness of his love; glorying in the defence of his brethren, and to expose his own life for theirs. He was, indeed, a genuine disciple of Christ, following the Lamb whithersoever He would go.

"After this, the others were also set apart, and the first martyrs came forth unhesitatingly, most cheerfully finishing the confession of martyrdom. They appeared, indeed, unprepared and inexperienced, and even weak, incapable of bearing the intensity of the mighty contest. Of these, indeed, about ten also fell away, causing great sorrow and excessive grief to our brethren, and damping the ardour of those who had not yet been taken. These, however, although they endured all manner of affliction, nevertheless were always present with the martyrs, and never left them. Then, indeed, we were all struck with great fear, on account of the uncertainty of their holding out in the profession, not indeed dreading the tortures inflicted, but looking at the end, and trembling lest they should apostatise. Those, indeed, that were worthy to fill up the number of the martyrs were seized from day to day, so that all the zealous members of the two Churches, and those by whose exertions the Church had been there established, were collected.

"Some domestics that were heathen, belonging to our brethren, were also seized, as the governor had publicly commanded search to be made for all of us. But these, at the instigation of Satan, fearing the tortures which they saw the saints suffering, and the soldiers beside this urging them, charged us with feasts of Thyestes, and the incests of Œdipus, and such crimes as are neither lawful for us to speak nor to think; and such, indeed, as we do not even believe were committed by men. These things being spread abroad among the people, all were so savage in their treatment of us, that, if before some had restrained themselves on account of some affinity, they now carried their cruelty and rage against us to a great excess. Then was fulfilled the declaration of our Lord, 'that the day would come when every one that slayeth you will think he is doing God service.'

"The holy martyrs, after this, finally endured tortures beyond all description; Satan striving with all his power that some blasphemy might be uttered by them. Most violently did the collective madness of the mob, the governor, and the soldiers, rage against Sanctus, the deacon of Vienne, and against Maturus a new convert, indeed, but a noble champion of the faith. Also against Attalus, a native of Pergamos, who was a pillar and foundation of the Church there. Against Blandina, also, in whom Christ made manifest that the things that appear mean and deformed and contemptible among men, are esteemed of great glory with God, on account of love to Him, which is really and powerfully displayed, and glories not in mere appearance. For whilst we were all trembling, and her earthly mistress, who was herself one of the contending martyrs, was apprehensive lest, through the weakness of the flesh, she should not be able to profess her faith with sufficient freedom, Blandina was filled with such power that her ingenious tormentors, who relieved and succeeded each other from morning till night, confessed that they were overcome, and had nothing more that they could inflict upon her. Only amazed that she still continued to breathe after her whole body had been torn asunder and pierced, they gave their testimony that one single kind of the torture inflicted was of itself sufficient to destroy life, without resorting to so many and such excruciating sufferings as these. But this blessed saint, as a noble wrestler, in the midst of her confession itself renewed her strength, and it was rest, refreshment, and relief from pain to her to repeat 'I am a Christian, no wickedness is carried on by us.'

"And Sanctus himself, also nobly sustaining beyond all measure and human power the various torments devised by men, whilst the wicked hoped that, by the continuance and the greatness of the tortures, they would get to hear something from him that he ought not to say, withstood them with so much firmness, that he did not even declare his name, nor that of his nation, nor the city whence he was, nor whether he was a slave or a freeman, but to all the questions that were proposed, he answered in the Latin tongue, 'I am a Christian.' For this he confessed instead of his name, his city, his race, and instead of everything. No other expression did the heathen hear from him. Whence, also, a great rivalry arose between the governor and the tormentors against him; so that when they had nothing further that they could inflict, they at last fastened red-hot plates of brass to the most tender parts of his body. But he continued unsubdued and unshaken, firm in his confession, refreshed and strengthened by the celestial fountain of living water that flows from Christ. But his body itself was evidence of his sufferings, as it was one continued wound, mangled and shrivelled, that had entirely lost the form of man to the external eye. Christ suffering in him exhibited wonders; defeating the adversary, and graphically presenting to the rest that nothing terrifies in presence of the love of the Father, nothing pains in presence of the glory of Christ. For when the wicked tortured the martyr again during the day, and supposed that whilst his members were swollen and inflamed, if they applied the same torments, they would subdue him, as if he would not then be able to bear even the touch of the hand, or else that, dying under his torture, he would strike a terror into the rest, not only was there no appearance like this, but, beyond all human expectation, the body raised itself, and stood erect amid the torments afterwards inflicted, and recovered the former shape and habits of the limbs; so that his second tortures became, through the grace of Christ, not his torment, but his cure.

"But the devil also led forth a certain Biblias to torture, who was one of those that had renounced the faith; thinking he had already consumed her, he was anxious to increase her condemnation by blasphemy, and constraining her as a frail and timid character, easily overpowered, to utter impieties against us. But in the midst of the torture she repented and recovered herself, and as if awakening out of a deep sleep, was reminded by the punishment before her of the eternal punishment in hell. And accordingly she contradicted the blasphemers in her declarations. 'How,' said she, 'could such as these devour children, who considered it unlawful even to taste the blood of irrational animals?' After that she professed herself a Christian, and was added to the number of martyrs.

"But as all the tortures of the tyrants were defeated by Christ, through the patience of the martyrs, the devil devised other machinations; among these were their confinement in prison, in a dark and most dismal place; their feet also stretched in the stocks, and extended to the fifth hole, and other torments, which the enraged minions of wickedness, especially when stimulated by the influence of Satan, are accustomed to inflict upon the prisoners. Numbers of them were therefore suffocated in prison, as many as the Lord would have to depart, thus showing forth His glory. Some of them, indeed, had been cruelly tormented, so that it appeared, even if every means were applied to recover them, they could scarcely live; though confined in prison, devoid of all human aid, they were strengthened by the Lord, and filled with power from Him both in body and mind, and they even stimulated and encouraged the rest. But the new converts, and those that were recently taken, whose bodies were not exercised in trial, did not bear the oppression of incarceration, but died within the prison.

"And the blessed Pothinus, who had faithfully performed the ministrations of the episcopate at Lyons, and who was past his ninetieth year, and very infirm in body; who, indeed, scarcely drew his breath, so weak was he in body at the time; yet in the ardour of his soul, and his eager desire for martyrdom, he roused his remaining strength, and was himself also dragged to the tribunal. Though his body, indeed, was already nearly dissolved, partly by age and partly by disease, yet he still retaining his life in him, that Christ might triumph by it. When carried by the soldiers to the tribunal, whither the public magistrates accompanied him, as if he were Christ himself, and when all the mob raised every outcry against him, he gave a noble testimony. When interrogated by the governor, who was the God of the Christians, he said, 'If thou art worthy, thou shalt know.' After this, he was unmercifully dragged away and endured many stripes, whilst those that were near abused him with their hands and feet in every possible way, not even regarding his age. But those at a distance, whatsoever they had at hand, every one hurled at him, all thinking it would be a great sin and impiety if they fell short of wanton abuse against him. For they supposed they would thus avenge their own gods. Thus, scarcely drawing breath, he was thrown into prison, and after two days he there expired.

"A wonderful interposition of God was then exhibited, and the boundless mercy of Jesus clearly displayed a thing that had rarely happened to the brotherhood, but by no means beyond the reach of the skill of Christ. For those that had fallen from the faith on the first seizure were also themselves imprisoned, and shared in the sufferings of the rest. Their renunciation did them no good at this time, but those that confessed what they really were, were imprisoned as Christians, no other charge being alleged against them. But these, at last, were confined as murderers and guilty culprits, and were punished with twice the severity of the rest. The former, indeed, were refreshed by the joy of martyrdom, the hope of the promises, the love of Christ, and the Spirit of the Father; but the latter were sadly tormented by their own conscience, so that the difference was obvious to all in their very countenances, when they were led forth. For the one went on joyful, much glory and grace being mixed in their faces, so that their bonds seemed to form noble ornaments, and, like those of a bride, adorned with various golden bracelets, and impregnated with the sweet odour of Christ, they appeared to some anointed with earthly perfumes. But the others, with downcast look, dejected, sad, and covered with every kind of shame, in addition to this, were reproached by the heathen as mean and cowardly, bearing the charge of murderers, and losing the honourable, glorious, and life-giving appellation of Christians. The rest, however, seeing these effects, were so much the more confirmed, and those that were taken immediately, confessed, not even admitting the thought suggested by diabolical objections."

Introducing some further remarks, they again proceed: "After these things their martyrdom was finally distributed into various kinds, for plaiting one crown of various colours and all kinds of flowers, they offered it to the Father. It was right, indeed, that these noble wrestlers, who had sustained a diversified contest, and had come off with a glorious victory, should bear away the great crown of immortality. Maturus, therefore, and Sanctus, and Blandina, and Attalus, were led into the amphitheatre to the wild beasts, and to the common spectacle of heathenish inhumanity, the day for exhibiting the fight with wild beasts being designedly published on our account. Maturus, however, and Sanctus, again passed through all the tortures in the amphitheatre, just as if they had suffered nothing at all before, or rather as those who in many trials before had defeated the adversary, and now contending for the crown itself; again, as they passed, bore the strokes of the scourge usually inflicted there, the draggings and lacerations from the beasts, and all that the madness of the people, one here and another there, cried for and demanded; and last of all the iron chair, upon which their bodies were roasted, whilst the fumes of their own flesh ascended to annoy them. The tormentors did not cease even then, but continued to rage so much the more, intending if possible to conquer their perseverance. They could not, however, elicit or hear anything from Sanctus, besides that confession which he had uttered from the beginning. They, therefore, in whom life for the most part had remained through the mighty conflict, were at last despatched. On that day they were made an exhibition to the world, in place of the variety of gladiatorial combats.

"Blandina, however, was bound and suspended on a stake, and thus exposed as food to the assaults of wild beasts, and as she thus appeared to hang after the manner of the cross, by her earnest prayers she infused much alacrity into the contending martyrs. For as they saw her in the contest, with the external eyes, through their sister they contemplated Him that was crucified for them, to persuade those that believe in Him, that every one who suffers for Christ will for ever enjoy communion with the living God. But as none of the beasts then touched her, she was taken down from the stake, and remanded back again to prison to be reserved for another contest, so that by gaining the victory in many conflicts she might render the condemnation of the wily serpent irrefragable, and though small and weak and contemptible, but yet clothed with the mighty and invincible wrestler Christ Jesus, might also encourage her brethren. Thus she overcame the enemy in many trials, and in the conflict received the crown of immortality.

"And Attalus himself too, being vehemently demanded by the populace, as he was a distinguished character, came well prepared for the conflict, conscious as he was of no evil done by him, and as one who had been truly exercised in Christian discipline, and had always been a witness of the truth with us. When led about in the theatre, with a tablet before him, on which was written in Latin : 'This is Attalus the Christian,' and the people were violently incensed against him, the governor, learning that he was a Roman, ordered him to be remanded back again to prison with the rest, concerning whom he had written to Cæsar, and was now awaiting his determination. And he in the meantime was neither idle nor unprofitable to them, but, by their patient endurance, the immeasurable mercy of Christ was manifested. For by means of those that were yet living, were things dead made to live. And the martyrs conferred benefits upon those that were no martyrs.[1] Much joy was also created in the virgin mother, for those whom she had brought forth as dead she recovered again as living. For by means of these the greater part of those that fell away again retraced their steps, were again conceived, were again endued with vital heat, and learned to make the confession of their faith. And now living again, and strengthened in their faith, they approached the tribunal, where that God that willeth not the death of the sinner, but inviteth all to repentance, sweetly regarding them, they were again

[1] *i.e.* on those that had fallen away.

interrogated by the governor. For as Cæsar had written that they should be beheaded, but if any renounced the faith these should be dismissed; at the commencement of the fair which is held here, which indeed is attended by an immense concourse of people from all nations, the governor led forth the martyrs, exhibiting them as a show and public spectacle to the crowd. Wherefore, he also examined them again, and as many as appeared to have the Roman citizenship, these he beheaded. The rest he sent away to the wild beasts. But Christ was wonderfully glorified in those that had before renounced Him, as they then, contrary to all suspicion, on the part of the Gentiles, confessed. And these indeed were separately examined, as if they were soon to be dismissed; but, as they confessed, they were added to the number of the martyrs. Those, however, who had never any traces of the faith, nor any conception of the marriage garment, nor any thought of the fear of God, remained without, who, as the sons of perdition, blasphemed the way by their apostasy.

"All the rest, however, were attached to the Church, of whom, when examined, a certain Alexander was found to be one, a Phrygian by birth, and physician by profession. Having passed many years in Gaul, and being well known for his love of God and his freedom in declaring the truth, for he was not destitute of apostolic grace, he stood before the tribunal, and by signs encouraged them to a good confession, appearing to those around the tribunal as one in the pains of childbirth. The mob, however, chagrined that those who had before renounced the faith were again confessing, cried out against Alexander, as if he had been the cause of this. And when the governor urged and asked him who he was, and he replied that he was a Christian, in his rage he condemned him to the wild beasts, and, accordingly, on the following day he entered the arena with Attalus. For the governor, to gratify the people, also gave up Attalus a second time to the beasts. Thus, enduring all the torments that were invented as punishment in the amphitheatre, and after sustaining the arduous conflict, these were likewise finally despatched. As to Alexander, he neither uttered a groan nor any moaning sound at all, but in his heart communed with God; and Attalus, when placed upon the iron chair, and the fumes from his roasting body rose upon him, said to the multitude in Latin: 'Lo, this is to devour men, what you are doing. But as to us, we neither devour men nor commit any other evil.' And when asked what was the name of God, he answered, 'God has no name like a man.'

"After all these, on the last day of the shows of gladiators, Blandina was again brought forth together with Ponticus, a youth about fifteen years old. These were brought in every day to see the tortures of the rest. Force was also used to make them swear by their idols; and when they continued firm and set them at nought, the multitude became outrageous at them, so that they neither compassionated the youth of the boy nor regarded the sex of the woman. Hence they subjected them to every horrible suffering, and led them through the whole round of torture, ever and anon striving to force them to swear, but were unable to effect it. Ponticus, indeed, encouraged by his sister, so that the heathen could see that she was encouraging and confirming him, nobly bore the whole of these sufferings, and gave up his life. But the blessed Blandina, last of all, as a noble mother that had animated her children, and sent them as victors to the King, herself retracing the ground of all the conflicts her children had endured, hastened at last, with joy and exultation at the issue, to them, as if she were invited to a marriage-feast, and not to be cast to wild beasts. And thus, after scourging, after exposure to the beasts, after roasting, she was finally thrown into a net and cast before a bull, and when she had been well tossed by the animal, and had now no longer any sense of what was done to her by reason of her firm hope, confidence, faith, and her communion with Christ, she too was despatched. Even the Gentiles confessed that no woman among them had ever endured sufferings as many and great as these.

"But not even then was their madness and cruelty to the saints satisfied; for these fierce and barbarous tribes, stimulated by the Savage Beast, were in a fury not easily to be assuaged, so that their abuse of the bodies assumed another novel and singular aspect. Not abashed when overcome by the martyrs, but evidently destitute of all reason, the madness both of the governor and the people, as of some savage beast, blazed forth so much the more, to exhibit the same unjust hostility against us,—that the Scriptures might be fulfilled, 'He that is unjust, let him be unjust still, and he that is righteous, let him be righteous still.' For those that were suffocating in the prison, they cast to the dogs, carefully watching them night and day, lest any should be buried by us, and then also cast away the remains left by the beasts and the fire, howsoever they had either been mangled or burnt. They also guarded the heads of the others, together with the trunks of their bodies, with military watches, for many days in succession, in order to prevent them from being buried. Some, indeed, raged and gnashed their teeth against them, anxious to find out some better way of punishment. Others, again, laughed at and insulted them, extolling their idols, and imputing to them the punishment of the martyrs. But others, more moderate, and who in some measure appeared to sympathise, frequently upbraided them, saying, 'Where is their God? and what benefit has their religion been to them, which they preferred to their own life?' Such was the variety of disposition among the Gentiles, but among our brethren, matters were in great affliction for want of liberty to commit the bodies to the earth. For neither did the night avail us for this purpose, nor had money any effect to persuade, nor could any prayers or entreaties move them. But they guarded them in every possible way, as if it were a great gain to prevent them from burial." To these they afterwards add other accounts, saying: "The bodies of the martyrs, after being abused in every possible manner, and thus exposed to the open air for six days, were at length burned and reduced to ashes by the wicked, and finally cast into the Rhone, that flows near at hand, that there might not be a vestige of them remaining on the land. These things they did as if they were able to overcome God, and destroy their resurrection ($\pi\alpha\lambda\iota\gamma\gamma\epsilon\nu\epsilon\sigma\iota\alpha$), as they themselves gave out, 'that they might not have any hope of rising again, in the belief of which they have introduced a new and strange religion, and contemn the most dreadful punishments, and are prepared to meet death even with joy. Now we shall see whether they will rise again; and whether their God is able to help them, and rescue them out of their hands.'"

B. Chronological Table.

Civil Affairs.	Date.	Ecclesiastical Leaders.	Works current before the end of the Period.	Historians and Historical References.
		Cerinth, fl.	Canonical Writings, Epistles of S. Clement and Ignatius (Syriac and short Greek), *Pastor of Hermas, First Apology* and *Dialogue* of Justin Martyr.	Hegesippus, Irenaeus, Hippolytus, Eusebius, Epiphanius.
Trajan.	100			
Pliny.	110			
Hadrian.	120	Ignatius, m.		
	130			
Antoninus Pius.	140			
	150	Marcion, fl. Montanus, fl.		
	160	Justin, m. Anicetus.	Martyrdom of Polycarp. Melito. Apollinaris, Athenagoras. Tertullian's and Irenaeus' earlier works.	
M. Aurelius.	170	Melito of Sardis. Polycarp, m.		
Commodus.	180	Pothinus, m. Athenagoras. Hegesippus.		
	190	Polycrates, fl.		
Severus.	200	Tertullian, fl. Victor. Irenaeus, fl. Zephyrinus.		

INDEX.

AARON, 25, 50, 227.
Abraham, 157.
Acts, Apocryphal, 19.
Acts of the Apostles, 16, 41, 44, 46, 57, 75, 113, 114, 119, 134, 136.
Adam, 160.
Aelia, 116.
Alexander, 287.
Alexandria, 11, 28, 87, 92, 94, 113, 116, 131, 209.
Ananias, 44, 186.
Anatolius, 205.
Anicetus, 206.
Antioch, 11, 91, 105, 228.
Apocalypse, 16, 49, 51, 52, 55, 57, 64, 65, 76, 85, 90, 99, 128.
Apollinaris, 208.
Apostles, 32, 42, 57, 80, 120, 122, 125, 132, 133, 185, 226, 227, 229, 231, 238, 248.
Apostolical Constitutions, 16, 81, 195, 221, 251.
Ascension, 39, 258.
Asia, 13, 18, 27, 47, 52, 55, 62, 64, 78, 82, 85, 100, 106, 108, 114, 121, 123, 129, 180, 195, 208, 221, 228, 250, 273.
Athanasian Creed, 183.
Athenagoras, 162, 179.
Attalus, 277, 285, 288.
Augustus, 128.
Aurelius, M., 144, 286.

BAPTISM, 35, 37, 42, 55, 63, 67, 109, 182, 210, 246.
Bar Cochab, 29, 90.
S. Barnabas, 105, 120.
S. Barnabas, Epistle of, 17, 65, 67, 87, 94, 97.
Baronius, 7.
Baur, 3, 5, 11, 62, 87, 140, 153, 155.
Bellermann, 79.
Berkeley, 87.
Biblias, 280.
Bishops. *See* Episcopate.
Bithynia, 142.
Blandina, 277, 285, 288.
Boehme, 87.
Bunsen, 87, 196, 221.
Butler, 156.

CAIN, 156.
Canon of Scripture, 14, 145.
Catechumens, 175, 256.
Cerinth, 95, 99, 103, 123.
Chronicon Paschale, 208.
Clarke, 88.
Clement, of Alexandria, 9, 87, 124.
S. Clement of Rome, 81, 217.
—— *Epistle of,* 17, 65, 72, 75, 76, 77, 78, 113, 124, 222.
Clementines, 19, 74, 95, 113, 160, 175.
Cleopas, 253.
Colosse, 57, 105, 122.

Colossians, Epistle to the, 56, 57, 65, 101.
Congregationalism, 135.
Consciousness, Christian, 12, 35, 48, 121, 134, 136, 146, 167, 172.
Corinth, 72, 77, 78, 105, 133, 182, 272.
Corinthians, S. Paul's Epistles to the, 61, 112, 115, 120, 163.
—— *S. Clement's. See* S. Clement.
Councils, 101, 102, 132, 134, 144, 145, 163, 180. *See also* Jerusalem, Laodicea.
Courts Christian, 182.
Crete, 105.
Crusé, 221.
Custom of the Church, 147, 167, 168, 171, 181, 210, 218.

DANIEL, 49, 53.
David, 24, 25, 103, 232.
Deacons, 44, 74, 81, 119, 126, 210, 226, 229, 238.
Demetrius, 141.
Deuteronomy, 161.
Diocletian, 112.
Diognetus, Epistle to, 72.
Drake, 72.
Dressel, 80.
Drummond, 28, 30.

EASTER, 194, 204, 206, 207, 254.
Ebionitism, 19, 86, 91, 94, 97, 103, 122, 127, 139, 215.
Elijah, 161.
Epaphroditus, 120.
Epaphras, 105.
Ephesians, Epistle to the, 56, 65, 77.
Ephesus, 17, 85, 90, 105, 120, 129, 138, 233.
Epiphanius, 95, 164, 196, 255.
Epiphany, 251.

Episcopate, Civic, 77, 81, 106, 113, 121, 125, 130, 145, 165, 180, 184, 210, 226, 281.
—— Viceregal, 46, 52, 74, 113, 115, 123, 130, 229, 230, 231, 238.
Erastus, 38.
Essenes, 27, 93, 94.
Eucharist, 60, 70, 72, 109, 177, 247.
Eunuch, Ethiopian, 174.
Eusebius, 15, 18, 95, 100, 115, 144, 145, 191, 273.
Ewald, 32.
Exodus, 50.
Ezekiel, 49, 53.

FICHTE, 87.
France, 23.

GAIUS, 95, 272.
Galatia, 91, 114, 120.
Galatians, Epistle to the, 45, 114, 134.
Gallio, 141.
Garucci, 80.
de Gebhardt, O., 18, 222, 259.
Gentiles, 32, 43, 44, 46, 90, 136, 254.
Germanicus, 261.
Gnosticism, 86 *seq.*, 215.
Gospels, Apocryphal, 18, 19.
—— Synoptic, 16, 33, 34, 41, 47, 57, 59 *seq.*, 188 *seq.*
Greek Civilisation, 104, 128.

HADRIAN, 113, 143, 250.
Hamilton, 159.
Harnack, 18, 222.
Hebrews, Epistle to the, 16, 51, 52, 54, 58.
Hegel, 5, 87.
Hegesippus, 115.
Heinichen, 273.
Herod, 26.
—— of Smyrna, 263, 269, 272.
Hierapolis, 208.

INDEX.

Hilgenfeld, 158, 193.
Hippolytus, 9, 95, 125, 153, 158, 186, 205.
Holy Office, 172.

S. IGNATIUS, 142, 228.
—— *Epistles of*, 17, 71, 72, 73, 76, 78, 79, 113, 125.
Innes, Alexander Taylor, 40.
Irenæus, 9, 71, 95, 153, 162, 207, 210, 272.
Isaiah, 50, 78, 226, 245.
Israel, 8, 24, 27, 30, 32, 42, 51, 54, 61, 227.

S. JAMES THE JUST, 45, 63, 74, 91, 114, 116, 119, 184.
S. James, Epistle of, 16, 48, 57.
S. Januarius, 80.
Jeremiah, 24, 161.
Jerusalem, 11, 31, 37, 41, 45, 47, 52, 57, 61, 63, 72, 73, 74, 92, 114, 116, 118, 121, 132, 204, 225.
—— New, 49.
—— Council of, 43, 44, 132, 134.
Jesus of Nazareth, 8, 24, 33, 34, 42, 50, 54, 61, 63, 74, 89, 91, 94, 95, 97, 105, 174, 214, 223, 226, 227, 228 *seq.*, 245 *seq.*, 259, 267, 273, 282.
—— doings of, 39, 48, 187 *seq.*, 249, 251 *seq.*
—— teaching of, 32, 36, 58 *seq.*, 165, 169, 245.
Jewish Christianity, 91, 136, 198.
—— Church, 24, 26.
Jews, 27, 30, 45, 51, 52, 58, 61, 67, 68, 71, 89 *seq.*, 103, 136, 141, 156, 174, 189, 198, 205, 254, 267, 270.
S. John the Baptist, 34.
S. John the Evangelist, 42, 47, 100, 106, 120, 123, 197, 202, 206.

S. John, Gospel of, 17, 35, 36, 40, 58, 87, 100, 138, 188 *seq.*, 252.
Judaisers, 6, 90, 127, 129, 139.
Judaism, 94, 102, 127, 200, 211, 215.
Judas Maccabæus, 103.
Julian, 112.
Justin Martyr, 66, 68, 69, 73, 76, 111, 112, 131, 143, 154, 162, 164, 177, 179, 244.

KEIM, 28.
Kirk Sessions, 182.

LAODICEA, 101, 102, 194, 205, 208.
Law, 25, 27, 45, 48, 92, 93, 94, 97, 102, 137, 190, 213.
Le Bas, 129.
Lent, 206, 251.
Leo, 217.
Levites, 25, 211, 225.
Leviticus, 50.
Lightfoot, Bishop, 28, 45, 102, 113, 116, 119, 122, 125, 228.
S. Luke, Gospel of, 36, 252.
Lyons, 18, 273, 281.
Lystra, 105.

MAGNESIANS, *Epistle to the*, 74.
Manasseh, 24.
Mansel, 159.
Marcion, 87, 153, 159, 166, 173, 216.
Marcionites, 41, 161, 176, 180, 215.
S. Mark, Gospel of, 25, 34.
S. Mary Magdalene, 253.
Mary, the mother of James, 253.
S. Mary the Virgin, 232.
Mary Tudor, 144.
Maturus, 277, 284.
S. Matthew, Gospel of, 32, 34, 35, 38, 40, 54, 59, 138, 161, 169.
Melito of Sardis, 144, 161, 167, 172, 194, 208.
Merivale, 129.

Messiah, 25, 29, 32, 34, 42, 52, 59, 89, 174.
Minucius Felix, 180.
—— Fundanus, 250.
Montanism, 86, 145, 180, 183, 196, 215.
Montanus, 160 *seq.*, 173, 216.
More, 87.
Moses, 226, 258.
Mithras, 248.

NAPLES, 79.
Nathanael, 60.
Nazarenes, 92, 103.
Neander, 6, 11, 143.
Nehemiah, 103.
Nero, 142, 143, 147.
Nicetas, 263, 269.
Nicodemus, 60.
Nicolaitans, 122.
Noah, 68, 157, 160.
Novatianism, 86.

OLSHAUSEN, 38.
Origen, 175, 176, 180.
Otto, 244.
Overbeck, 138, 139.

PALESTINE, 2 9.
Papias, 65.
Paschal Lamb, 61, 188, 201.
Passover, 61, 188 *seq.*, 251.
Pastor of Hermas, 17, 65, 67, 78, 79, 124, 179, 235.
S. Paul, 31, 42, 46, 47, 55, 58, 90, 105, 106, 112, 136, 165, 201, 216.
—— Epistles of, 16, 55, 58, 67, 106, 113, 120.
Pella, 115.
Pentecost, 37, 42, 57, 131, 214, 258.
Pergamos, 85, 277.
S. Peter, 37, 38, 42, 44, 74, 106, 183, 252.

S. Peter, First Epistle of, 16, 53, 57, 64, 67, 113.
Pharisees, 32, 91, 165, 190.
Philemon, Epistle to, 57.
Philadelphia, 85.
S. Philip, 174, 202.
Philip the Trallian, 266.
Philippi, 76, 77, 120.
Philippians, Epistle of S. Paul to the, 120.
Philomelium, 259.
Philochristus, 30.
Phrygia, 105, 114, 120, 129, 261, 273, 287.
Pilate, 232, 246, 256.
Pionius, 193, 272.
Platonism, 96.
Pliny, 142.
Plotinus, 88.
Polybius, 229.
S. Polycarp, 77, 126, 147, 192, 206.
—— *Epistle of*, 17, 76, 79.
—— *Epistle to*, 72.
—— *Martyrdom of*, 71, 76, 169, 191, 259.
Polycrates, 145, 208.
Ponticus, 288.
Pontus, 154, 159.
Pothinus, 281.
Presbyters, 46, 55, 74, 75, 78, 81, 106, 115, 118, 120, 121, 125, 126, 183, 184, 210, 228, 229, 231, 233.
Presbyterianism, 88, 135, 172.
Priestley, 88.
Prophets, Hebrew, 25, 256.
—— in the Church, 167 *seq.*

QUARTO-DECIMAN, 62, 186 *seq.*, 255.
Quintus, 169, 261.

RATIONALISM, 88.
Resurrection, 39, 48, 186 *seq.*, 211, 259.

INDEX.

Ritschl, 5, 44, 79, 119, 161, 165.
Romans, 32, 36, 104, 110, 128.
Romans, Epistle to the, 114.
Rome, 11, 69, 77, 78, 80, 122, 124, 201, 205, 206.
Rothe, 25, 32, 38, 132, 175, 179.
Routh, 65.

SADDUCEES, 31.
Sagaris, 208.
Samaria, 60.
Samuel, First Book of, 25.
Sanctus, 278, 284.
Sanday, 158.
Sanhedrin, 26, 31, 38, 45, 74, 230.
Sardis, 144, 167, 172, 208.
Satan, 51, 61, 103, 261, 276.
Schwegler, 5, 167.
Scythia, 116.
Serenius Granianus, 250.
Sergilius Paulus, 208.
Sidon, 74.
Simon Magus, 44.
Smyrna, 79, 191, 193, 229, 233, 259.
Smyrnœans, Epistle to the, 74.
Solomon, 24, 32, 103.
de Soyres, 164, 170.
Sozomen, 116.
The Spirit of God, 12, 37, 97, 108, 121, 154, 157, 160 *seq.*, 226, 245 *seq.*, 268, 283.

Stations, 168, 187, 253, 257.
Statius Quadratus, 272.
Steitz, 194, 195.
Symeon, 115.
Syria, 87, 116, 131, 233.

TACITUS, 142, 147.
Talmud, 28.
Tertullian, 9, 124, 153, 161, 162 *seq.*, 176, 180, 182, 183, 184.
Testaments of the Twelve Patriarchs, 92.
Timothy, Epistles to, 120, 123.
Titus, 105.
Trallians, Epistle to the, 73, 228.
Tripolis, 74.
Trypho, 66.
Trajan, 142.

UELTZEN, 251.

VALENS, 76.
Valentin, 87, 96.
Vitringa, 38.

WADDINGTON, 17, 129.
Westcott, 191.
de Wette, 138.
Whiston, 221.

ZACHARIAS, 275.
Zahn, 18, 192, 222.
Zephyrinus, 182, 183, 184.

BY THE SAME AUTHOR.

The Influence of Descartes on Metaphysical Speculation in England.

'Mr. Cunningham's treatise on Descartes and English speculation is a model in its kind; it is clear, penetrating, succinct, and trustworthy. . . . Mr. Cunningham writes from the point of view of those who hold that Kant and Hegel have constructed the final transcendental justification for sound common sense. . . . He corrects very happily K. Fischer's attempt to derive all English thinking from Bacon, bringing out the direct relation of Locke and indirect relation of his successors to Descartes.'—*Academy.*

'Mr. Cunningham has read carefully, and thought much upon the philosophical writings of England and Scotland from the seventeenth century to the beginning of the nineteenth. . . . His results are well calculated to stimulate thought, as they are certain to interest all independent thinkers.'—*Nonconformist.*

'Displays a range of reading and an amount of careful thinking which render it deserving of high praise.'—*Scotsman.*

'An excellent monograph, which shows both powers of thought and a philosophical erudition very unusual in the English metaphysical literature of the present time. . . . An acquaintance with the best German works which treat of his subject is a leading feature.'—(*American*) *Journal of Speculative Philosophy.*

A Dissertation on the Epistle of S. Barnabas:

To this are added a Greek Text, the Latin Version, with a new English Translation and Commentary, by G. H. Rendall, M.A., Fellow of Trinity College, Cambridge.

Dr. Donaldson writes :—

'It is with peculiar pleasure that we note among the monographs on Barnabas one from an English scholar. Mr. Cunningham's treatise is a valuable contribution to the discussion of the questions connected with the Epistle of Barnabas. It is well written, and marked by thorough independence, mastery of all requisite knowledge, and a genuine spirit of investigation. Mr. Rendall's edition of the epistle is also worthy of great praise. The editor shows conspicuous ability in dealing with his authorities and in his selection of readings.'—*Theological Review.*

Dr. Sanday writes :—
'His dissertation is very fairly exhaustive. . . . It is clearly and neatly written; it shows considerable skill in tracing the relations of thought and doctrine, and a laudable desire to hold the balance evenly in the discussion of controverted questions. . . . The two fellow-workers have achieved a success. . . . We wish we could hope that there would be more among us in England who at the same stage in their career could look back upon a like account of work done and well done.'—*Academy.*

'Very scholarly and complete.'—*John Bull.*

'A very useful monograph.'—*Church Times.*

'A more exhaustive critical performance than this has rarely been produced even in this age of exhaustive criticism.'—*Nonconformist.*

'Mr. Cunningham has gained distinction among metaphysicians by his essay on "Descartes," and he is no less painstaking and skilful in this discussion of a very different subject. . . . The Greek text has been very carefully edited by Mr. Rendall, whose critical and expository notes are admirable, and add greatly to the value of the work.'—*Freeman.*

Christian Civilisation: with special reference to India.

LONDON: MACMILLAN AND CO.

June, 1880.

A CATALOGUE of THEOLOGICAL BOOKS,

Published by

MACMILLAN AND CO.

Bedford Street, Strand, London, W.C.

Abbott (Rev. E. A.)—Works by the Rev. E. A. ABBOTT, D.D., Head Master of the City of London School:

BIBLE LESSONS. Second Edition. Crown 8vo. 4s. 6d.
"*Wise, suggestive, and really profound initiation into religious thought.*"
—Guardian. *The Bishop of St. David's, in his speech at the Education Conference at Abergwilly, says he thinks "nobody could read them without being the better for them himself, and being also able to see how this difficult duty of imparting a sound religious education may be effected."*

THE GOOD VOICES: A Child's Guide to the Bible. With upwards of 50 Illustrations. Crown 8vo. cloth gilt. 5s.
"*It would not be easy to combine simplicity with fulness and depth of meaning more successfully than Mr. Abbott has done.*"—Spectator. *The Times says—"Mr. Abbott writes with clearness, simplicity, and the deepest religious feeling."*

CAMBRIDGE SERMONS PREACHED BEFORE THE UNIVERSITY. Second Edition. 8vo. 6s.

OXFORD SERMONS PREACHED BEFORE THE UNIVERSITY. 8vo. 7s. 6d.

ABBOTT (Rev. E. A.)—*continued.*

THROUGH NATURE TO CHRIST; or, The Ascent of Worship through Illusion to the Truth. 8vo. 12s. 6d.

"*The beauty of its style, its tender feeling, and its perfect sympathy, the originality and suggestiveness of many of its thoughts, would of themselves go far to recommend it. But far besides these, it has a certain value in its bold, comprehensive, trenchant method of apology, and in the adroitness with which it turns the flank of the many modern fallacies that caricature in order to condemn Christianity.*"—Church Quarterly Review.

Ainger (Rev. Alfred).—SERMONS PREACHED IN THE TEMPLE CHURCH. By the Rev. ALFRED AINGER, M.A. of Trinity Hall, Cambridge, Reader at the Temple Church. Extra fcap. 8vo. 6s.

"*It is,*" *the* British Quarterly *says,* "*the fresh unconventional talk of a clear independent thinker, addressed to a congregation of thinkers.... Thoughtful men will be greatly charmed by this little volume.*"

Alexander.—THE LEADING IDEAS of the GOSPELS. Five Sermons preached before the University of Oxford in 1870—71. By WILLIAM ALEXANDER, D.D., Brasenose College; Lord Bishop of Derry and Raphoe; Select Preacher. Cr. 8vo. 4s. 6d.

"*Eloquence and force of language, clearness of statement, and a hearty appreciation of the grandeur and importance of the topics upon which he writes, characterize his sermons.*"—Record.

Arnold.—Works by MATTHEW ARNOLD:

A BIBLE READING FOR SCHOOLS. THE GREAT PROPHECY OF ISRAEL'S RESTORATION (Isaiah, Chapters 40—66). Arranged and Edited for Young Learners. By MATTHEW ARNOLD, D.C.L., formerly Professor of Poetry in the University of Oxford, and Fellow of Oriel. Third Edition. 18mo. cloth. 1s.

The Times *says*—"*Whatever may be the fate of this little book in Government Schools, there can be no doubt that it will be found excellently calculated to further instruction in Biblical literature in any school into which it may be introduced.... We can safely say that whatever school uses this book, it will enable its pupils to understand Isaiah, a great advantage compared with other establishments which do not avail themselves of it.*"

ISAIAH XL.—LXVI., with the Shorter Prophecies allied to it. Arranged and Edited with Notes. Crown 8vo. 5s.

Bather.—ON SOME MINISTERIAL DUTIES, CATECHISING, PREACHING, &c. Charges by the late Archdeacon BATHER. Edited, with Preface, by Dr. C. J. VAUGHAN. Extra fcap. 8vo. 4s. 6d.

Bernard.—THE PROGRESS OF DOCTRINE IN THE NEW TESTAMENT. By THOMAS D. BERNARD, M.A., Rector of Walcot and Canon of Wells. Third and Cheaper Edition. Crown 8vo. 5s. (Bampton Lectures for 1864.)

"*We lay down these lectures with a sense not only of being edified by sound teaching and careful thought, but also of being gratified by conciseness and clearness of expression and elegance of style.*"—Churchman.

Binney.—SERMONS PREACHED IN THE KING'S WEIGH HOUSE CHAPEL, 1829—69. By THOMAS BINNEY, D.D. New and Cheaper Edition. Extra fcap. 8vo. 4s. 6d.

"*Full of robust intelligence, of reverent but independent thinking on the most profound and holy themes, and of earnest practical purpose.*"—London Quarterly Review.

A SECOND SERIES OF SERMONS. Edited, with Biographical and Critical Sketch, by the Rev. HENRY ALLON, D.D. With Portrait of Dr. Binney engraved by JEENS. 8vo. 12s.

Birks.—Works by T. R. BIRKS, M.A., Professor of Moral Philosophy, Cambridge :

THE DIFFICULTIES OF BELIEF in connection with the Creation and the Fall, Redemption and Judgment. Second Edition, enlarged. Crown 8vo. 5s.

AN ESSAY ON THE RIGHT ESTIMATION OF MSS. EVIDENCE IN THE TEXT OF THE NEW TESTAMENT. Crown 8vo. 3s. 6d.

COMMENTARY ON THE BOOK OF ISAIAH, Critical, Historical and Prophetical; including a Revised English Translation. With Introduction and Appendices on the Nature of Scripture Prophecy, the Life and Times of Isaiah, the Genuineness of the Later Prophecies, the Structure and History of the whole Book, the Assyrian History in Isaiah's Days, and various Difficult Passages. Second Edition, revised. 8vo. 12s. 6d.

SUPERNATURAL REVELATION, or First Principles of Moral Theology. 8vo. 8s.

Bradby.—SERMONS PREACHED AT HAILEYBURY. By E. H. BRADBY, M.A., Master. 8vo. 10s. 6d.

"*He who claims a public hearing now, speaks to an audience accustomed to Cotton, Temple, Vaughan, Bradley, Butler, Farrar, and others...... Each has given us good work, several, work of rare beauty, force, or originality ; but we doubt whether any one of them has touched deeper chords, or brought more freshness and strength into his sermons, than the last of their number, the present Head Master of Haileybury.*"—Spectator.

Butcher.—THE ECCLESIASTICAL CALENDAR; its Theory and Construction. By SAMUEL BUTCHER, D.D., late Bishop of Meath. 4to. 14*s.*

Butler (G.)—Works by the Rev. GEORGE BUTLER, M.A., Principal of Liverpool College:

FAMILY PRAYERS. Crown 8vo. 5*s.*

SERMONS PREACHED in CHELTENHAM COLLEGE CHAPEL. Crown 8vo. 7*s.* 6*d.*

Butler (Rev. H. M.)—SERMONS PREACHED in the CHAPEL OF HARROW SCHOOL. By H. MONTAGU BUTLER, Head Master. Crown 8vo. 7*s.* 6*d.*

"*These sermons are adapted for every household. There is nothing more striking than the excellent good sense with which they are imbued.*"—Spectator.

A SECOND SERIES. Crown 8vo. 7*s.* 6*d.*

"*Excellent specimens of what sermons should be—plain, direct, practical, pervaded by the true spirit of the Gospel, and holding up lofty aims before the minds of the young.*"—Athenæum.

Butler (Rev. W. Archer).—Works by the Rev. WILLIAM ARCHER BUTLER, M.A., late Professor of Moral Philosophy in the University of Dublin:

SERMONS, DOCTRINAL AND PRACTICAL. Edited, with a Memoir of the Author's Life, by THOMAS WOODWARD, Dean of Down. With Portrait. Ninth Edition. 8vo. 8*s.*

The Introductory Memoir narrates in considerable detail and with much interest, the events of Butler's brief life; and contains a few specimens of his poetry, and a few extracts from his addresses and essays, including a long and eloquent passage on the Province and Duty of the Preacher.

A SECOND SERIES OF SERMONS. Edited by J. A. JEREMIE, D.D., Dean of Lincoln. Seventh Edition. 8vo. 7*s.*

The North British Review *says,* "*Few sermons in our language exhibit the same rare combination of excellencies: imagery almost as rich as Taylor's; oratory as vigorous often as South's; judgment as sound as Barrow's; a style as attractive but more copious, original, and forcible than Atterbury's; piety as elevated as Howe's, and a fervour as intense at times as Baxter's. Mr. Butler's are the sermons of a true poet.*"

BUTLER (Rev. W. Archer)—*continued.*

LETTERS ON ROMANISM, in reply to Dr. Newman's Essay on Development. Edited by the Dean of Down. Second Edition, revised by Archdeacon HARDWICK. 8vo. 10s. 6d.

These Letters contain an exhaustive criticism of Dr. Newman's famous "Essay on the Development of Christian Doctrine." "A work which ought to be in the Library of every student of Divinity."—BP. ST. DAVID'S.

Campbell.—Works by JOHN M'LEOD CAMPBELL:

THE NATURE OF THE ATONEMENT AND ITS RELATION TO REMISSION OF SINS AND ETERNAL LIFE. Fourth and Cheaper Edition, crown 8vo. 6s.

"Among the first theological treatises of this generation."—Guardian.

"One of the most remarkable theological books ever written."—Times.

CHRIST THE BREAD OF LIFE. An Attempt to give a profitable direction to the present occupation of Thought with Romanism. Second Edition, greatly enlarged. Crown 8vo. 4s. 6d.

"Deserves the most attentive study by all who interest themselves in the predominant religious controversy of the day."—Spectator.

REMINISCENCES AND REFLECTIONS, referring to his Early Ministry in the Parish of Row, 1825—31. Edited with an Introductory Narrative by his Son, DONALD CAMPBELL, M.A., Chaplain of King's College, London. Crown 8vo. 7s. 6d.

These 'Reminiscences and Reflections,' written during the last year of his life, were mainly intended to place on record thoughts which might prove helpful to others. "We recommend this book cordially to all who are interested in the great cause of religious reformation."—Times. *"There is a thoroughness and depth, as well as a practical earnestness, in his grasp of each truth on which he dilates, which make his reflections very valuable."*—Literary Churchman.

THOUGHTS ON REVELATION, with Special Reference to the Present Time. Second Edition. Crown 8vo. 5s.

RESPONSIBILITY FOR THE GIFT OF ETERNAL LIFE. Compiled by permission of the late J. M'LEOD CAMPBELL, D.D., from Sermons preached chiefly at Row in 1829—31. Crown 8vo. 5s.

"There is a healthy tone as well as a deep pathos not often seen in sermons. His words are weighty and the ideas they express tend to perfection of life."—Westminster Review.

THEOLOGICAL BOOKS.

Campbell (Lewis).—SOME ASPECTS OF THE CHRISTIAN IDEAL. Sermons by the Rev. L. CAMPBELL, M.A., LL.D., Professor of Greek in the University of Glasgow. Crown 8vo. 6s.

Canterbury.—Works by ARCHIBALD CAMPBELL, Archbishop of Canterbury:

THE PRESENT POSITION OF THE CHURCH OF ENGLAND. Seven Addresses delivered to the Clergy and Churchwardens of his Diocese, as his Charge, at his Primary Visitation, 1872. Third Edition. 8vo. cloth. 3s. 6d.

SOME THOUGHTS ON THE DUTIES OF THE ESTABLISHED CHURCH OF ENGLAND AS A NATIONAL CHURCH. Seven Addresses delivered at his Second Visitation. 8vo. 4s. 6d.

Cheyne.—Works by T. K. CHEYNE, M.A., Fellow of Balliol College, Oxford:

THE BOOK OF ISAIAH CHRONOLOGICALLY ARRANGED. An Amended Version, with Historical and Critical Introductions and Explanatory Notes. Crown 8vo. 7s. 6d.

The Westminster Review *speaks of it as "a piece of scholarly work, very carefully and considerately done." The* Academy *calls it "a successful attempt to extend a right understanding of this important Old Testament writing."*

NOTES AND CRITICISMS on the HEBREW TEXT OF ISAIAH. Crown 8vo. 2s. 6d.

Choice Notes on the Four Gospels, drawn from Old and New Sources. Crown 8vo. 4s. 6d. each Vol. (St. Matthew and St. Mark in one Vol. price 9s.)

Church.—Works by the Very Rev. R. W. CHURCH, M.A., D.C.L., Dean of St. Paul's:

ON SOME INFLUENCES OF CHRISTIANITY UPON NATIONAL CHARACTER. Three Lectures delivered in St. Paul's Cathedral, Feb. 1873. Crown 8vo. 4s. 6d.

"Few books that we have met with have given us keener pleasure than this....... It would be a real pleasure to quote extensively, so wise and so true, so tender and so discriminating are Dean Church's judgments, but the limits of our space are inexorable. We hope the book will be bought."
—Literary Churchman.

CHURCH (Very Rev. R. W.)—*continued.*

THE SACRED POETRY OF EARLY RELIGIONS. Two Lectures in St. Paul's Cathedral. 18mo. 1s. I. The Vedas. II. The Psalms.

ST. ANSELM. Second Edition. Crown 8vo. 6s.
"*It is a sketch by the hand of a master, with every line marked by taste, learning, and real apprehension of the subject.*"—Pall Mall Gazette.

HUMAN LIFE AND ITS CONDITIONS. Sermons preached before the University of Oxford, 1876—78, with Three Ordination Sermons. Crown 8vo. 6s.

THE GIFTS OF CIVILIZATION, and other Sermons and Lectures delivered at Oxford and in St. Paul's Cathedral. New Edition. Crown 8vo. 7s. 6d.

Clergyman's Self-Examination concerning the APOSTLES' CREED. Extra fcap. 8vo. 1s. 6d.

Colenso.—THE COMMUNION SERVICE FROM THE BOOK OF COMMON PRAYER; with Select Readings from the Writings of the Rev. F. D. MAURICE, M.A. Edited by the Right Rev. J. W. COLENSO, D.D., Lord Bishop of Natal. New Edition. 16mo. 2s. 6d.

Collects of the Church of England. With a beautifully Coloured Floral Design to each Collect, and Illuminated Cover. Crown 8vo. 12s. Also kept in various styles of morocco.
The distinctive characteristic of this edition is the coloured floral design which accompanies each Collect, and which is generally emblematical of the character of the day or saint to which it is assigned; the flowers which have been selected are such as are likely to be in bloom on the day to which the Collect belongs. The Guardian *thinks it "a successful attempt to associate in a natural and unforced manner the flowers of our fields and gardens with the course of the Christian year."*

Congreve.—HIGH HOPES, AND PLEADINGS FOR A REASONABLE FAITH, NOBLER THOUGHTS, LARGER CHARITY. Sermons preached in the Parish Church of Tooting Graveney, Surrey. By J. CONGREVE, M.A., Rector. Cheaper Issue. Crown 8vo. 5s.

Cotton.—Works by the late GEORGE EDWARD LYNCH COTTON, D.D., Bishop of Calcutta:

THEOLOGICAL BOOKS.

COTTON (Bishop)—*continued.*

SERMONS PREACHED TO ENGLISH CONGREGATIONS IN INDIA. Crown 8vo. 7s. 6d.

EXPOSITORY SERMONS ON THE EPISTLES FOR THE SUNDAYS OF THE CHRISTIAN YEAR. Two Vols. Crown 8vo. 15s.

Curteis.—DISSENT in its RELATION to the CHURCH OF ENGLAND. Eight Lectures preached before the University of Oxford, in the year 1871, on the foundation of the late Rev. John Bampton, M.A., Canon of Salisbury. By GEORGE HERBERT CURTEIS, M.A., late Fellow and Sub-Rector of Exeter College; Principal of the Lichfield Theological College, and Prebendary of Lichfield Cathedral; Rector of Turweston, Bucks. New Edition. Crown 8vo. 7s. 6d.

"*Mr. Curteis has done good service by maintaining in an eloquent, temperate, and practical manner, that discussion among Christians is really an evil, and that an intelligent basis can be found for at least a proximate union.*"—Saturday Review. "*A well timed, learned, and thoughtful book.*"

Davies.—Works by the Rev. J. LLEWELYN DAVIES, M.A., Rector of Christ Church, St. Marylebone, etc.:

THE GOSPEL AND MODERN LIFE; with a Preface on a Recent Phase of Deism. Second Edition. To which is added Morality according to the Sacrament of the Lord's Supper, or Three Discourses on the Names, Eucharist, Sacrifice, and Communion. Extra fcap. 8vo. 6s.

WARNINGS AGAINST SUPERSTITION, IN FOUR SERMONS FOR THE DAY. Extra fcap. 8vo. 2s. 6d.

"*We have seldom read a wiser little book. The Sermons are short, terse, and full of true spiritual wisdom, expressed with a lucidity and a moderation that must give them weight even with those who agree least with their author....... Of the volume as a whole it is hardly possible to speak with too cordial an appreciation.*"—Spectator.

THE CHRISTIAN CALLING. Sermons. Extra fcap. 8vo. 6s.

Donaldson.—THE APOSTOLICAL FATHERS: a Critical Account of their Genuine Writings and of their Doctrines. By JAMES DONALDSON, LL.D. Crown 8vo. 7s. 6d.

DONALDSON (J., LL.D.)—*continued.*

This book was published in 1864 as the first volume of a 'Critical History of Christian Literature and Doctrine from the death of the Apostles to the Nicene Council.' The intention was to carry down the history continuously to the time of Eusebius, and this intention has not been abandoned. But as the writers can be sometimes grouped more easily according to subject or locality than according to time, it is deemed advisable to publish the history of each group separately. The Introduction to the present volume serves as an introduction to the whole period.

Drake.—THE TEACHING OF THE CHURCH DURING THE FIRST THREE CENTURIES ON THE DOCTRINES OF THE CHRISTIAN PRIESTHOOD AND SACRIFICE. By the Rev. C. B. DRAKE, M.A., Warden of the Church of England Hall, Manchester. Crown 8vo. 4s. 6d.

Eadie.—Works by JOHN EADIE, D.D., LL.D., Professor of Biblical Literature and Exegesis, United Presbyterian Church:

THE ENGLISH BIBLE. An External and Critical History of the various English Translations of Scripture, with Remarks on the Need of Revising the English New Testament. Two vols. 8vo. 28s.

"*Accurate, scholarly, full of completest sympathy with the translators and their work, and marvellously interesting.*"—Literary Churchman.

"*The work is a very valuable one. It is the result of vast labour, sound scholarship, and large erudition.*"—British Quarterly Review.

ST. PAUL'S EPISTLES TO THE THESSALONIANS. A Commentary on the Greek Text. Edited by the Rev. W. YOUNG, M.A., with a Preface by the Rev. Professor CAIRNS, D.D. 8vo. 12s.

Ecce Homo. A SURVEY OF THE LIFE AND WORK OF JESUS CHRIST. Fourteenth Edition. Crown 8vo. 6s.

"*A very original and remarkable book, full of striking thought and delicate perception; a book which has realised with wonderful vigour and freshness the historical magnitude of Christ's work, and which here and there gives us readings of the finest kind of the probable motive of His individual words and actions.*"—Spectator. "*The best and most established believer will find it adding some fresh buttresses to his faith.*"—Literary Churchman. "*If we have not misunderstood him, we have before us a writer who has a right to claim deference from those who think deepest and know most.*"—Guardian.

Faber.—SERMONS AT A NEW SCHOOL. By the Rev. ARTHUR FABER, M.A., Head Master of Malvern College. Cr. 8vo. 6s.

"*These are high-toned, earnest Sermons, orthodox and scholarlike, and laden with encouragement and warning, wisely adapted to the needs of school-life.*"—Literary Churchman.

Farrar.—Works by the Rev. F. W. FARRAR, D.D., F.R.S., Canon of Westminster, late Head Master of Marlborough College:

THE FALL OF MAN, AND OTHER SERMONS. Fourth Edition. Crown 8vo. 6s.

The Nonconformist *says of these Sermons,* "*Mr. Farrar's Sermons are almost perfect specimens of one type of Sermons, which we may concisely call beautiful. The style of expression is beautiful—there is beauty in the thoughts, the illustrations, the allusions—they are expressive of genuinely beautiful perceptions and feelings.*" *The* British Quarterly *says,* "*Ability, eloquence, scholarship, and practical usefulness, are in these Sermons combined in a very unusual degree.*"

THE WITNESS OF HISTORY TO CHRIST. Being the Hulsean Lectures for 1870. Fifth Edition. Crown 8vo. 5s.

The following are the subjects of the Five Lectures:—I. "*The Antecedent Credibility of the Miraculous.*" *II.* "*The Adequacy of the Gospel Records.*" *III.* "*The Victories of Christianity.*" *IV.* "*Christianity and the Individual.*" *V.* "*Christianity and the Race.*" *The subjects of the four Appendices are:—A.* "*The Diversity of Christian Evidences.*" *B.* "*Confucius.*" *C.* "*Buddha.*" *D.* "*Comte.*"

SEEKERS AFTER GOD. The Lives of Seneca, Epictetus, and Marcus Aurelius. New Edition. Crown 8vo. 6s.

"*A very interesting and valuable book.*"—Saturday Review.

THE SILENCE AND VOICES OF GOD: University and other Sermons. Fifth Edition. Crown 8vo. 6s.

"*We can most cordially recommend Dr. Farrar's singularly beautiful volume of Sermons...... For beauty of diction, felicity of style, aptness of illustration and earnest loving exhortation, the volume is without its parallel.*"—John Bull. "*They are marked by great ability, by an honesty which does not hesitate to acknowledge difficulties and by an earnestness which commands respect.*"—Pall Mall Gazette.

"IN THE DAYS OF THY YOUTH." Sermons on Practical Subjects, preached at Marlborough College from 1871—76. Fifth Edition. Crown 8vo. 9s.

THEOLOGICAL BOOKS.

FARRAR (Rev. F. W.)—*continued.*

"*All Dr. Farrar's peculiar charm of style is apparent here, all that care and subtleness of analysis, and an even-added distinctness and clearness of moral teaching, which is what every kind of sermon wants, and especially a sermon to boys.*"—Literary Churchman.

ETERNAL HOPE. Five Sermons preached in Westminster Abbey, in 1876. With Preface, Notes, etc. Contents: What Heaven is.—Is Life Worth Living?—'Hell,' What it is not.—Are there few that be saved?—Earthly and Future Consequences of Sin. Seventeenth Thousand. Crown 8vo. 6s.

SAINTLY WORKERS. Lenten Lectures delivered in St. Andrew's, Holborn, March and April, 1878. Crown 8vo. 6s.

EPHPHATHA; or the Amelioration of the World. Sermons preached at Westminster Abbey. With Two Sermons at St. Margaret's, Westminster, on the Opening of Parliament. Crown 8vo. 6s.

Fellowship: LETTERS ADDRESSED TO MY SISTER MOURNERS. Fcap. 8vo. cloth gilt. 3s. 6d.

Ferrar.—A COLLECTION OF FOUR IMPORTANT MSS. OF THE GOSPELS, viz., 13, 69, 124, 346, with a view to prove their common origin, and to restore the Text of their Archetype. By the late W. H. FERRAR, M.A., Professor of Latin in the University of Dublin. Edited by T. K. ABBOTT, M.A., Professor of Biblical Greek, Dublin. 4to., half morocco. 10s. 6d.

Forbes.—Works by GRANVILLE H. FORBES, Rector of Broughton:

THE VOICE OF GOD IN THE PSALMS. Cr. 8vo. 6s. 6d.

VILLAGE SERMONS. By a Northamptonshire Rector. Crown 8vo. 6s.

"*Such a volume as the present ... is as great an accession to the cause of a deep theology as the most refined exposition of its fundamental principles ... We heartily accept his actual teaching as a true picture of what revelation teaches us, and thank him for it as one of the most profound that was ever made perfectly simple and popular.... It is part of the beauty of these sermons that while they apply the old truth to the new modes of feeling they seem to preserve the whiteness of its simplicity.... There will be plenty of critics to accuse this volume of inadequacy of doctrine because it says no more than Scripture about vicarious suffering* and external retribution. For ourselves we welcome it most cordially as expressing adequately what we believe to be the true burden of the Gospel in a manner which may take hold either of the least or the most cultivated intellect."—Spectator.

Gaskoin.—CHILDREN'S TREASURY OF BIBLE STORIES. By Mrs. HERMAN GASKOIN. Edited with Preface by the Rev. G. F. MACLEAR, D.D.
PART I.—Old Testament. 18mo. 1s.
PART II.—New Testament. 18mo. 1s.
PART III.—The Apostles. 18mo. 1s.

Hardwick.—Works by the Ven. ARCHDEACON HARDWICK:
CHRIST AND OTHER MASTERS. A Historical Inquiry into some of the Chief Parallelisms and Contrasts between Christianity and the Religious Systems of the Ancient World. New Edition, revised, and a Prefatory Memoir by the Rev. FRANCIS PROCTER, M.A. New Edition. Cr. 8vo. 10s. 6d.

A HISTORY OF THE CHRISTIAN CHURCH. Middle Age. From Gregory the Great to the Excommunication of Luther, Edited by WILLIAM STUBBS, M.A., Regius Professor of Modern History in the University of Oxford. With Four Maps constructed for this work by A. KEITH JOHNSTON. New Edition. Crown 8vo. 10s. 6d.

"As a Manual for the student of ecclesiastical history in the Middle Ages, we know no English work which can be compared to Mr. Hardwick's book."—Guardian.

A HISTORY of the CHRISTIAN CHURCH DURING THE REFORMATION. New Edition, revised by Professor STUBBS. Crown 8vo. 10s. 6d.

This volume is intended as a sequel and companion to the "History of the Christian Church during the Middle Age."

Hare.—Works by the late ARCHDEACON HARE:
THE VICTORY OF FAITH. By JULIUS CHARLES HARE, M.A., Archdeacon of Lewes. Edited by Prof. PLUMPTRE. With Introductory Notices by the late Prof. MAURICE and Dean STANLEY. Third Edition. Crown 8vo. 6s. 6d.

THE MISSION OF THE COMFORTER. With Notes. New Edition, edited by Prof. E. H. PLUMPTRE. Crn. 8vo. 7s. 6d.

Harris.—SERMONS. By the late GEORGE COLLYER HARRIS, Prebendary of Exeter, and Vicar of St. Luke's, Torquay. With Memoir by CHARLOTTE M. YONGE, and Portrait. Extra fcap. 8vo. 6s.

Hervey.—THE GENEALOGIES OF OUR LORD AND SAVIOUR JESUS CHRIST, as contained in the Gospels of St. Matthew and St. Luke, reconciled with each other, and shown to be in harmony with the true Chronology of the Times. By Lord ARTHUR HERVEY, Bishop of Bath and Wells. 8vo. 10s. 6d.

Hort.—TWO DISSERTATIONS. I. On ΜΟΝΟΓΕΝΗΣ ΘΕΟΣ in Scripture and Tradition. II. On the "Constantinopolitan" Creed and other Eastern Creeds of the Fourth Century. By F. J. A. HORT, D.D., Fellow and Divinity Lecturer of Emmanuel College, Cambridge. 8vo. 7s. 6d.

Howson (Dean)—Works by:

BEFORE THE TABLE. An Inquiry, Historical and Theological, into the True Meaning of the Consecration Rubric in the Communion Service of the Church of England. By the Very Rev. J. S. HOWSON, D.D., Dean of Chester. With an Appendix and Supplement containing Papers by the Right Rev. the Bishop of St. Andrew's and the Rev. R. W. KENNION, M.A. 8vo. 7s. 6d.

THE POSITION OF THE PRIEST DURING CONSECRATION IN THE ENGLISH COMMUNION SERVICE. A Supplement and a Reply. Crown 8vo. 2s. 6d.

Hughes.—THE MANLINESS OF CHRIST. By THOMAS HUGHES, Author of "Tom Brown's School Days." Cr. 8vo. 4s. 6d.

"*Mr. Hughes makes no profession of scholarship or critical ability, but his pages bear the impress of much careful reading and thoughtful study; and accordingly although he limits himself, in set terms, to the consideration of the character of Christ in what he calls its 'manly' aspect he has given to the world a volume, which so truly, and in some places so picturesquely and strikingly, represents the life of our Lord, that we can only express the hope that it may find its way into the hands of thousands of English working men.*"—Spectator.

Hutton.—ESSAYS: THEOLOGICAL AND LITERARY. By RICHARD HUTTON, M.A. New and cheaper issue. 2 vols. 8vo. 18s.

Hymni Ecclesiæ.—Fcap. 8vo. 7s. 6d.

This collection was edited by Dr. Newman while he lived at Oxford.

Hyacinthe.—CATHOLIC REFORM. By FATHER HYACINTHE. Letters, Fragments, Discourses. Translated by Madame HYACINTHE-LOYSON. With a Preface by the Very Rev. A. P. STANLEY, D.D., Dean of Westminster. Cr. 8vo. 7s. 6d.

"A valuable contribution to the religious literature of the day, and is especially opportune at a time when a controversy of no ordinary importance upon the very subject it deals with is engaged in all over Europe."— Daily Telegraph.

Imitation of Christ.—FOUR BOOKS. Translated from the Latin, with Preface by the Rev. W. BENHAM, B.D., Vicar of Margate. Printed with Borders in the Ancient Style after Holbein, Dürer, and other Old Masters. Containing Dances of Death, Acts of Mercy, Emblems, and a variety of curious ornamentation. Cr. 8vo. gilt edges. 7s. 6d.

Also in Latin, uniform with the above. New Edition. 7s. 6d.

Jacob.—BUILDING IN SCIENCE, AND OTHER SERMONS. By J. A. JACOB, M.A., Minister of St. Thomas's, Paddington. Extra fcap. 8vo. 6s.

Jellett.—THE EFFICACY OF PRAYER : being the Donnellan Lectures for 1877. By J. H. JELLETT, B.D., Senior Fellow of Trinity College, Dublin, formerly President of the Royal Irish Academy. Second Edition. 8vo. 5s.

Jennings and Lowe.—THE PSALMS, with Introductions and Critical Notes. By A. C. JENNINGS, B.A., Jesus College, Cambridge, Tyrwhitt Scholar, Crosse Scholar, Hebrew University Scholar, and Fry Scholar of St. John's College ; helped in parts by W. H. LOWE, M.A., Hebrew Lecturer and late Scholar of Christ's College, Cambridge, and Tyrwhitt Scholar. Complete in two vols, crown 8vo. 10s. 6d. each. Vol. 1, Psalms i.—lxxii., with Prolegomena ; Vol. 2, Psalms lxxiii.—cl.

Killen.—THE ECCLESIASTICAL HISTORY OF IRELAND from the Earliest Period to the Present Time. By W. D. KILLEN, D.D., President of Assembly's College, Belfast, and Professor of Ecclesiastical History. Two vols. 8vo. 25s.

" Those who have the leisure will do well to read these two volumes. They are full of interest, and are the result of great research." - Spectator.

Kingsley.—Works by the late Rev. CHARLES KINGSLEY. M.A., Rector of Eversley, and Canon of Westminster :

THE WATER OF LIFE, AND OTHER SERMONS. New Edition. Crown 8vo. 6s.

KINGSLEY (Rev. Charles)—*continued.*
> THE GOSPEL OF THE PENTATEUCH ; AND DAVID. New Edition. Crown. 8vo. 6s.
>
> GOOD NEWS OF GOD. Ninth Edition. Crown 8vo. 6s.
>
> SERMONS FOR THE TIMES. New Edition. Crown 8vo. 6s.
>
> VILLAGE AND TOWN AND COUNTRY SERMONS. New Edition. Crown 8vo. 6s.
>
> SERMONS on NATIONAL SUBJECTS. Second Edition. Fcap. 8vo. 3s. 6d.
>
> THE KING OF THE EARTH, and other Sermons, a Second Series of Sermons on National Subjects. Second Edition. Fcap. 8vo. 3s. 6d.
>
> DISCIPLINE, AND OTHER SERMONS. Second Edition. Fcap. 8vo. 3s. 6d.
>
> WESTMINSTER SERMONS. With Preface. New Edition. Crown 8vo. 6s.

Kynaston.—SERMONS PREACHED IN THE COLLEGE CHAPEL, CHELTENHAM, during the First Year of his Office. By the Rev. HERBERT KYNASTON, M.A., Principal of Cheltenham College. Crown 8vo. 6s.

Lightfoot.—Works by J. B. LIGHTFOOT, D.D., Bishop of Durham.
> S. PAUL'S EPISTLE TO THE GALATIANS. A Revised Text, with Introduction, Notes, and Dissertations. Fifth Edition, revised. 8vo. cloth. 12s.

While the Author's object has been to make this commentary generally complete, he has paid special attention to everything relating to St. Paul's personal history and his intercourse with the Apostles and Church of the Circumcision, as it is this feature in the Epistle to the Galatians which has given it an overwhelming interest in recent theological controversy. The Spectator *says, " There is no commentator at once of sounder judgment and more liberal than Dr. Lightfoot."*

> ST. PAUL'S EPISTLE TO THE PHILIPPIANS. A Revised Text, with Introduction, Notes, and Dissertations. Fourth Edition, revised. 8vo. 12s.

"No commentary in the English language can be compared with it in regard to fulness of information, exact scholarship, and laboured attempts to settle everything about the epistle on a solid foundation."—Athenæum.

LIGHTFOOT (Dr.)—*continued.*

ST. PAUL'S EPISTLES TO THE COLOSSIANS AND TO PHILEMON. A Revised Text with Introduction, Notes, etc. Third Edition, revised. 8vo. 12s.

"*It bears marks of continued and extended reading and research, and of ampler materials at command. Indeed, it leaves nothing to be desired by those who seek to study thoroughly the epistles contained in it, and to do so with all known advantages presented in sufficient detail and in convenient form.*"—Guardian.

S. CLEMENT OF ROME. An Appendix containing the newly discovered portions of the two Epistles to the Corinthians with Introductions and Notes, and a Translation of the whole. 8vo. 8s. 6d.

ON A FRESH REVISION OF THE ENGLISH NEW TESTAMENT. Second Edition. Crown 8vo. 6s.

The Author shews in detail the necessity for a fresh revision of the authorized version on the following grounds:—1. *False Readings.* 2. *Artificial distinctions created.* 3. *Real distinctions obliterated.* 4. *Faults of Grammar.* 5. *Faults of Lexicography.* 6. *Treatment of Proper Names, official titles, etc.* 7. *Archaisms, defects in the English, errors of the press, etc.* "*The book is marked by careful scholarship, familiarity with the subject, sobriety, and circumspection.*"—Athenæum.

Lorne.—THE PSALMS LITERALLY RENDERED IN VERSE. By the MARQUIS OF LORNE. With three Illustrations. New Edition. Crown 8vo. 7s. 6d.

Maclaren.—SERMONS PREACHED at MANCHESTER. By ALEXANDER MACLAREN. Sixth Edition. Fcap. 8vo. 4s. 6d.

These Sermons represent no special school, but deal with the broad principles of Christian truth, especially in their bearing on practical, every-day life. A few of the titles are:—"*The Stone of Stumbling,*" "*Love and Forgiveness,*" "*The Living Dead,*" "*Memory in Another World,*" "*Faith in Christ,*" "*Love and Fear,*" "*The Choice of Wisdom,*" "*The Food of the World.*"

A SECOND SERIES OF SERMONS. Fourth Edition. Fcap. 8vo. 4s. 6d.

The Spectator *characterises them as "vigorous in style, full of thought, rich in illustration, and in an unusual degree interesting."*

A THIRD SERIES OF SERMONS. Third Edition. Fcap. 8vo. 4s. 6d.

MACLAREN (A.)—*continued.*

"*Sermons more sober and yet more forcible, and with a certain wise and practical spirituality about them it would not be easy to find.*"—Spectator.

WEEK-DAY EVENING ADDRESSES. Delivered in Manchester. Extra Fcap. 8vo. 2s. 6d.

Maclear.—Works by the Rev. G. F. MACLEAR, D.D., Head Master of King's College School:

A CLASS-BOOK OF OLD TESTAMENT HISTORY. With Four Maps. New Edition. 18mo. 4s. 6d.

"*The present volume,*" says the Preface, "*forms a Class-Book of Old Testament History from the Earliest Times to those of Ezra and Nehemiah. In its preparation the most recent authorities have been consulted, and wherever it has appeared useful, Notes have been subjoined illustrative of the Text, and, for the sake of more advanced students, references added to larger works. The Index has been so arranged as to form a concise Dictionary of the Persons and Places mentioned in the course of the Narrative.*" The *Maps, prepared by Stanford, materially add to the value and usefulness of the book.* The British Quarterly Review *calls it* "*A careful and elaborate, though brief compendium of all that modern research has done for the illustration of the Old Testament. We know of no work which contains so much important information in so small a compass.*"

A CLASS-BOOK OF NEW TESTAMENT HISTORY. Including the Connexion of the Old and New Testament. New Edition. 18mo. 5s. 6d.

The present volume forms a sequel to the Author's Class-Book of Old Testament History, and continues the narrative to the close of S. Paul's second imprisonment at Rome. The work is divided into three Books— I. The Connection between the Old and New Testament. II. The Gospel History. III. The Apostolic History. In the Appendix are given Chronological Tables. The Clerical Journal *says,* "*It is not often that such an amount of useful and interesting matter on biblical subjects is found in so convenient and small a compass as in this well-arranged volume.*"

A CLASS-BOOK OF THE CATECHISM OF THE CHURCH OF ENGLAND. New and Cheaper Edition. 18mo. 1s. 6d.

The present work is intended as a sequel to the two preceding books. "*Like them, it is furnished with notes and references to larger works, and it is hoped that it may be found, especially in the higher forms of our*

MACLEAR (Dr. G. F.)—*continued.*

Public Schools, to supply a suitable manual of instruction in the chief doctrines of our Church, and a useful help in the preparation of Candidates for Confirmation." The Literary Churchman *says, "It is indeed the work of a scholar and divine, and as such, though extremely simple, it is also extremely instructive. There are few clergy who would not find it useful in preparing Candidates for Confirmation; and there are not a few who would find it useful to themselves as well."*

A FIRST CLASS-BOOK OF THE CATECHISM OF THE CHURCH OF ENGLAND, with Scripture Proofs for Junior Classes and Schools. New Edition. 18mo. 6*d*.

This is an epitome of the larger Class-book, meant for junior students and elementary classes. The book has been carefully condensed, so as to contain clearly and fully, the most important part of the contents of the larger book.

A SHILLING-BOOK of OLD TESTAMENT HISTORY. New Edition. 18mo. cloth limp. 1*s*.

This Manual bears the same relation to the larger Old Testament History, that the book just mentioned does to the larger work on the Catechism. It consists of Ten Books, divided into short chapters, and subdivided into sections, each section treating of a single episode in the history, the title of which is given in bold type.

A SHILLING-BOOK of NEW TESTAMENT HISTORY. New Edition. 18mo. cloth limp. 1*s*.

A MANUAL OF INSTRUCTION FOR CONFIRMATION AND FIRST COMMUNION, with Prayers and Devotions. 32mo. cloth extra, red edges. 2*s*.

This is an enlarged and improved edition of 'The Order of Confirmation.' To it have been added the Communion Office, with Notes and Explanations, together with a brief form of Self Examination and Devotions selected from the works of Cosin, Ken, Wilson, and others.

THE ORDER OF CONFIRMATION, with Prayers and Devotions. 32mo. cloth. 6*d*.

THE FIRST COMMUNION, with Prayers and Devotions for the Newly Confirmed. 32mo. 6*d*.

THE HOUR OF SORROW; or, The Order for the Burial of the Dead. With Prayers and Hymns. 32mo. cloth extra. 2*s*.

MACLEAR (Dr. G. F.)—*continued.*

APOSTLES OF MEDIÆVAL EUROPE. Cr. 8vo. 4s. 6d.

"*Mr. Maclear will have done a great work if his admirable little volume shall help to break up the dense ignorance which is still prevailing among people at large.*"—Literary Churchman.

Macmillan.—Works by the Rev. HUGH MACMILLAN, LL.D. F.R.S.E. (For other Works by the same Author, see CATALOGUE OF TRAVELS and SCIENTIFIC CATALOGUE).

THE TRUE VINE; or, the Analogies of our Lord's Allegory. Third Edition. Globe 8vo. 6s.

The Nonconformist *says,* "*It abounds in exquisite bits of description, and in striking facts clearly stated.*" *The* British Quarterly *says,* "*Readers and preachers who are unscientific will find many of his illustrations as valuable as they are beautiful.*"

BIBLE TEACHINGS IN NATURE. Twelfth Edition. Globe 8vo. 6s.

In this volume the author has endeavoured to shew that the teaching of Nature and the teaching of the Bible are directed to the same great end: that the Bible contains the spiritual truths which are necessary to make us wise unto salvation, and the objects and scenes of Nature are the pictures by which these truths are illustrated. "*He has made the world more beautiful to us, and unsealed our ears to voices of praise and messages of love that might otherwise have been unheard.*"—British Quarterly Review. "*Dr. Macmillan has produced a book which may be fitly described as one of the happiest efforts for enlisting physical science in the direct service of religion.*"—Guardian.

THE SABBATH OF THE FIELDS. A Sequel to "Bible Teachings in Nature." Second Edition. Globe 8vo. 6s.

"*This volume, like all Dr. Macmillan's productions, is very delightful reading, and of a special kind. Imagination, natural science, and religious instruction are blended together in a very charming way.*"—British Quarterly Review.

THE MINISTRY OF NATURE. Fourth Edition. Globe 8vo. 6s.

"*Whether the reader agree or not with his conclusions, he will acknowledge he is in the presence of an original and thoughtful writer.*"—Pall Mall Gazette. "*There is no class of educated men and women that will not profit by these essays.*"—Standard.

OUR LORD'S THREE RAISINGS FROM THE DEAD. Globe 8vo. 6s.

Maurice.—Works by the late Rev. F. DENISON MAURICE, M.A., Professor of Moral Philosophy in the University of Cambridge :

The Spectator *says,—"Few of those of our own generation whose names will live in English history or literature have exerted so profound and so permanent an influence as Mr. Maurice."*

THE PATRIARCHS AND LAWGIVERS OF THE OLD TESTAMENT. Third and Cheaper Edition. Crown 8vo. 5s.

The Nineteen Discourses contained in this volume were preached in the chapel of Lincoln's Inn during the year 1851. *The texts are taken from the books of Genesis, Exodus, Numbers, Deuteronomy, Joshua, Judges, and Samuel, and involve some of the most interesting biblical topics discussed in recent times.*

THE PROPHETS AND KINGS OF THE OLD TESTAMENT. New Edition. Crown 8vo. 10s. 6d.

Mr. Maurice, in the spirit which animated the compilers of the Church Lessons, has in these Sermons regarded the Prophets more as preachers of righteousness than as mere predictors—an aspect of their lives which, he thinks, has been greatly overlooked in our day, and than which, there is none we have more need to contemplate. He has found that the Old Testament Prophets, taken in their simple natural sense, clear up many of the difficulties which beset us in the daily work of life; make the past intelligible, the present endurable, and the future real and hopeful.

THE GOSPEL OF THE KINGDOM OF HEAVEN. A Series of Lectures on the Gospel of St. Luke. New Edition. Crown 8vo. 9s.

Mr. Maurice, in his Preface to these Twenty-eight Lectures, says,— "In these Lectures I have endeavoured to ascertain what is told us respecting the life of Jesus by one of those Evangelists who proclaim Him to be the Christ, who says that He did come from a Father, that He did baptize with the Holy Spirit, that He did rise from the dead. I have chosen the one who is most directly connected with the later history of the Church, who was not an Apostle, who professedly wrote for the use of a man already instructed in the faith of the Apostles. I have followed the course of the writer's narrative, not changing it under any pretext. I have adhered to his phraseology, striving to avoid the substitution of any other for his."

THE GOSPEL OF ST. JOHN. A Series of Discourses. New Edition. Crown 8vo. 6s.

MAURICE (Rev. F. D.)—*continued.*

The Literary Churchman *thus speaks of this volume:* "*Thorough honesty, reverence, and deep thought pervade the work, which is every way solid and philosophical, as well as theological, and abounding with suggestions which the patient student may draw out more at length for himself.*"

THE EPISTLES OF ST. JOHN. A Series of Lectures on Christian Ethics. Second and Cheaper Edition. Cr. 8vo. 6s.

These Lectures on Christian Ethics were delivered to the students of the Working Men's College, Great Ormond Street, London, on a series of Sunday mornings. Mr. Maurice believes that the question in which we are most interested, the question which most affects our studies and our daily lives, is the question, whether there is a foundation for human morality, or whether it is dependent upon the opinions and fashions of different ages and countries. This important question will be found amply and fairly discussed in this volume, which the National Review *calls "Mr. Maurice's most effective and instructive work. He is peculiarly fitted by the constitution of his mind, to throw light on St. John's writings." Appended is a note on "Positivism and its Teacher."*

EXPOSITORY SERMONS ON THE PRAYER-BOOK. The Prayer-book considered especially in reference to the Romish System; and the Lord's Prayer. Crown 8vo. 9s.

After an Introductory Sermon, Mr. Maurice goes over the various parts of the Church Service, expounds in eighteen Sermons, their intention and significance, and shews how appropriate they are as expressions of the deepest longings and wants of all classes of men.

WHAT IS REVELATION? A Series of Sermons on the Epiphany; to which are added, Letters to a Theological Student on the Bampton Lectures of Mr. Mansel. Crown 8vo. 10s. 6d.

Both Sermons and Letters were called forth by the doctrine maintained by Mr. Mansel in his Bampton Lectures, that Revelation cannot be a direct Manifestation of the Infinite Nature of God. Mr. Maurice maintains the opposite doctrine, and in his Sermons explains why, in spite of the high authorities on the other side, he must still assert the principle which he discovers in the Services of the Church and throughout the Bible.

SEQUEL TO THE INQUIRY, "WHAT IS REVELATION?" Letters in Reply to Mr. Mansel's Examination of "Strictures on the Bampton Lectures." Crown 8vo. 6s.

This, as the title indicates, was called forth by Mr. Mansel's examination of Mr. Maurice's Strictures on his doctrine of the Infinite.

MAURICE (Rev. F. D.)—*continued.*

THEOLOGICAL ESSAYS. Third Edition. Crown 8vo. 10s. 6d.

"*The book,*" *says Mr. Maurice,* "*expresses thoughts which have been working in my mind for years; the method of it has not been adopted carelessly; even the composition has undergone frequent revision.*"

THE DOCTRINE OF SACRIFICE DEDUCED FROM THE SCRIPTURES. New Edition. Crown 8vo. 7s. 6d.

THE RELIGIONS OF THE WORLD, AND THEIR RELATIONS TO CHRISTIANITY. Fifth Edition. Crown 8vo. 5s.

ON THE SABBATH DAY; the Character of the Warrior, and on the Interpretation of History. Fcap. 8vo. 2s. 6d.

THE LORD'S PRAYER, THE CREED, AND THE COMMANDMENTS. A Manual for Parents and Schoolmasters. To which is added the Order of the Scriptures. 18mo. cloth limp. 1s.

DIALOGUES ON FAMILY WORSHIP. Crown 8vo. 6s.

SOCIAL MORALITY. Twenty-one Lectures delivered in the University of Cambridge. New and Cheaper Edition. Cr. 8vo. 10s. 6d.

"*Whilst reading it we are charmed by the freedom from exclusiveness and prejudice, the large charity, the loftiness of thought, the eagerness to recognise and appreciate whatever there is of real worth extant in the world, which animates it from one end to the other. We gain new thoughts and new ways of viewing things, even more, perhaps, from being brought for a time under the influence of so noble and spiritual a mind.*"
—Athenæum.

THE CONSCIENCE: Lectures on Casuistry, delivered in the University of Cambridge. Second and Cheaper Edition. Crown 8vo. 5s.

The Saturday Review *says:* "*We rise from the perusal of these lectures with a detestation of all that is selfish and mean, and with a living impression that there is such a thing as goodness after all.*"

LECTURES ON THE ECCLESIASTICAL HISTORY OF THE FIRST AND SECOND CENTURIES. 8vo. 10s. 6d.

MAURICE (Rev. F. D.)—*continued.*

LEARNING AND WORKING. Six Lectures delivered in Willis's Rooms, London, in June and July, 1854.—THE RELIGION OF ROME, and its Influence on Modern Civilisation. Four Lectures delivered in the Philosophical Institution of Edinburgh, in December, 1854. Crown 8vo. 5s.

SERMONS PREACHED IN COUNTRY CHURCHES. New Edition. Crown 8vo. 10s. 6d.

"*Earnest, practical, and extremely simple.*"—Literary Churchman.

"*Good specimens of his simple and earnest eloquence. The Gospel incidents are realized with a vividness which we can well believe made the common people hear him gladly. Moreover they are sermons which must have done the hearers good.*"—John Bull.

Moorhouse.—Works by JAMES MOORHOUSE, M.A., Bishop of Melbourne:

SOME MODERN DIFFICULTIES RESPECTING the FACTS OF NATURE AND REVELATION. Fcap. 8vo. 2s. 6d.

JACOB. Three Sermons preached before the University of Cambridge in Lent 1870. Extra fcap. 8vo. 3s. 6d.

O'Brien.—PRAYER. Five Sermons preached in the Chapel of Trinity College, Dublin. By JAMES THOMAS O'BRIEN, D.D., Bishop of Ossory and Ferns. 8vo. 6s.

"*It is with much pleasure and satisfaction that we render our humble tribute to the value of a publication whose author deserves to be remembered with such deep respect.*"—Church Quarterly Review.

Palgrave.—HYMNS. By FRANCIS TURNER PALGRAVE. Third Edition, enlarged. 18mo. 1s. 6d.

This is a collection of twenty original Hymns, which the Literary Churchman *speaks of as "so choice, so perfect, and so refined,—so tender in feeling, and so scholarly in expression."*

Paul of Tarsus. An Inquiry into the Times and the Gospel of the Apostle of the Gentiles. By a GRADUATE. 8vo. 10s. 6d.

"*Turn where we will throughout the volume, we find the best fruit of patient inquiry, sound scholarship, logical argument, and fairness of conclusion. No thoughtful reader will rise from its perusal without a real and lasting profit to himself, and a sense of permanent addition to the cause of truth.*"—Standard.

THEOLOGICAL BOOKS.

Philochristus.—MEMOIRS OF A DISCIPLE OF THE LORD. Second Edition. 8vo. 12s.

"*The winning beauty of this book and the fascinating power with which the subject of it appeals to all English minds will secure for it many readers.*"—Contemporary Review.

Picton.—THE MYSTERY OF MATTER; and other Essays. By J. ALLANSON PICTON, Author of "New Theories and the Old Faith." Cheaper Edition. With New Preface. Crown 8vo. 6s.

Contents—The Mystery of Matter: The Philosophy of Ignorance: The Antithesis of Faith and Sight: The Essential Nature of Religion: Christian Pantheism.

Plumptre.—MOVEMENTS IN RELIGIOUS THOUGHT. Sermons preached before the University of Cambridge, Lent Term, 1879. By E. H. PLUMPTRE, D.D., Professor of Divinity, King's College, London, Prebendary of St. Paul's, etc. Fcap. 8vo. 3s. 6d.

Prescott.—THE THREEFOLD CORD. Sermons preached before the University of Cambridge. By J. E. PRESCOTT, B.D. Fcap. 8vo. 3s. 6d.

Procter.—A HISTORY OF THE BOOK OF COMMON PRAYER: With a Rationale of its Offices. By FRANCIS PROCTER, M.A. Fourteenth Edition, revised and enlarged. Cr. 8vo. 10s. 6d.

The Athenæum *says:—"The origin of every part of the Prayer-book has been diligently investigated,—and there are few questions or facts connected with it which are not either sufficiently explained, or so referred to that persons interested may work out the truth for themselves.*"

Procter and Maclear.—AN ELEMENTARY INTRODUCTION TO THE BOOK OF COMMON PRAYER. Re-arranged and Supplemented by an Explanation of the Morning and Evening Prayer and the Litany. By F. PROCTER, M.A., and G. F. MACLEAR, D.D. New Edition. Enlarged by the addition of the Communion Service and the Baptismal and Confirmation Offices. 18mo. 2s. 6d.

The Literary Churchman *characterises it as "by far the completest and most satisfactory book of its kind we know. We wish it were in the hands of every schoolboy and every schoolmaster in the kingdom.*"

Psalms of David CHRONOLOGICALLY ARRANGED. An Amended Version, with Historical Introductions and Explanatory Notes. By FOUR FRIENDS. Second and Cheaper Edition, much enlarged. Crown 8vo. 8s. 6d.

One of the chief designs of the Editors, in preparing this volume, was to restore the Psalter as far as possible to the order in which the Psalms were written. They give the division of each Psalm into strophes, and of each strophe into the lines which composed it, and amend the errors of translation. *The* Spectator *calls it "one of the most instructive and valuable books that have been published for many years."*

Psalter (Golden Treasury).—THE STUDENT'S EDITION. Being an Edition of the above with briefer Notes. 18mo. 3s. 6d.

The aim of this edition is simply to put the reader as far as possible in possession of the plain meaning of the writer. "It is a gem," the Nonconformist *says.*

Pulsford.—SERMONS PREACHED IN TRINITY CHURCH, GLASGOW. By WILLIAM PULSFORD, D.D. Cheaper Edition. Crown 8vo. 4s. 6d.

Ramsay.—THE CATECHISER'S MANUAL; or, the Church Catechism Illustrated and Explained, for the Use of Clergymen, Schoolmasters, and Teachers. By ARTHUR RAMSAY, M.A. Second Edition. 18mo. 1s. 6d.

Rays of Sunlight for Dark Days. A Book of Selections for the Suffering. With a Preface by C. J. VAUGHAN, D.D. 18mo. Eighth Edition. 3s. 6d. Also in morocco, old style.

Dr. Vaughan says in the Preface, after speaking of the general run of Books of Comfort for Mourners, "It is because I think that the little volume now offered to the Christian sufferer is one of greater wisdom and of deeper experience, that I have readily consented to the request that I would introduce it by a few words of Preface." The book consists of a series of very brief extracts from a great variety of authors, in prose and poetry, suited to the many moods of a mourning or suffering mind. "Mostly gems of the first water."—Clerical Journal.

Reynolds.—NOTES OF THE CHRISTIAN LIFE. A Selection of Sermons by HENRY ROBERT REYNOLDS, B.A., President of Cheshunt College, and Fellow of University College, London. Crown 8vo. 7s. 6d.

Roberts.—DISCUSSIONS ON THE GOSPELS. By the Rev. ALEXANDER ROBERTS, D.D. Second Edition, revised and enlarged. 8vo. 16s.

THEOLOGICAL BOOKS.

Robinson.—MAN IN THE IMAGE OF GOD; and other Sermons preached in the Chapel of the Magdalen, Streatham, 1874—76. By H. G. ROBINSON, M.A., Prebendary of York. Crown 8vo. 7s. 6d.

Romanes.—CHRISTIAN PRAYER AND GENERAL LAWS, being the Burney Prize Essay for 1873. With an Appendix, examining the views of Messrs. Knight, Robertson, Brooke, Tyndall, and Galton. By GEORGE J. ROMANES, M.A. Crown 8vo. 5s.

Rushbrooke.—SYNOPTICON: An Exposition of the Common Matter of the Synoptic Gospels. By W. G. RUSHBROOKE, M.L., Fellow of St. John's College, Cambridge. Printed in colours. To be completed in Six Parts. 4to. Part I. 3s. 6d. Parts II. and III. 7s.

Salmon.—THE REIGN OF LAW, and other Sermons, preached in the Chapel of Trinity College, Dublin. By the Rev. GEORGE SALMON, D.D., Regius Professor of Divinity in the University of Dublin. Crown 8vo. 6s.

"*Well considered, learned, and powerful discourses.*"—Spectator.

Sanday.—THE GOSPELS IN THE SECOND CENTURY. An Examination of the Critical part of a Work entitled "Supernatural Religion." By WILLIAM SANDAY, M.A., late Fellow of Trinity College, Oxford. Crown 8vo. 8s. 6d.

"*A very important book for the critical side of the question as to the authenticity of the New Testament, and it is hardly possible to conceive a writer of greater fairness, candour, and scrupulousness.*"—Spectator.

Scotch Sermons, 1880.—By Principal CAIRD; Rev. J. CUNNINGHAM, D.D.; Rev. D. J. FERGUSON, B.D.; Professor WM. KNIGHT, LL.D.; Rev. W. MACKINTOSH, D.D.; Rev. W. L. M'FARLAN; Rev. ALLAN MENZIES, B.D.; Rev. T. NICOLL; Rev. T. RAIN, M.A.; Rev. A. SEMPLE, B.D.; Rev. J. STEVENSON; Rev. PATRICK STEVENSON; Rev. R. H. STORY, D.D. 8vo. 10s. 6d.

Selborne.—THE BOOK OF PRAISE: From the Best English Hymn Writers. Selected and arranged by Lord SELBORNE. With Vignette by WOOLNER. 18mo. 4s. 6d.

THEOLOGICAL BOOKS. 27

SELBORNE (Lord)—*continued.*

It has been the Editor's desire and aim to adhere strictly, in all cases in which it could be ascertained, to the genuine uncorrupted text of the authors themselves. The names of the authors and date of composition of the hymns, when known, are affixed, while notes are added to the volume, giving further details. The Hymns are arranged according to subjects. "There is not room for two opinions as to the value of the 'Book of Praise.'"
—Guardian. *"Approaches as nearly as one can conceive to perfection."*
—Nonconformist.

BOOK OF PRAISE HYMNAL. *See* end of this Catalogue.

Service.—SALVATION HERE AND HEREAFTER. Sermons and Essays. By the Rev. JOHN SERVICE, D.D., Minister of Inch. Fourth Edition. Crown 8vo. 6s.

"*We have enjoyed to-day a rare pleasure, having just closed a volume of sermons which rings true metal from title page to finis, and proves that another and very powerful recruit has been added to that small band of ministers of the Gospel who are not only abreast of the religious thought of their time, but have faith enough and courage enough to handle the questions which are the most critical, and stir men's minds most deeply, with frankness and thoroughness.*"—Spectator.

Shipley.—A THEORY ABOUT SIN, in relation to some Facts of Daily Life. Lent Lectures on the Seven Deadly Sins. By the Rev. ORBY SHIPLEY, M.A. Crown 8vo. 7s. 6d.

"*Two things Mr. Shipley has done, and each of them is of considerable worth. He has grouped these sins afresh on a philosophic principle..... and he has applied the touchstone to the facts of our moral life... so wisely and so searchingly as to constitute his treatise a powerful antidote to self-deception.*"—Literary Churchman.

Smith.—PROPHECY A PREPARATION FOR CHRIST. Eight Lectures preached before the University of Oxford, being the Bampton Lectures for 1869. By R. PAYNE SMITH, D.D., Dean of Canterbury. Second and Cheaper Edition. Crown 8vo. 6s.

The author's object in these Lectures is to shew that there exists in the Old Testament an element, which no criticism on naturalistic principles can either account for or explain away: that element is Prophecy. The author endeavours to prove that its force does not consist merely in its predictions. "*These Lectures overflow with solid learning.*"—Record.

Smith.—CHRISTIAN FAITH. Sermons preached before the University of Cambridge. By W. SAUMAREZ SMITH, M.A., Principal of St. Aidan's College, Birkenhead. Fcap. 8vo. 3s. 6d.

THEOLOGICAL BOOKS.

Stanley.—Works by the Very Rev. A. P. STANLEY, D.D., Dean of Westminster:

THE ATHANASIAN CREED, with a Preface on the General Recommendations of the RITUAL COMMISSION. Cr. 8vo. 2s.

"*Dr. Stanley puts with admirable force the objections which may be made to the Creed; equally admirable, we think, in his statement of its advantages.*"—Spectator.

THE NATIONAL THANKSGIVING. Sermons preached in Westminster Abbey. Second Edition. Crown 8vo. 2s. 6d.

ADDRESSES AND SERMONS AT ST. ANDREW'S in 1872, 1875 and 1876. Crown 8vo. 5s.

Stewart and Tait.—THE UNSEEN UNIVERSE; or, Physical Speculations on a Future State. By Professors BALFOUR STEWART and P. G. TAIT. Sixth Edition, Revised and Enlarged. Crown 8vo. 6s.

"*A most remarkable and most interesting volume, which, probably more than any that has appeared in modern times, will affect religious thought on many momentous questions—insensibly it may be, but very largely and very beneficially.*"—Church Quarterly. "*This book is one which well deserves the attention of thoughtful and religious readers...... It is a perfectly safe enquiry, on scientific grounds, into the possibilities of a future existence.*"—Guardian.

Swainson.—Works by C. A. SWAINSON, D.D., Canon of Chichester:

THE CREEDS OF THE CHURCH in their Relations to Holy Scripture and the Conscience of the Christian 8vo. cloth. 9s.

THE AUTHORITY OF THE NEW TESTAMENT, and other LECTURES, delivered before the University of Cambridge. 8vo. cloth. 12s.

Taylor.—THE RESTORATION OF BELIEF. New and Revised Edition. By ISAAC TAYLOR, Esq. Crown 8vo. 8s. 6d.

Temple.—SERMONS PREACHED IN THE CHAPEL of RUGBY SCHOOL. By F. TEMPLE, D.D., Bishop of Exeter. New and Cheaper Edition. Extra fcap. 8vo. 4s. 6d.

This volume contains Thirty-five Sermons on topics more or less intimately connected with every-day life. The following are a few of the subjects discoursed upon:—"*Love and Duty;*" "*Coming to Christ;*"

THEOLOGICAL BOOKS. 29

TEMPLE (Dr.)—*continued.*

"Great Men;" "Faith;" "Doubts;" "Scruples;" "Original Sin;" "Friendship;" "Helping Others;" "The Discipline of Temptation;" "Strength a Duty;" "Worldliness;" "Ill Temper;" "The Burial of the Past."

A SECOND SERIES OF SERMONS PREACHED IN THE CHAPEL OF RUGBY SCHOOL. Second Edition. Extra fcap. 8vo. 6s.

This Second Series of Forty-two brief, pointed, practical Sermons, on topics intimately connected with the every-day life of young and old, will be acceptable to all who are acquainted with the First Series. The following are a few of the subjects treated of:—"Disobedience," "Almsgiving," "The Unknown Guidance of God," "Apathy one of our Trials," "High Aims in Leaders," "Doing our Best," "The Use of Knowledge," "Use of Observances," "Martha and Mary," "John the Baptist," "Severity before Mercy,". "Even Mistakes Punished," "Morality and Religion," "Children," "Action the Test of Spiritual Life," "Self-Respect," "Too Late," "The Tercentenary."

A THIRD SERIES OF SERMONS PREACHED IN RUGBY SCHOOL CHAPEL IN 1867—1869. Extra fcap. 8vo. 6s.

This Third Series of Bishop Temple's Rugby Sermons, contains thirty-six brief discourses, including the "Good-bye" sermon preached on his leaving Rugby to enter on the office he now holds.

Thring.—Works by Rev. EDWARD THRING, M.A.:

SERMONS DELIVERED AT UPPINGHAM SCHOOL. Crown 8vo. 5s.

THOUGHTS ON LIFE-SCIENCE. New Edition, enlarged and revised. Crown 8vo. 7s. 6d.

Thrupp.—AN INTRODUCTION TO THE STUDY AND USE OF THE PSALMS. By the Rev. J. F. THRUPP, M.A., late Fellow of Trinity College, Cambridge. New Edition. 2 vols. 8vo. 25s.

Trench.—Works by R. CHENEVIX TRENCH, D.D., Archbishop of Dublin:

NOTES ON THE PARABLES OF OUR LORD. Thirteenth Edition. 8vo. 12s.

This work has taken its place as a standard exposition and interpretation of Christ's Parables. The book is prefaced by an Introductory Essay in four chapters:—I. On the definition of the Parable. II. On Teaching by Parables. III. On the Interpretation of the Parables. IV. On

TRENCH (Archbishop)—*continued.*

other Parables besides those in the Scriptures. The author then proceeds to take up the Parables one by one, and by the aid of philology, history, antiquities, and the researches of travellers, shews forth the significance, beauty, and applicability of each, concluding with what he deems its true moral interpretation. In the numerous Notes are many valuable references, illustrative quotations, critical and philological annotations, etc., and appended to the volume is a classified list of fifty-six works on the Parables.

NOTES ON THE MIRACLES OF OUR LORD. Eleventh Edition, revised. 8vo. 12s.

*In the 'Preliminary Essay' to this work, all the momentous and interesting questions that have been raised in connection with Miracles, are discussed with considerable fulness. The Essay consists of six chapters:—I. On the Names of Miracles, i.e. the Greek words by which they are designated in the New Testament. II. The Miracles and Nature—What is the difference between a Miracle and any event in the ordinary course of Nature? III. The Authority of Miracles—Is the Miracle to command absolute obedience? IV. The Evangelical, compared with the other cycles of Miracles. V. The Assaults on the Miracles—*1. *The Jewish.* 2. *The Heathen (Celsus, etc.).* 3. *The Pantheistic (Spinosa, etc.).* 4. *The Sceptical (Hume).* 5. *The Miracles only relatively miraculous (Schleiermacher).* 6. *The Rationalistic (Paulus).* 7. *The Historico-Critical (Woolston, Strauss).* VI. *The Apologetic Worth of the Miracles. The author then treats the separate Miracles as he does the Parables.*

SYNONYMS OF THE NEW TESTAMENT. Eighth Edition, enlarged. 8vo. cloth. 12s.

This Edition has been carefully revised, and a considerable number of new Synonyms added. Appended is an Index to the Synonyms, and an Index to many other words alluded to or explained throughout the work. "He is," the Athenæum *says, "a guide in this department of knowledge to whom his readers may intrust themselves with confidence. His sober judgment and sound sense are barriers against the misleading influence of arbitrary hypotheses."*

ON THE AUTHORIZED VERSION OF THE NEW TESTAMENT. Second Edition. 8vo. 7s.

After some Introductory Remarks, in which the propriety of a revision is briefly discussed, the whole question of the merits of the present version is gone into in detail, in eleven chapters. Appended is a chronological list of works bearing on the subject, an Index of the principal Texts considered, an Index of Greek Words, and an Index of other Words referred to throughout the book.

STUDIES IN THE GOSPELS. Fourth Edition, revised. 8vo. 10s. 6d.

TRENCH (Archbishop)—*continued.*

This book is published under the conviction that the assertion often made is untrue,—viz. that the Gospels are in the main plain and easy, and that all the chief difficulties of the New Testament are to be found in the Epistles. These "Studies," sixteen in number, are the fruit of a much larger scheme, and each Study deals with some important episode mentioned in the Gospels, in a critical, philosophical, and practical manner. Many references and quotations are added to the Notes. Among the subjects treated are:—The Temptation; Christ and the Samaritan Woman; The Three Aspirants; The Transfiguration; Zacchæus; The True Vine; The Penitent Malefactor; Christ and the Two Disciples on the way to Emmaus.

COMMENTARY ON THE EPISTLES to the SEVEN CHURCHES IN ASIA. Third Edition, revised. 8vo. 8s. 6d.

The present work consists of an Introduction, being a commentary on Rev. i. 4—20, a detailed examination of each of the Seven Epistles, in all its bearings, and an Excursus on the Historico-Prophetical Interpretation of the Epistles.

THE SERMON ON THE MOUNT. An Exposition drawn from the writings of St. Augustine, with an Essay on his merits as an Interpreter of Holy Scripture. Third Edition, enlarged. 8vo. 10s. 6d.

The first half of the present work consists of a dissertation in eight chapters on "Augustine as an Interpreter of Scripture," the titles of the several chapters being as follow:—I. Augustine's General Views of Scripture and its Interpretation. II. The External Helps for the Interpretation of Scripture possessed by Augustine. III. Augustine's Principles and Canons of Interpretation. IV. Augustine's Allegorical Interpretation of Scripture. V. Illustrations of Augustine's Skill as an Interpreter of Scripture. VI. Augustine on John the Baptist and on St. Stephen. VII. Augustine on the Epistle to the Romans. VIII. Miscellaneous Examples of Augustine's Interpretation of Scripture. The latter half of the work consists of Augustine's Exposition of the Sermon on the Mount, not however a mere series of quotations from Augustine, but a connected account of his sentiments on the various passages of that Sermon, interspersed with criticisms by Archbishop Trench.

SHIPWRECKS OF FAITH. Three Sermons preached before the University of Cambridge in May, 1867. Fcap. 8vo. 2s. 6d.

These Sermons are especially addressed to young men. The subjects are "Balaam," "Saul," and "Judas Iscariot." These lives are set forth as beacon-lights, "to warn us off from perilous reefs and quicksands, which have been the destruction of many, and which might only too easily be ours." The John Bull *says, "they are, like all he writes, affectionate and earnest discourses."*

TRENCH (Archbishop)—*continued.*

SERMONS Preached for the most part in Ireland. 8vo. 10s. 6d.

This volume consists of Thirty-two Sermons, the greater part of which were preached in Ireland; the subjects are as follow:—Jacob, a Prince with God and with Men—Agrippa—The Woman that was a Sinner—Secret Faults—The Seven Worse Spirits—Freedom in the Truth—Joseph and his Brethren—Bearing one another's Burdens—Christ's Challenge to the World—The Love of Money—The Salt of the Earth—The Armour of God—Light in the Lord—The Jailer of Philippi—The Thorn in the Flesh—Isaiah's Vision—Selfishness—Abraham interceding for Sodom—Vain Thoughts—Pontius Pilate—The Brazen Serpent—The Death and Burial of Moses—A Word from the Cross—The Church's Worship in the Beauty of Holiness—Every Good Gift from Above—On the Hearing of Prayer—The Kingdom which cometh not with Observation—Pressing towards the Mark—Saul—The Good Shepherd—The Valley of Dry Bones—All Saints.

LECTURES ON MEDIEVAL CHURCH HISTORY. Being the Substance of Lectures delivered in Queen's College, London. Second Edition, revised. 8vo. 12s.

Contents:—The Middle Ages Beginning—The Conversion of England—Islam—The Conversion of Germany—The Iconoclasts—The Crusades—The Papacy at its Height—The Sects of the Middle Ages—The Mendicant Orders—The Waldenses—The Revival of Learning—Christian Art in the Middle Ages, &c. &c.

Tulloch.—THE CHRIST OF THE GOSPELS AND THE CHRIST OF MODERN CRITICISM. Lectures on M. RENAN's "Vie de Jésus." By JOHN TULLOCH, D.D., Principal of the College of St. Mary, in the University of St. Andrew's. Extra fcap. 8vo. 4s. 6d.

Vaughan.—Works by the very Rev. CHARLES JOHN VAUGHAN, D.D., Dean of Llandaff and Master of the Temple:

CHRIST SATISFYING THE INSTINCTS OF HUMANITY. Eight Lectures delivered in the Temple Church. Second Edition. Extra fcap. 8vo. 3s. 6d.

"*We are convinced that there are congregations, in number unmistakably increasing, to whom such Essays as these, full of thought and learning, are infinitely more beneficial, for they are more acceptable, than the recognised type of sermons.*"—John Bull.

THE BOOK AND THE LIFE, and other Sermons, preached before the University of Cambridge. Third Edition. Fcap. 8vo. 4s. 6d.

VAUGHAN (Dr. C. J.)—*continued.*

TWELVE DISCOURSES on SUBJECTS CONNECTED WITH THE LITURGY and WORSHIP of the CHURCH OF ENGLAND. Fcap. 8vo. 6s.

LESSONS OF LIFE AND GODLINESS. A Selection of Sermons preached in the Parish Church of Doncaster. Fourth and Cheaper Edition. Fcap. 8vo. 3s. 6d.

This volume consists of Nineteen Sermons, mostly on subjects connected with the every-day walk and conversation of Christians. The Spectator *styles them "earnest and human. They are adapted to every class and order in the social system, and will be read with wakeful interest by all who seek to amend whatever may be amiss in their natural disposition or in their acquired habits."*

WORDS FROM THE GOSPELS. A Second Selection of Sermons preached in the Parish Church of Doncaster. Third Edition. Fcap. 8vo. 4s. 6d.

The Nonconformist *characterises these Sermons as "of practical earnestness, of a thoughtfulness that penetrates the common conditions and experiences of life, and brings the truths and examples of Scripture to bear on them with singular force, and of a style that owes its real elegance to the simplicity and directness which have fine culture for their roots."*

LIFE'S WORK AND GOD'S DISCIPLINE. Three Sermons. Third Edition. Fcap. 8vo. 2s. 6d.

THE WHOLESOME WORDS OF JESUS CHRIST. Four Sermons preached before the University of Cambridge in November 1866. Second Edition. Fcap. 8vo. 3s. 6d.

Dr. Vaughan uses the word "Wholesome" here in its literal and original sense, the sense in which St. Paul uses it, as meaning healthy, sound, conducing to right living; *and in these Sermons he points out and illustrates several of the "wholesome" characteristics of the Gospel,—the Words of Christ. The* John Bull *says this volume is "replete with all the author's well-known vigour of thought and richness of expression."*

FOES OF FAITH. Sermons preached before the University of Cambridge in November 1868. Second Edition. Fcap. 8vo. 3s. 6d.

The "Foes of Faith" preached against in these Four Sermons are:— I. "Unreality." II. "Indolence." III. "Irreverence." IV. "Inconsistency."

LECTURES ON THE EPISTLE to the PHILIPPIANS. Third and Cheaper Edition. Extra fcap. 8vo. 5s.

Each Lecture is prefaced by a literal translation from the Greek of the paragraph which forms its subject, contains first a minute explanation

VAUGHAN (Dr. C. J.)—*continued.*
of the passage on which it is based, and then a practical application of the verse or clause selected as its text.

LECTURES ON THE REVELATION OF ST. JOHN.
Fourth Edition. Two Vols. Extra fcap. 8vo. 9s.

In this Edition of these Lectures, the literal translations of the passages expounded will be found interwoven in the body of the Lectures themselves. "Dr. Vaughan's Sermons," the Spectator *says, "are the most practical discourses on the Apocalypse with which we are acquainted." Prefixed is a Synopsis of the Book of Revelation, and appended is an Index of passages illustrating the language of the Book.*

EPIPHANY, LENT, AND EASTER. A Selection of
Expository Sermons. Third Edition. Crown 8vo. 10s. 6d.

THE EPISTLES OF ST. PAUL. For English Readers.
PART I., containing the FIRST EPISTLE TO THE THESSALONIANS. Second Edition. 8vo. 1s. 6d.

It is the object of this work to enable English readers, unacquainted with Greek, to enter with intelligence into the meaning, connexion, and phraseology of the writings of the great Apostle.

ST. PAUL'S EPISTLE TO THE ROMANS. The Greek
Text, with English Notes. Fourth Edition. Crown 8vo. 7s. 6d.

The Guardian *says of the work,—"For educated young men his commentary seems to fill a gap hitherto unfilled. . . . As a whole, Dr. Vaughan appears to us to have given to the world a valuable book of original and careful and earnest thought bestowed on the accomplishment of a work which will be of much service and which is much needed."*

THE CHURCH OF THE FIRST DAYS.
Series I. The Church of Jerusalem. Third Edition.
,, II. The Church of the Gentiles. Third Edition.
,, III. The Church of the World. Third Edition.
Fcap. 8vo. 4s. 6d. each.

The British Quarterly *says, "These Sermons are worthy of all praise, and are models of pulpit teaching."*

COUNSELS for YOUNG STUDENTS. Three Sermons
preached before the University of Cambridge at the Opening of the Academical Year 1870-71. Fcap. 8vo. 2s. 6d.

The titles of the Three Sermons contained in this volume are:—I. "The Great Decision." II. "The House and the Builder." III. "The Prayer and the Counter-Prayer." They all bear pointedly, earnestly, and sympathisingly upon the conduct and pursuits of young students and young men generally.

VAUGHAN (Dr. C. J.)—*continued.*

NOTES FOR LECTURES ON CONFIRMATION, with suitable Prayers. Tenth Edition. Fcap. 8vo. 1*s.* 6*d.*

THE TWO GREAT TEMPTATIONS. The Temptation of Man, and the Temptation of Christ. Lectures delivered in the Temple Church, Lent 1872. Second Edition. Extra fcap. 8vo. 3*s.* 6*d.*

WORDS FROM THE CROSS : Lent Lectures, 1875 ; and Thoughts for these Times: University Sermons, 1874. Extra fcap. 8vo. 4*s.* 6*d.*

ADDRESSES TO YOUNG CLERGYMEN, delivered at Salisbury in September and October, 1875. Extra fcap. 8vo. 4*s.* 6*d.*

HEROES OF FAITH : Lectures on Hebrews xi. Extra fcap. 8vo. 6*s.*

THE YOUNG LIFE EQUIPPING ITSELF FOR GOD'S SERVICE : Sermons before the University of Cambridge. Sixth Edition. Extra fcap. 8vo. 3*s.* 6*d.*

THE SOLIDITY OF TRUE RELIGION ; and other Sermons. Second Edition. Extra fcap. 8vo. 3*s.* 6*d.*

SERMONS IN HARROW SCHOOL CHAPEL (1847). 8vo. 10*s.* 6*d.*

NINE SERMONS IN HARROW SCHOOL CHAPEL (1849). Fcap. 8vo. 5*s.*

"MY SON, GIVE ME THINE HEART," SERMONS Preached before the Universities of Oxford and Cambridge, 1876—78. Fcap. 8vo. 5*s.*

THE LORD'S PRAYER. Second Edition. Extra fcap. 8vo. 3*s.* 6*d.*

REST AWHILE : Addresses to Toilers in the Ministry. Extra fcap. 8vo. 5*s.*

Vaughan (E. T.)—SOME REASONS OF OUR CHRISTIAN HOPE. Hulsean Lectures for 1875. By E. T. VAUGHAN, M.A., Rector of Harpenden. Crown 8vo. 6*s.* 6*d.*

"*His words are those of a well-tried scholar and a sound theologian, and they will be read widely and valued deeply by an audience far beyond the range of that which listened to their masterly pleading at Cambridge.*"—Standard.

Vaughan (D. J.)—Works by Canon Vaughan, of Leicester:
SERMONS PREACHED IN ST. JOHN'S CHURCH, LEICESTER, during the Years 1855 and 1856. Cr. 8vo. 5s. 6d.
CHRISTIAN EVIDENCES AND THE BIBLE. New Edition, revised and enlarged. Fcap. 8vo. cloth. 5s. 6d.
THE PRESENT TRIAL OF FAITH. Sermons preached in St. Martin's Church, Leicester. Crown 8vo. 9s.

Venn.—ON SOME OF THE CHARACTERISTICS OF BELIEF, Scientific and Religious. Being the Hulsean Lectures for 1869. By the Rev. J. Venn, M.A. 8vo. 6s. 6d.
These discourses are intended to illustrate, explain, and work out into some of their consequences, certain characteristics by which the attainment of religious belief is prominently distinguished from the attainment of belief upon most other subjects.

Warington.—THE WEEK OF CREATION; or, The Cosmogony of Genesis considered in its Relation to Modern Science. By George Warington, Author of "The Historic Character of the Pentateuch vindicated." Crown 8vo. 4s. 6d.
"A very able vindication of the Mosaic Cosmogony by a writer who unites the advantages of a critical knowledge of the Hebrew text and of distinguished scientific attainments."—Spectator.

Westcott.—Works by Brooke Foss Westcott, D.D., Regius Professor of Divinity in the University of Cambridge; Canon of Peterborough:
The London Quarterly, *speaking of Mr. Westcott, says, "To a learning and accuracy which command respect and confidence, he unites what are not always to be found in union with these qualities, the no less valuable faculties of lucid arrangement and graceful and facile expression."*
AN INTRODUCTION TO THE STUDY OF THE GOSPELS. Fifth Edition. Crown 8vo. 10s. 6d.
The author's chief object in this work has been to shew that there is a true mean between the idea of a formal harmonization of the Gospels and the abandonment of their absolute truth. After an Introduction on the General Effects of the course of Modern Philosophy on the popular views of Christianity, he proceeds to determine in what way the principles therein indicated may be applied to the study of the Gospels.
A GENERAL SURVEY OF THE HISTORY OF THE CANON OF THE NEW TESTAMENT during the First Four Centuries. Fourth Edition, revised, with a Preface on "Supernatural Religion." Crown 8vo. 10s. 6d.

WESTCOTT (Dr.)—*continued*.

The object of this treatise is to deal with the New Testament as a whole, and that on purely historical grounds. The separate books of which it is composed are considered not individually, but as claiming to be parts of the apostolic heritage of Christians. The Author has thus endeavoured to connect the history of the New Testament Canon with the growth and consolidation of the Catholic Church, and to point out the relation existing between the amount of evidence for the authenticity of its component parts and the whole mass of Christian literature. "*The treatise,*" *says the* British Quarterly, "*is a scholarly performance, learned, dispassionate, discriminating, worthy of his subject and of the present state of Christian literature in relation to it.*"

THE BIBLE IN THE CHURCH. A Popular Account of the Collection and Reception of the Holy Scriptures in the Christian Churches. Sixth Edition. 18mo. 4s. 6d.

A GENERAL VIEW OF THE HISTORY OF THE ENGLISH BIBLE. Second Edition. Crown 8vo. 10s. 6d.

The Pall Mall Gazette *calls the work "A brief, scholarly, and, to a great extent, an original contribution to theological literature."*

THE CHRISTIAN LIFE, MANIFOLD AND ONE. Six Sermons preached in Peterborough Cathedral. Crown 8vo. 2s. 6d.

The Six Sermons contained in this volume are the first preached by the author as a Canon of Peterborough Cathedral. The subjects are:— I. "Life consecrated by the Ascension." II. "Many Gifts, One Spirit." III. "The Gospel of the Resurrection." IV. "Sufficiency of God." V. "Action the Test of Faith." VI. "Progress from the Confession of God."

THE GOSPEL OF THE RESURRECTION. Thoughts on its Relation to Reason and History. Fourth Edition, revised. Crown 8vo. 6s.

The present Essay is an endeavour to consider some of the elementary truths of Christianity, as a miraculous Revelation, from the side of History and Reason. The author endeavours to shew that a devout belief in the Life of Christ is quite compatible with a broad view of the course of human progress and a frank trust in the laws of our own minds. In the third edition the author has carefully reconsidered the whole argument, and by the help of several kind critics has been enabled to correct some faults and to remove some ambiguities, which had been overlooked before.

ON THE RELIGIOUS OFFICE OF THE UNIVERSITIES. Crown 8vo. 4s. 6d.

"*There is certainly no man of our time—no man at least who has obtained the command of the public ear—whose utterances can compare with* those of Professor Westcott for largeness of views and comprehensiveness of grasp...... There is wisdom, and truth, and thought enough, and a harmony and mutual connection running through them all, which makes the collection of more real value than many an ambitious treatise."—Literary Churchman.

Wilkins.—THE LIGHT OF THE WORLD. An Essay, by A. S. WILKINS, M.A., Professor of Latin in Owens College, Manchester. Second Edition. Crown 8vo. 3s. 6d.

"*It would be difficult to praise too highly the spirit, the burden, the conclusions, or the scholarly finish of this beautiful Essay.*"—British Quarterly Review.

Wilson.—THE BIBLE STUDENT'S GUIDE TO THE MORE CORRECT UNDERSTANDING of the ENGLISH TRANSLATION OF THE OLD TESTAMENT, by Reference to the Original Hebrew. By WILLIAM WILSON, D.D., Canon of Winchester. Second Edition, carefully revised. 4to. 25s.

The author believes that the present work is the nearest approach to a complete Concordance of every word in the original that has yet been made: and as a Concordance, it may be found of great use to the Bible student, while at the same time it serves the important object of furnishing the means of comparing synonymous words, and of eliciting their precise and distinctive meaning. The knowledge of the Hebrew language is not absolutely necessary to the profitable use of the work.

Worship (The) of God and Fellowship among Men. Sermons on Public Worship. By Professor MAURICE, and others. Fcap. 8vo. 3s. 6d.

Yonge (Charlotte M.)—Works by CHARLOTTE M. YONGE, Author of "The Heir of Redclyffe :"

SCRIPTURE READINGS FOR SCHOOLS AND FAMILIES. 5 vols. Globe 8vo. 1s. 6d. With Comments, 3s. 6d. each.

FIRST SERIES. Genesis to Deuteronomy.
SECOND SERIES. From Joshua to Solomon.
THIRD SERIES. The Kings and Prophets.
FOURTH SERIES. The Gospel Times.
FIFTH SERIES. Apostolic Times.

Actual need has led the author to endeavour to prepare a reading book convenient for study with children, containing the very words of the Bible, with only a few expedient omissions, and arranged in Lessons of such length as by experience she has found to suit with children's ordinary

YONGE (Charlotte M.)—*continued.*

power of accurate attentive interest. The verse form has been retained because of its convenience for children reading in class, and as more resembling their Bibles; but the poetical portions have been given in their lines. Professor Huxley at a meeting of the London School-board, particularly mentioned the Selection made by Miss Yonge, as an example of how selections might be made for School reading. "Her Comments are models of their kind."—Literary Churchman.

THE PUPILS OF ST. JOHN THE DIVINE. New Edition. Crown 8vo. 6s.

"*Young and old will be equally refreshed and taught by these pages, in which nothing is dull, and nothing is far-fetched.*"—Churchman.

PIONEERS AND FOUNDERS; or, Recent Workers in the Mission Field. With Frontispiece and Vignette Portrait of Bishop HEBER. Crown 8vo. 6s.

The missionaries whose biographies are here given, are—John Eliot, the Apostle of the Red Indians; David Brainerd, the Enthusiast; Christian F. Schwartz, the Councillor of Tanjore; Henry Martyn, the Scholar-Missionary; William Carey and Joshua Marshman, the Serampore Missionaries; the Judson Family; the Bishops of Calcutta—Thomas Middleton, Reginald Heber, Daniel Wilson; Samuel Marsden, the Australian Chaplain and Friend of the Maori; John Williams, the Martyr of Erromango; Allen Gardener, the Sailor Martyr; Charles Frederick Mackenzie, the Martyr of Zambesi.

THE "BOOK OF PRAISE" HYMNAL,

COMPILED AND ARRANGED BY
LORD SELBORNE.

In the following four forms:—

A. Beautifully printed in Royal 32mo., limp cloth, price 6d.
B.   ,,   ,, Small 18mo., larger type, cloth limp, 1s.
C. Same edition on fine paper, cloth, 1s. 6d.
Also an edition with Music, selected, harmonized, and composed by JOHN HULLAH, in square 18mo., cloth, 3s. 6d.

The large acceptance which has been given to "The Book of Praise" by all classes of Christian people encourages the Publishers in entertaining the hope that this Hymnal, which is mainly selected from it, may be extensively used in Congregations, and in some degree at least meet the desires of those who seek uniformity in common worship as a means towards that unity which pious souls yearn after, and which our Lord prayed for in behalf of his Church. "The office of a hymn is not to teach controversial Theology, but to give the voice of song to practical religion. No doubt, to do this, it must embody sound doctrine; but it ought to do so, not after the manner of the schools, but with the breadth, freedom, and simplicity of the Fountain-head." On this principle has Sir R. Palmer proceeded in the preparation of this book.

The arrangement adopted is the following :—

PART I. *consists of Hymns arranged according to the subjects of the Creed—"God the Creator," "Christ Incarnate," "Christ Crucified," "Christ Risen," "Christ Ascended," "Christ's Kingdom and Judgment," etc.*

PART II. *comprises Hymns arranged according to the subjects of the Lord's Prayer.*

PART III. *Hymns for natural and sacred seasons.*

There are 320 Hymns in all.

CAMBRIDGE: PRINTED BY J. PALMER.

www.ingramcontent.com/pod-product-compliance
Lightning Source LLC
Chambersburg PA
CBHW020321240426
43673CB00039B/884